Teachers and Their Unions

Teachers and Their Unions

Labor Relations in Uncertain Times

Todd A. DeMitchell

ROWMAN & LITTLEFIELD
Lanham • Boulder • New York • London

Published by Rowman & Littlefield
An imprint of The Rowman & Littlefield Publishing Group, Inc.
4501 Forbes Boulevard, Suite 200, Lanham, Maryland 20706
www.rowman.com

6 Tinworth Street, London SE11 5AL, United Kingdom

British Library Cataloguing in Publication Information Available

Library of Congress Cataloging-in-Publication Data

Library of Congress Control Number: 2019956009

ISBN: 978-1-4758-5427-5 (cloth)
ISBN: 978-1-4758-5428-2 (pbk.)
ISBN: 978-1-4758-5429-9 (electronic)

Contents

Preface

Labor Unrest, or Unrest with Labor?

The 2018 teacher-strike tsunami was decades in the making. State budget cuts, especially after the Great Recession, squeezed school spending and teacher salaries.[1]

Like blindfolded partygoers swinging at a piñata, state legislatures took multiple swipes at their respective collective bargaining laws in 2011.[2]

In the last five years (2010–2015), three states—Wisconsin, Indiana, and Michigan—have eliminated many of the rights conveyed to public employees through state labor law, and this has resulted in a substantial decline in public-employee union membership.[3]

The challenge and uncertainty of labor relations in American public education can be captured in the following question: Can teacher unions remain relevant in the lives of teachers and in the work of America's public schools in the twenty-first century? Many assert that teachers, their unions, and the institution of public education itself are under assault. Rolling back mandatory subjects of bargaining, while expanding prohibited ones, reducing tenure protections, starving unions financially through judicial challenges to agency fees, and passing right-to-work legislation have been decried as wrongful attacks by some, but lauded by others as necessary and about time!

While supporters of these policy initiatives consider them as needed and long overdue reforms, opponents suggest that they are undermining public education and the profession of teaching. For example, during the decade of 2010–2019, many welcomed the actions of the legislatures in Indiana, Idaho, Tennessee, and Wisconsin when they passed laws substantially restricting the collective bargaining rights of public employees.[4] In short, these policy challenges have created a time of challenge and uncertainty for teachers and their unions.

ix

Daniel Disalvo, in the fall of 2010, published an article titled "The Trouble with Public Sector Unions" in *National Affairs*.[5] Earlier in the same year, Chris Edwards, writing for the *Cato Institute Tax & Budget Bulletin* and focusing on public sector unions, asserted, "Collective bargaining is a misguided labor policy because it violates civil liberties and gives unions excessive power to block needed reforms."[6] He called for a ban on collective bargaining in the public sector.

Four years later, Charles Lane in a *Washington Post* Op-Ed piece asked, "Is public sector collective bargaining in the public interest?" His answer was "no."[7] In 2015, an article in *The American Spectator* written by Gary Shapiro lamented that public unions are so powerful that they harm the public they are supposed to serve.[8] The effect is that public school teachers and their unions feel under siege from attacks that often seem virulent and personal.

The question of whether government workers, including teachers, should have the opportunity to continue to engage in collective bargaining has reopened. Many governors, state legislatures, policymakers, research-ers, and commentators are inclined to answer no; things must change. The trend to limit public sector bargaining rights and reduce, if not eliminate, the power of public sector unions was energized in the second decade of the twenty-first century. The pendulum that provided collective bargain-ing rights in the second half of the twentieth century has now swung back and is limiting those rights legislatively and through the courts. Law professor Joseph Slater stated that the most striking political development of 2011 was the "widespread and aggressive assault on public sector bar-gaining rights."[9] However, following a series of statewide teacher strikes in traditionally red states starting in 2018 and a widespread support for increased teacher compensation and school support, maybe a corner is being turned.

A lot has happened since January 2010, when I published *Labor Relations in Education: Policies, Politics, and Practices* (Rowman & Littlefield). The impact of the Great Recession rippled through public education with large effects. A total of 135,000 education positions lost in 2008 have still not been filled as of 2017, yet there are 1,419,000 more students in the schools.[10] Funding for public education dropped precipitously starting in 2008 and as of 2015 has not fully rebounded.[11] The loss of positions and the loss of funding add stress to an already stressed system of public schools.

Against this backdrop of financial distress teacher unions are under attack, tenure is threatened, and bargaining rights are being rolled back, or attempts have been made to roll them back. Stephen Sawchuk noted in 2011 that lawmakers in several states were challenging bargaining, "the foundation of unionism" in several states.[12]

In a *Newsweek* point/counterpoint discussion and written against this backdrop of attacks, Ezra Klein writing under the banner "Do We Still Need Unions?" argues that unions give workers a voice and are the counterweight to "moneyed, organized interests who lobby strategically and patiently to get their way."[13] Bringing law suits against educational policies/practices such tenure (*Vergara v. State of California* discussed in chapter 8) is one of the examples of moneyed organized special interest groups lobbying for significant change. Should they be the dominant or the only voice on policy issues, or should the teaching profession also add their voice to these important issues? Klein answers yes to the voice of the teachers.

In response, Mark McKinnon, referring to public employee union members as the "privileged class" and public union bosses as running a "racket," wrote, "the primary purpose of public unions today, as ugly as it sounds, is to work against the financial interests of taxpayers."[14] The words were sharp as were the elbows that were metaphorically heaved about in the larger public debate. Teacher unions were portrayed as being cast from the same mold as the most negative stereotypes of industrial unions.

This retrenchment of unions and their ability to represent their members occurred several years into the Great Recession of 2008. The economy's slow rebound devastated many jobs, including public sector jobs. Teachers were singled out as doing well, while others in the private sector lost their jobs. A "beggar-thy-neighbor" response of "I don't have what you have, therefore you should not have it" seemed to underlie the criticism of teachers. However, while many teachers survived the flurry of pink slips, a significant number did not. As revenues dwindled for state government, cuts were made to public K–12 education, resulting in a nationwide "lay off [of] teachers at a scale previously unseen."[15]

Governors and their legislatures went after unions seeking to reduce, if not eliminate, their influence and power, asserting that it was a necessary cost savings measure to balance budgets and a reasonable response to the outsized influence public sector unions had on public policy. The resurgence of right-to-work legislation in multiple states underscores this policy approach to reducing the role of unions.[16]

Probably no state better exemplified the charge to fundamentally change the relationship between teachers and their school districts than Wisconsin's governor Scott Walker and his fight with the teacher unions. The state that led the way in granting public-sector unions the right to negotiate with their public employees, nearly six decades later led the way to reduce and eliminate those rights. Eliminating tenure was a shared goal for many governors. Former Texas governor Rick Perry told the Greater Miami Chamber of Commerce, "Good teachers know they don't need tenure. There is no reason to have it except to protect those that don't perform as they should."[17]

Republican governor of New Jersey, Chris Christie, at the State of the State Address on January 11, 2011, declared, "[t]he time to eliminate teacher tenure is now."

Diane D'Amico, "NJEA Plans to Fight Gov. Christie Over Plans to Eliminate Teacher Tenure," *Press of Atlantic City* (Jan. 13, 2011). Site visited December 12, 2018, at http://www.pressofatlanticcity.com/education/njea-plans-to-fight-gov-christie-over-plan-to-eliminate/article_52062a 6e-1eaf-11e0-9f79-001cc4c002e0.html.

However, not all governors prevailed in their bid to reduce the power and influence of public sector unions. "Voters in Ohio, sent an unequivocal message to that state's Republican governor [John Kasich] and lawmakers last week that they went too far in reining in collective bargaining for teachers and other public employees."[18] In New Hampshire, Republican governor John Sununu with a Republican House could not muster the votes necessary to pass right-to-work legislation in 2017. He stated that he is "deeply disappointed" that the House voted to kill his bill, which was a priority for his first term as governor.[19]

In addition to many state governors and legislators taking on unions, the courts, most notably in California, have also been a venue for the policy debate. In the summer of 2014 a trial court in Los Angeles County California rocked the national debate by declaring that four of California's tenure laws were unconstitutional as well as its layoff law, commonly called Last-In-First-Out.[20] Superior Court judge Rolf Michael Treu held that these five statutes violated California students' fundamental right to equality of educational opportunity, especially for minority students and students from poor communities.[21] Even though the decision was later overturned on appeal in the spring of 2016,[22] the courts continue to play a large part in shaping the labor relations in public education.

Conservatives seek to allow teacher unions to be present in the public schools but to be functionally irrelevant. Teacher union supporters recognize the ebbing tide and seek to adjust and thrive—and not just survive. Teachers, their unions, their tenure, and their wages, benefits, and terms and conditions of employment are under scrutiny, and, some would consider, under assault.

Terry Moe, a professor of political science and a senior fellow at the Hoover Institution at Stanford University, stated, "The pivotal question for the future of American education is, will the problem of union power ever get resolved so that the nation's schools can actually be organized in the best interests of children."

Terry Moe, *Special Interests: Teacher Unions and America's Public Schools* (Washington, DC: Brookings Institution Press, 2011), 14.

This volume explores the contours and the relevance of public teachers unions in an uncertain time. The history of teachers and the rise of teacher unions, legal framework for bargaining, the practice of bargaining, provide the backdrop upon which I discuss the tumultuous decade of labor relations change, and of power played, and power misplayed. Discussing the political fights with teacher unions, Sarah Butrymowicz, in a 2013 *Hechinger Report*, wrote that "the fights are about the relevance and future of teacher unions and, by extension, the labor movement itself."[23]

It is an uncertain time for teachers and their unions. Will antiunion forces continue to reduce the influence of teacher unions through an expansion of prohibited subjects of bargaining and the shrinking of mandatory subjects of bargaining? Will the agenda of "starve the beast" under the argument for eliminating agency fees and the institution of right-to-work legislation prevail? Will the buffer of tenure from the changing winds of politics be eliminated? And the most important question is whether these policy changes will benefit children.

Lest I give the impression that all challenges to achieving labor peace, a central tenet of public sector bargaining,[24] is the legislative agenda to weaken the power of unions to possibly make them irrelevant; teacher unions have not been idle pushing back with some using industrial style union tactics. For example, there were strikes, walkouts, and threats of strikes, as well as work-to-rule actions occurring across the nation.

Teachers and Their Unions: Labor Relations in Uncertain Times builds on and uses my earlier work *Labor Relations in Education: Policies, Politics, and Practices* (Lanham, MD: Rowman & Littlefield, 2010) as a foundation. New chapters and sections were written, existing chapters were revised, and some chapters were rewritten and moved to a companion book, *Educators at the Bargaining Table: Successfully Negotiating a Contract That Works for All* (2018), including the Arroyo Wells School District simulation. The *Educators at the Bargaining Table* book can be used with this volume or used separately.

Teachers and Their Unions focuses on the broad legal and political force that impacts the labor relations aspects of teacher unionization and the impact of collective bargaining. *Educators at the Bargaining Table, including the Arroyo Wells School District simulation,* explores the specific actions/tasks necessary to prepare for bargaining, bargaining at the table, and implementing and enforcing the contract. They fit together and they can stand alone.

It is my hope that this volume, *Teachers and Their Unions*, adds to your understanding of the policies, politics, and practices that structure public sector labor relations in education.

Todd A. DeMitchell
John & H. Irene Peters,
Professor of Education
Professor and Coordinator of
Graduate Studies, Justice Studies Program
University of New Hampshire
Durham, New Hampshire
December 2019

NOTES

1. Andrew Van Dam, "Teacher Strikes Made 2018 the Biggest Year for Worker Protest in a Generation," *Washington Post* (February 14, 2019). Site visited April 29, 2019, at https://www.washingtonpost.com/us-policy/2019/02/14/with-teachers-lead-more-workers-went-strike-than-any-year-since/?utm_term=.8595f4a709f2.

2. Mark Paige, "Applying the 'Paradox' Theory: A Law and Policy Analysis of Collective Bargaining Rights and Teacher Evaluation Reform from Selected States," *Brigham Young University Education and Law Journal* 21 (2013): 42.

3. Jeffrey Keefe, "Laws Enabling Public-Sector Collective Bargaining Have Not Led to Excessive Public-Sector Pay," *Economic Policy Institute* Briefing Paper #409 (October 16, 2015). Site visited February 2, 2016, at http://www.epi.org/publication/laws-enabling-public-sector-collective-bargaining-have-not-led-to-excessive-public-sector-pay/.

4. Eunice A. Han, "The Myth of Union's Overprotection of Bad Teachers: Evidence from the District-Teacher Matched Panel Data on Teacher Turnover," Wellesley College (February 27, 2016): 16. Site visited April 5, 2016, at http://haveyouheardblog.com/wpcontent/uploads/2016/07/Han_Teacher_dismissal_Feb_16.pdf.

5. Daniel Disalvo, "The Trouble with Public Sector Unions," *National Affairs* 5 (Fall 2010). Site visited February 21, 2016, at http://www.nationalaffairs.com/publications/detail/the-trouble-with-public-sector-unions.

6. Chris Edwards, "Public Sector Unions," *Cato Institute, Tax & Budget Bulletin* 61 (March 2010). Site visited at February 20, 2016, at http://object.cato.org/sites/cato.org/files/pubs/pdf/tbb_61.pdf.

7. Charles Lane, "Public-Sector Unions Interfere With the Public Interest," *The Washington Post* (January 27, 2014). Site visited June 5, 2016, at https://www.washingtonpost.com/opinions/charles-lane-public-sector-unions-interfere-with-the-public-interest/2014/01/27/e4214f84-877d-11e3-833c-33098f9e5267_story.html. Lane continues, "The fundamental problem is collective bargaining. It is appropriate in the private sector, where workers bargain with private, profit-making corporations,

not the taxpaying citizenry—and where market forces provide an independent check on both sides' demands. In the public sector, however, it means higher costs, lower efficiency and, worst of all, less democracy." Ibid.

8. Gary Shapiro, "Should SCOTUS Limit the Power of Public Sector Unions?" *The American Spectator* (July 7 2015). Site visited September 4, 2017, at https://sp ectator.org/63363_should-scotus-limit-power-public-sector-unions/.

9. Joseph E. Slater, "The Assault on Public Sector Collective Bargaining: Real Harms and Imaginary Benefits," *American Constitution Society for Law and Policy* Issue Brief (June 2011). Site visited December 8, 2015, at https://www.acslaw.org/si tes/default/files/Slater_Collective_Bargaining.pdf.

10. Michael Leachman, Kathleen Masterson, & Eric Figueroa, A *"Punishing Decade for School Funding"* (Washington, DC: Center on Budget and Policy Priorities, November 29, 2017). Site visited on April 29, 2019, at https://www.cbpp.org/site s/default/files/atoms/files/11-29-17sfp.pdf.

11. Ibid.

12. Stephen Sawchuk, "States Eye Curbs on Collective Bargaining by Teachers," *Education Week* 1 (February 9, 2011): 20, at 1.

13. Ezra Klein, "YES, Why They're Worth Fighting For," *Newsweek* 18 (March 7, 2011).

14. Mark McKinnon, "NO, Let's End a Privileged Class," *Newsweek* 19 (March 7, 2011).

15. Dan Goldhaber, Katharine O. Strunk, Nate Brown, & David S. Knight, *Lessons Learned From the Great Recession: Layoffs and the RIF-Induced Teacher Shuffle* (Working Paper No. 129) (Washington, DC: National Center for Analysis of Longitudinal Data in Educational Research, July 2015), 3. The study found that the large-scale layoffs increase the likelihood that teachers will leave their jobs inducing a "structural churn" within the schools. The researchers studied layoffs in Los Angeles and Washington and found the mere receipt of a RIF notice—even when it is rescinded—induces a good deal of teacher churn.

16. For an example of legislative responses to Right-to-Work legislation since 2010, see George Leef, "Indiana, Michigan, Now Wisconsin: What the Right-to-Work Momentum Means," *Forbes* (March 11, 2015). Site visited June 28, 2016, at http://www.forbes.com/sites/georgeleef/2015/03/11/indiana-michigan-now-wisc onsin-what-the-right-to-work-momentum-means/#dbe9dfb944e5.

17. Trip Gabriel & Sam Dillon, "G.O.P. Governors Take Aim at Teacher Tenure," *New York Times* (Jan. 31, 2011). Site visited May 30, 2016, at http://www.nytimes.c om/2011/02/01/us/01tenure.html?_r=1.

18. Michele McNeil, "Ohio Vote to Scrap Bargaining Law a Labor Victory—For Now," *Education Week* (November 16, 2011): 26–27.

19. Allie Morris, "Right to Work Fails in NH House, 200-177," *Concord Monitor* (Concord, NH, February 16, 2017). Site visited July 2, 2017, at http://www.conc ordmonitor.com/Right-to-work-updates-on-house-vote-day-8137054

20. *Vergara v. State of California*, No. BC484642, 2014 WL 2598719 (Cal. Super. Ct. L.A. Cty. June 10, 2014).

21. See Todd A. DeMitchell & Joseph J. Onosko, *"Vergara v. State of California*: The End of Teacher Tenure or a Flawed Ruling?" *Southern California Interdisciplinary Law Journal* 25, no. 589 (2016).

22. *Vergara v. State of California*, 246 Cal.App.4th 619 (2016).

23. Sarah Butrymowicz, "Under Siege—and In Bid to Stay Relevant—Teacher Unions Evolve," at Hechinger Report (June, 9, 2013). Site visited May 29, 2016, http://hechingerreport.org/under-siege-and-in-bid-to-stay-relevant-teacher-unions-evolve/.

24. The National Labor Relations Act, the template for many public sector bargaining laws, stated:

> Experience has proved that protection by law of the right of employees to organize and bargain collectively safeguards commerce from injury, impairment, or interruption, and promotes the flow of commerce by removing recognized sources of industrial strife and unrest, by encouraging practices fundamental to the friendly adjustment of industrial disputes arising out of differences as to wages, hours, or other working conditions.

29 U.S.C. § 151 (1970).

See also, *Abood v. Detroit Board of Education*, 431 U.S. 209, 224 (1977), the seminal case supporting fair share agreements among public employees. Justice Stewart writing for the majority stated, "The desirability of labor peace is no less important in the public sector, nor is the risk of 'free riders any smaller.'"

Chapter 1

Introduction

2010 to the Present, Teachers and Their Unions

Over the past five years in particular, public workers have endured a vicious and unprecedented attack not only on their wages and benefits but also on their right to bargain over the terms and conditions of their employment.[1]

To the extent teachers benefit from more generous pay and benefits, less-demanding work conditions, and higher job security, the unions will pursue those goals, even if achieving them comes at the expense of students.[2]

Teachers and their unions have for over a century had a storied but influential past with public education. Recently both teachers and their unions have been the subject of scrutiny, and in some cases ridicule. Dana Goldstein, in her work *The Teacher Wars: A History of America's Most Embattled Profession*, wrote, "Public school teaching had become the most controversial profession in America."[3] Public policy in these uncertain times of the second decade of the twenty-first century has focused on teachers and their unions.

Critics argue that unions must be constrained and incompetent teachers should, for the benefit of students, be easily removed. However, should the collective voice of employees be diminished leaving the employing school board to dictate the terms of employment without regard for the employees who do the central work of educating the community's children? This is particularly salient when the workforce is a professional one with a certain amount of necessary autonomy to engage students and develop lessons. This book explores teacher unions and the policies and practices that influence their labor relations with public school districts.

In the last fifty-plus years teacher unions have impacted the governance of America's public schools through the rise of public sector collective bargaining legislation. The two teacher unions, the National Education Association (NEA) and the American Federation of Teachers (AFT), have become major policy and political players not only at the local school district level but also at the national level.

In those states that have public sector collective bargaining laws, governance has become bilateral on issues of wages, benefits, and terms and conditions of employment. Reform strategies must also come to the bargaining table because real reform impacts the terms and conditions of employment. The trend over time has been to expand the subjects of bargaining, thus increasing the impact of collective bargaining and the influence of unions.

"Although the teachers unions have tremendous influence over the nation's schools, they have been poorly studied."[4] Teachers bargain collectively in approximately 90 percent of the states, yet instead of using a robust research base upon which to base policy decisions, "deeply held beliefs and largely untested assumptions" are used as proxies.[5] Understanding unions, their history, and their work is important for effective school stewardship. This is true for all educators. Administrators must work with unions, and teachers work in a collective bargaining environment and need to understand how their union works and what a collective bargaining environment means to their professional practice.

A telling aspect of this period from 2010 to the publication of this book is the targeting of teachers. Causal linkage is asserted between bad teachers and the union that protects their incompetence, with little to no regard for what is best for students. If only, the argument goes, we could get rid of these rotten apples, educational reform would move forward and our children will learn. More specifically, critics argue that teacher tenure protects bad teachers and unions protect tenure; therefore, students lose out and communities cannot offer high-quality education to its citizens.

Get rid of bad teachers, and, if not possible, eliminate unions or at least render them irrelevant, and then students win. To many this calculus is simple and accurate: hobble unions and we can fire our way to excellence.

Two major national magazines reported on this approach in their cover stories. *Newsweek*'s March 15, 2010, cover read, "The Key to Saving American Education," with an old-fashioned chalkboard in the background that read "We must fire bad teachers" written in chalk. These nine lines on the chalkboard are reminiscent of the misbehaving child who writes over and over on the blackboard how he/she will improve their behavior.

Four years later, the cover of *Time* (November 3, 2014) showed the iconic education apple with an imposing gavel poised above it and this caption read, "ROTTEN APPLES: It's Nearly Impossible to Fire a Bad Teacher. Some Tech Millionaires May Have Found a Way to Change That." The calculus is articulated again; the system in which bad teachers are protected by tenure and supported by unions must end, and the interests of children and not the interests of adults must be established.

THE LEGISLATIVE RESPONSE

As discussed in the preface, teachers and their unions have come under increased scrutiny and have been the subject of political controversy, legislative initiatives, and court cases. Throughout the nation governors support legislative acts to reduce the impact of bargaining by limiting the scope of bargaining, targeting the financial support of unions through eliminating dues deductions,[6] and establishing a state as a Right-to-Work (RtW) state in which members of a bargaining unit cannot be compelled to pay a fee to the union for the work of the union to secure and enforce the contract that they would then get for free, prompting the derisive description of free-riders. A consequence of RtW in Michigan was the loss of union membership.[7]

State legislatures have also reduced due process protections (tenure). Florida, Indiana, Kansas, and North Carolina passed legislation repealing tenure. Alaska, Colorado, Connecticut, Delaware, Florida, Illinois, Indiana, Louisiana, Michigan, Nevada, Oklahoma, Rhode Island, Tennessee, Washington, and Wyoming passed legislation requiring that performance evaluations be considered before granting tenure.[8]

New York passed legislation in which the timeline for tenure eligibility was extended to four years and requires a candidate for tenure to have effective or highly effective rating in three of the four years of probation "and was not [rated] ineffective in the final year."[9] Legislative change regarding tenure is afoot across the nation.

However, teachers in both Indiana and North Carolina turned to the courts. In Indiana, tenure could be changed for new teachers but not teachers already employed under the tenure legislation. The 2013 suit in North Carolina reached a similar decision.[10]

THE JUDICIAL RESPONSE

Tenure

The courts have also been active in the field of education labor relations since 2010. For example, Judge Treu, a superior court judge in Los Angeles County, California, issued a tentative ruling on June 10, 2014, followed by his judgment on August 27, 2014.[11] He found four California statutes on tenure and dismissal plus a fifth statute on Last-In-First-Out layoffs to be unconstitutional.[12] A *Huffington Post, The Blog*, article phrased the question before the court thusly, "Are job protections for teachers to blame for educational underachievement among low-income students of color?"[13] Judge Treu's decision was later overturned by a California Court of Appeals.[14] This case sparked controversy and follow-on lawsuits in New York and Minnesota.[15]

Agency Fees: Subsidized Compelled Speech

A second major case out of California addressed the issue of fair share agreements, or often called agency shop agreements. Agency fees arise out of the concept that a unit of employees may elect a union to act as their exclusive representative in bargaining for their interests with the employer. The cost of the service rendered on their behalf is borne by the employees receiving the benefit. All members of the bargaining unit must be fairly represented. The U.S. Supreme Court in *Vaca v. Sipes*, 386 U.S. 171, 177 (1967) held that a union must serve all employees in good faith and without hostility or discrimination.[16]

The Supreme Court had previously held in *Abood v. Detroit Board of Education*[17] that such agency shop agreements requiring that nonunion members covered under the collective bargaining agreement pay their fair share for the service rendered by the union. This is often called the "free rider" principle. A second argument advanced by the Supreme Court is that agency fees supports labor peace in that it reduces conflict between competing unions bargaining for the same set of employees at the same time.

However, the nonunion member cannot be charged for union activities unrelated to bargaining or enforcing the contract. In other words, the teacher cannot be compelled to subsidize the political speech of the union with which she/he disagrees. This is one of the major arguments of the RtW legislation started the 1940s as an employer response to the growing labor movement.[18]

Opponents of public sector agency fees brought suit to overturn the practice in *Friedrichs v. California Teachers Association*. The plaintiffs argued that *Abood v. Detroit Board of Education* should be overturned, which found agency fees to be constitutional and second, they argued that an agency shop violated their "First Amendment rights by requiring that public employees affirmatively object to subsidizing nonchargeable speech by public sector unions, rather than requiring that employees affirmatively consent to subsidizing such speech."[19]

The Ninth Circuit Court of Appeals in a two-paragraph ruling affirmed the district court judgment in favor of the defendant teachers' union. The Appellate Court considered the questions presented in the appeal to be "insubstantial" and already to be settled law. Similarly, the U.S. Supreme Court in March 2016, in a terse one sentence per curiam decision stated, "The judgment is affirmed by an equally divided Court," affirming the Ninth Circuit, thus upholding the practice.[20] Justice Anton Scalia died earlier in the year leaving the court with eight members. The court was evenly divided (4–4) on the issue, thus upholding the lower court's ruling. This split decision did not resolve the issue of the constitutionality of agency fees; it merely postponed it.

The Supreme Court in a 5–4 decision, with a full bench of nine Justices, revisited the issue two years later. The Supreme Court in *Janus v. American*

Federation of State, County, and Municipal Employees Council, 31[21] overturned *Abood* and the concept that agency fees promote labor peace, and found that public employees', including teachers', free speech is abridged when they are required to pay a fee to the union for bargaining and that they have not affirmatively agreed to—the employee no longer has to seek an exemption with the default being no payment without explicit assent. This ruling overturned nearly fifty years of labor law and upset countless public sector bargain agreements.

Following the *Janus* decision several cases were brought in federal courts regarding agency fees. A number of cases were filed in which teachers who were required to pay a fair share for the union's work on bargaining and implementing the collective bargaining agreement (CBA), sought to have their agency fee refunded to them. For example in *Mooney v. Illinois Education Association*, the federal Central District Court joined the "growing consensus" denying relief to these plaintiffs.[22] Essentially, the court held that the agency fees paid under *Abood* were constitutional at that time and thus retrospective relief based on constitutional conduct should not be available.[23]

The union acted in good faith following the lead of *Abood*.[24] The court noted the "potential that some unions might face an existential threat from lawsuits such as the present one."[25] The unions were not "unjustly enriched" by the agency fee arrangement. The fees that they received covered the costs of representation for nonunion members. The court furthermore cited a 1989 Seventh Circuit Court of Appeals on this point writing:

> [T]he union negotiated on behalf of these employees as it is required by law to do, adjusted grievances for them as it was required by law to do, and incurred expenses in doing these things. . . . The plaintiffs do not propose to give back the benefits that the union's efforts bestowed on them.[26]

In a second case out of Ohio, the plaintiff teacher sought an injunction preventing the union and school board from recognizing the union as her representative on bargainable issues.[27] The plaintiff alleged that the selection of an exclusive representative unconstitutionally compelled association with the union and that it unconstitutionally allowed the union to speak for her on bargainable issues.[28]

The court cited earlier Supreme Court precedent in *Minnesota State Board of Education for Community Colleges v. Knight*[29] to *Janus* finding that "the nonmembers associational freedom was not impaired because the nonmembers were both 'free to form whatever advocacy groups they like' and were 'not required to become members of the union.'"[30] Furthermore, while *Janus* found that an agency fee amounts to unconstitutional subsidization of private speech, an exclusive representative who speaks for members of the bargaining unit does not amount to a violation of free speech rights. Unions are required to provide fair representation for all bargaining unit members; this furthers a compelling state interest, thus unit members' free speech rights are not abridged by an exclusive representative.

At this point the federal courts are not inclined to expand the constitutional rights of nonunion employees. There appears to be a recognition at the lower court level that *Janus* has limits. They seem unwilling to totally unravel the threads that have supported the rights of employees to associate and pursue mutually important conditions of employment.

TEACHERS, THEIR UNIONS, AND POLITICS

Public sector collective bargaining in the second decade of the twenty-first century is characterized by legislative and judicial actions designed to weaken public sector collective bargaining. The decade also turned a glaring spotlight on teachers. While legislative action focused on institutional aspects of unionization, issues of who is teaching our children and are they getting the job done emerged capturing the policy dialogue and debate about how to improve educational outcomes for students. While the evaluation of teachers has long been part of the educational system, the fervor of the twenty-first century reducing teacher effectiveness to a number—a number that tells us all we need to know about this teacher's skills and abilities—swept the nation.

Harvard education professor Susan Moore Johnson writes, "Who teaches matters."[31] While teachers have always stood at the crossroads of education this is an unprecedented time in that policymakers are seeking to hold teachers individually accountable in very public ways for the achievement of students.[32]

If teachers are considered central to education, why during this period, 2010–2019, were they targets with little regard for whether they were competent or not? A *New York Times* headline asked, "Teachers Wonder, Why the Scorn."[33] Teacher unions have faced attacks since their beginning, but many teachers believed that they were personally spared the vitriol because the public valued their work; but now they appear to have a target on their back. "Pathetic," "glorified babysitters," "parasites," and "union thugs" are terms that were written online, on placards, and voiced in commentaries.[34] Writing a year later in 2011, Christine Emmons stated, "The current educational climate seems riddled with blame, especially blame of teachers. Teacher-bashing is very much in favor."[35]

In today's climate, firing teachers takes precedence over issues of rising poverty rates among public school students, students entering school with a limited vocabulary thus impacting language and pre-reading skills, out-of-date textbooks, and underfunded school systems with crumbling infrastructures. Unfortunately many influential leaders in society still believe the mantra, "Those who can do, those who can't teach." And those that can't teach must be identified and rooted out.

The courts, along with governors, legislatures, and special interest groups, including unions and taxpayer associations, Save our Schools,[36] Students Matter,[37] and 50Can,[38] for example, will most likely continue the discussion about how best to organize and deliver an education for the public. The cases cited earlier will likely reenter the court systems. The political arena will continue to focus on public education with varying degrees of intensity. And special interests always pursue their special interests.

Teachers in the late 1800s came together in association in response to the emergence of a public school system prompted by the Common School movement. Two models of association emerged with the establishment of the NEA and AFT. The legislative enactment of public sector bargaining starting in the second half of the twentieth century sharpened the differences between the two; the realities of collective bargaining that recognition revealed and dulled the sharp edges of distinction. With the power of unions and the influence of the CBA on the rhythm of schools and the classroom practices, a retrenchment of labor laws emerged after the publication of *A Nation at Risk: The Imperative for Educational Reform* (1983).[39]

The year 2018, under the *Janus* decision,[40] ushered in a fundamental change in the relationship between the union and the teachers they represent. Unions as an exclusive representative of the "members of the unit" covered by a collective bargaining agreement lost the ability to require nonunion members without the employees' explicit permission to pay a fee to the union for bargaining their wages, benefits, and terms and conditions of employment. A union is required as the exclusive representative to equally enforce the provisions of the contract for the benefit of those who pay for the service and for those who do not (the free-rider concept).

In addition in some states, teachers must reaffirm each year whether they wish to remain as a member of the union. Against this winter of disillusion, teachers in a number of states rose up, left their classrooms and schools and descended on state capitals first in West Virginia, then spreading to Oklahoma, Kentucky, Arizona, and North Carolina—an unprecedented spring of resolution with changing the conditions of public education. These statewide strikes are noteworthy for the fact that they arose in red states with little union support. Their issues were not just the typical personal bread-and-butter issues of salary and benefits.

These teachers raised their united voices demanding a greater investment in public education. They wanted their state to replace outdated and deteriorated textbooks. They spoke for the replacement and maintenance of aging and sometimes dangerous school facilities. They pointed out the need to lower growing class sizes. And they underscored the need to hire more school nurses and counselors. Teachers were "mad as hell, and they weren't going to take it anymore."[41]

By 2010, teachers, their unions, and their tenure were already under assault from coast to coast. The pace soon quickened. "Republican governors and legislatures sounded their trumpets rallying the public against public employees and their unions."[42] The story of labor relations in education after 2010 is explored.

THE BOOK

Teachers and Their Unions: Labor Relations in Uncertain Times focuses on the policies and laws that gave rise to public sector bargaining, the politics that accompany the competition for scarce resources—who gets what?—and the practices of bargaining and managing a contract. The following eight chapters are divided into four sections.

Section 1. Teacher Unions asks such questions as what do unions do and what gave rise to public sector teacher unions. Chapter 2 traces early education in the colonies through the Common School movement, which formed the basis for our current system of public education. It concludes by posing the question, "What do unions do?" Chapter 3 explores the legal framework that structures public sector unions and the duty of fair representation that the union must afford to all members as their exclusive representative. The mid to late 1800s to the advent of public sector collective bargaining based on the National Labor Relations Act (NLRA) is discussed. A sidebar by Jacob A. Bennett applies National Labor Relations Board decisions to the unionization of charter schools. In chapter 4, the consequences of using the private sector NLRA as a template of industrial unionism for public sector bargaining are explored.

The next section, *Transitions: The Impact of Unionization*, reviews how a CBA impacts the relationships between employee and employer (chapter 5). Nathan Fellman provides insight into the transitions from union president to school administrator in his sidebar.

Chapter 6 reviews the conundrum of being a member of a profession and being a member of a union—the issue of whether the organization is called an association or a union underscores this paradox. Teachers want to be seen as members of a profession but may be willing to engage in union activities (strikes, work-to-rule, etc.) to achieve their self-interests or when they perceive threats to their wages, hours, and working conditions.

The next section, *Law and Politics in Uncertain Times: Retrenchment and Assault*, explores the legal and political challenges faced by teachers and their unions focusing primarily on the start of the second decade of the twenty-first century (2010–2016). Specifically, I explore the efforts to starve the beast of unionization (chapter 7), with a focus on the state (Wisconsin) movement against public sector unions that captured the national attention and elevated its governor within the Republican Party and the emergence of RtW. Value-added modeling, as a means of identifying and firing the incompetent, and the teacher strikes of 2018–2019 are discussed.

Professor Joseph J. Onosko and I explore in chapter 8 the question of whether tenure is a boondoggle for the incompetent or a public good providing necessary protection for teachers. It reviews the California *Vergara* decision which found five statutes relating to tenure and seniority unconstitutional, which was later overturned at the appellate level. It also reviews legislation aimed at eliminating or constraining tenure and asks the question whether tenure needs to change.

The last section, *Thoughts on an Uncertain Future*, explores the uncertain future. It asks, where do we go from here? The "we" is not just the teacher unions—it is the public school teachers, the school districts, and the communities that are served by public schools and their educators.

Throughout the book the terms "union" and "management" are used. These are terms that are used in private sector labor relations, neither are perjoratives, they are accepted descriptors of parties n labor relations. The book does not specifically discuss public sector unions that include custodians, clerks, secretaries, bus drivers, or maintenance workers. This does not mean that these unions and the labor relations that characterize those employees are not important—they are important. But the limited space does not allow for an exploration of those specific labor relations (however state law applies equally to these unionized employees). The public sector collective bargain laws that pertain to teachers also pertain to other unions in a school district including administrator unions, which I will not be able to discuss in this volume.

Using *Getting Together*[43] and *Getting to Yes*[44] as conceptual frameworks, my focus is not on just getting a contract. The success of bargaining is not predicated upon signing the contract. Success is determined by whether the labor relations—employee/employer relations—are enhanced and improved, or at a minimum, not harmed.

Bargaining is not a success if one side or the other is angry at the end of bargaining and has a score to settle in the next round. An example is found in Rhode Island in 2017. The teachers in East Greenwich, Rhode Island, voted to approve a contract with the school board. However, immediately following the bilateral approval of the CBA, the union instituted work-to-rule. A union official stated, "We will teach. We will continue to put East Greenwich students and families first, but we will no longer undertake the many extra activities we have historically done."[45] If you can't live with the contract, don't sign it. That goes for both sides of the bargaining table. A contract that ends in anger does not bode well for the "harmonious relations public sector collective bargaining laws envisioned."

Fisher and Brown in *Getting Together* write, "If we don't feel positive after the last transaction, we may dread the next and have more difficulty dealing with it."[46] Collective bargaining that does not solve problems, but rather creates or perpetuates them, cannot be considered successful just because two reluctant or angry parties signed the last page of the contract.

Labor relations can be viewed as a reel of film. One end is blank waiting to be imprinted by the actions of the major players. The other is the history of the working relations of the educators, teachers and administrators, union and management. Consequently, bargaining is not an unconnected event; it is part of the reel of labor relations. The bargaining of a contract is tied to the past, impacts the present, and helps to structure the future.

What happens at the bargaining table, and how the participants treat each other, has consequences for the present and for the future. Administrator trashing and union bashing at the table spill over to the schools and the relations outside of the table. This leaves the public with the perception that the callous and inept are led by the indifferent and incompetent. Public education loses its public in this situation.

This book seeks to help the readers build a knowledge base about unions and collective bargaining, and to provide some practical suggestions about bargaining that leads to improved labor relations between educators. As stated earlier, signing a contract is not the measure of the success of collective bargaining. If the ink has not even dried on the signature page and vows of "just wait until the next round of negotiations" are uttered, the coming success of relations is in serious doubt. The measure of success is whether the relationship in this people-intensive activity of teaching has been strengthened or harmed. The collective bargaining agreement is a guiding paper for action but it is the individuals who give it substance through their relationships.

NOTES

1. Deborah Prokopf, "Public Employees at the School of Hard Knox: How the Supreme Court is Turning Public-Sector Unions Into a History Lesson," *William Mitchell Law Review* 39 (2013): 1370.

2. Jay P. Greene, "Unions and the Public Interest: Is Collective Bargaining Good for Students?" *Education Next* (Winter 2012): 64.

3. Dana Goldstein, *The Teacher Wars: A History of America's Most Embattled Profession* (New York: Doubleday 2014), 1.

4. Terry M. Moe, *Special Interest: Teachers Unions and America's Public Schools* (Washington, DC: Brookings Institution Press 2011), 18.

5. Morgaen L. Donaldson, Anysia P. Mayer, Casey D. Cobb, Kimberly LeChasseur, and Anjale Welton, "New Roles for Teacher Unions? Reform Unionism in School Decentralization," *Journal of Educational Change* 14 (2013): 501–525, 522.

6. In Michigan, a 2013 Sixth Circuit Court of Appeals decision upheld Public Law 53, which prohibits school districts from deducting union dues from teachers' paychecks and sending them to their union. Michigan Radio Newsroom, "Understanding the New Ruling on Teachers' Union Dues," *Michigan Radio* (May 13, 2013). Site visited June 27, 2016, at http://michiganradio.org/post/understanding-n ew-ruling-teachers-union-dues#stream/0.

7. Jonathan Oosting, "Michigan Union Membership Dropped Significantly in 2014, First Full Year Under Right-to-Work Law," *MLive Michigan* (January 23, 2015). Site visited June 27, 2016, at http://www.mlive.com/lansing-news/index.ssf/2 015/01/michigan_union_membership_down.html.

8. Julie Underwood, "The State of Teacher Tenure," *Phil Delta Kappan* (March 26, 2018). Site visited May 1, 2019, at https://www.kappanonline.org/underwood-s tate-teacher-tenure/.

9. N.Y.S. C.L., EDN § 3012(2)(b). Site visited May 30, 2019, at https://codes.f indlaw.com/ny/education-law/edn-sect-3012.html.

10. Underwood, "The State of Teacher Tenure."

11. *Vergara v. State*, No. BC484642, 2014 WL 2598719 (Cal. Super. Ct. L.A. Cty. June 10, 2014).

12. For a discussion of this case, see Todd A. DeMitchell and Joseph J. Onosko, "*Vergara v. State of California*: The End of Teacher Tenure or a Flawed Ruling," *Southern California Interdisciplinary Law Journal* 25 (2016): 589–624.

13. Julie Gutman Dickinson, "Children Last: California Trail Showcases the Corporate War on Teachers and Public Education," *Huffington Post, The Blog* (April 21, 2014). Site visited June 28, 2016, at http://www.huffingtonpost.com/julie-b-gutman/ children-last-california-_b_4809068.html.

14. *Vergara v. State of California*, No. B258589 (Cal. Ct. App., 2d Dist., April 14, 2016). See also Jennifer Medina and Motko Rich, "California Appeals Court Reverses Decision to Overturn Teacher Tenure Rules," *New York Times* (April 14, 2016). Site visited June 28, 2016, at http://www.nytimes.com/2016/04/15/us/californ iaappealscourt-reverses-decision-to-overturn-teacher-tenure-rules.html?smprod=ny tcore-iphone&smid=nytcore-iphone-share&_r=1.

15. Motoko Rich, "Teacher Tenure Is Challenged Again in a Minnesota Lawsuit," *New York Times* (April 13, 2016). Site visited on June 28, 2016, at http://www.nyti mes.com/2016/04/14/us/teacher-tenure-is-challenged-again-in-a-minnesota-lawsuit. html.

16. *Vaca v. Sipes*, 386 U.S. 171, 177 (1967).

17. *Abood v. Detroit Board of Education*, 431 U.S. 209 (1971).

18. One commentator characterizes right-to-work in the following manner:

Under Right-to-Work, employees can opt out and free-ride at any time. And when some do, there are fewer union resources available to file grievances, represent employees, and bargain with employers. This slowly starves the union of their ability to bargain, where unions with fewer resources become less effective and less attractive to existing members, who then opt out. That's the point.

Marc Dixon, "Right-to-Work's Big Moment," *The Hill* (June 15, 2015). Site visited July 2, 2019, at https://thehill.com/blogs/congress-blog/labor/244882-right-to-works-big-moment.

19. *Friederichs v. California Teachers Association*, Petition for a writ of Certiorari to the U.S. Supreme Court (January 26, 2015).

20. *Friedrichs v. California Teachers Association*, 136 S.Ct. 1083, 1083 (2016).

21. *Janus v. American Federation of State, County, and Municipal Employees Council, 31*, 138 S.Ct. 2448 (2018).

22. *Mooney v. Illinois Education Association*, 372 F.Supp. 3d 690, 697 (C.D. Ill. 2019).

23. Ibid., 707.

24. Ibid., "Prudence, equity, and fairness would have counseled the same result absent the good faith defense."

25. Ibid.

26. Ibid., 701, citing *Gilpin v. AFSCME, AFL-CIO*, 875 F.2d 1310, 1316 (7th Cir. 1989).

27. *Thompson v. Marietta Education Association*, 371 F. Supp. 3d 431 (S.D. Ohio 2019).

28. Ibid., 440.

29. *Minnesota State Board of Education for Community Colleges v. Knight*, 465 U.S. 271 (1984).

30. *Thompson, supra* note 27 at 436.

31. Susan Moore Johnson, *Teachers at Work: Achieving Success in Our Schools* (New York: Basic Books, 1990), xiii.

32. Clarin Collins and Audrey Amrein-Beardsley, "Putting Growth and Value-Added Models On the Map: A National Overview," *Teachers College Record* 1 (2014): 116.

33. Trip Gabriel, "Teachers Wonder, Why the Scorn?" *The New York Times* (March 2, 2011). Site visited January 10, 2016, at http://www.nytimes.com/2011/03/03/education/03teacher.html?_r=0.

34. See Sam Dillon, "Teachers' Union Shuns Obama Aides at Convention," *The New York Times* (July 4, 2010): A8 (head of nation's largest teacher union stating today's teachers "face the most anti-educator, anti-union, anti-student environment" ever).

35. Christine Emmons, "No Teacher Is an Island," *Education Week* 44 (April 6, 2011).

36. See "Save Our Schools," at http://saveourschoolsmarch.org/. Site visited July 3, 2016.

37. See http://studentsmatter.org/.

38. See Joy Resmovits, "Michelle Rhee's StudentsFirst will Merge with Education Advocacy Group 50Can," *Los Angeles Times* (March 29, 2016). Site visited July 2, 2016, at http://touch.latimes.com/#section/-1/article/p2p-86372761/.

39. Author, *A Nation at Risk: The Imperative for Educational Reform* (Washington, DC: The National Commission on Excellence in Education, April 1983).

40. *Janus v. American Federation of State, County, and Municipal Employees Council, 31*, 138 S.Ct. 2448 (2018).

41. See Pamela Mahabeer, "'I'm Mad as Hell' Familiar Quotes about the Workplace," *AOL* (March 11, 2011). Site visited August 11, 2019, at https://www.aol.com/2011/03/24/im-mad-as-hell-famous-movie-quotes-about-the-workplace/.

42. Todd A. DeMitchell and Martha Parker-Magagna, "A 'Law too Far?' The Wisconsin Budget Act: Point," *Education Law Reporter* 275 (2012): 1–15, 6.

43. Roger Fisher and Scott Brown, *Getting Together: Building Relationships As We Negotiate* (New York: Penguin Books, 1988).

44. Roger Fisher and William Ury, *Getting to Yes: Negotiating Agreement Without Giving In* (New York: Penguin Books, 1981).

45. Brenda Lasevoli, "Fed-Up Teachers in R.I. Town Say They Will Teach, But No More 'Extras,'" *Education Week's Blogs, Teacher Beat* (June 22, 2017). Site visited July 2, 2017, at http://blogs.edweek.rg/edweek/teacherbeat/2017/fed-up_teachers_n_ri_town_say.html.

46. Fischer and Brown, *Getting Together*, at 8.

Section 1

TEACHER UNIONS

Chapter 2

Teachers, Their Work, and Their Union

I am not saying—and do not think—that teachers unions are solely responsible for the nation's educational problems. I *am* saying that the teachers unions are at the heart of these problems and, therefore, that the unions themselves and the various roles they play in collective bargaining and politics need to be much better studied and understood.[1]

Education Secretary Rod Paige said on February 23, 2004, that the National Education Association, one of the nation's largest labor unions, was like "a terrorist organization" because of the way it was resisting many provisions of a school improvement law (No Child Left Behind) pushed through Congress by President Bush in 2001.[2]

Teachers have a history that influences who they are today, what they do, and how they do it. That history is not just a history of teachers; it is a history of how America sought to develop an educated populace to preserve the republic and its underlying democratic principles. Noted professors of education David Tyack and Larry Cuban write, "Whether they are aware of it or not, all people use history (defined as an interpretation of past events) when they make choices about the present and future."[3] We begin with a brief history of our educational roots so as to assist the review of the present and help to provide a pathway to the future regarding teachers and their unions.

FROM COLONIES TO A REPUBLIC:
A GLIMPSE AT EARLY AMERICAN EDUCATION

Schooling was not a transplanted institution in the early days of the migration of Europeans seeking to colonize North America. The New England colonies of New Hampshire, Connecticut, and Massachusetts (which included Maine) were the crucible for the development of the American system of education.[4] The middle colonies and the colonies of the South largely followed the English model that education was a private matter. The earliest governmental action to install education into the evolving society occurred on April 14, 1642, when the Massachusetts General Court, twelve years after its founding in 1630, passed the Massachusetts Bay School Law (1642).[5]

This law laid the early foundation for a state-supported system of compulsory education. Parents and masters were required to ensure that their children were educated to understand the religious principles and the written laws of the community. The responsibility of an education was placed on parents and masters.

The law required, "[A]ll parents and masters do breed & bring up their children & apprentices in some honest lawful calling, labour or imployment, either in husbandry, or some other trade profitable for themselves, and the Common-wealth."[6] Failure on the part of parents and masters to "fit" them for "higher employments" whereby they become "rude, stubborn & unruly" could result in the children being removed from them.[7] Not quite compulsory schooling but a forerunner for the Common School movement of the early to late nineteenth century.

Five years later, Massachusetts enacted the Old Deluder Act (1647).[8] The 1642 Act required that children receive an education, the 1647 meeting required townships with at least fifty households to "forthwith appoint one within their town to teach all such children as shall resort to him to write and read."[9] The teachers were to be paid by either parents or the students' masters. For townships with 100 families, a grammar school with a master was to be established. Failure to meet the requirement resulted in a fine of five pounds to be paid to the next school that was established.

The beginning of American education that requires children to be educated to support the society—education as a public good—started in the rocky soil of New England. A schoolmaster was required and schools established were paid for by parents and masters. Failure to provide an education resulted in a fine (1647) and removal of the child (1642).

The Massachusetts government used schooling to support the good of the public. It was not just the wealthy and powerful who were being educated, although they went on to Harvard College to assume positions of leadership in the clergy and government; the worth of educated citizens in general was deemed important to the community as a whole. Education of the public to achieve and support the goals of government took root and flourished. But the rise of a public education as a compulsory and state-supported institution had not yet grown from this Puritan beginning.

The concept of an educated populace gained traction with a number of prominent colonists advocating for the public support of schools. For example, Thomas Jefferson wrote *A Bill for the More General Diffusion of Knowledge* in 1779 calling for the public support of education. Literacy, computational skills, and civic literacy were the mainstays of the publically supported schools.

THE COMMON SCHOOL MOVEMENT:
SETTING THE TABLE FOR BARGAINING

The Common School movement that Horace Mann and others sought to implement in the decades following the War of 1812 provides the blueprint in many ways for the public school system that exists in the twenty-first century. Schooling in the early days of the republic was rudimentary, irregularly attended, and received a hodgepodge of support. Most education ended at the elementary school level with few students going on to academies, let alone to college. Education was neither universal nor compulsory.

Great skepticism about a state-supported education through taxation was evident. Many believed that education was a frill and a luxury to be borne by parents who wanted it for their children. Opponents argued that the masses would not benefit from a free public education. Furthermore, they asserted that the "thrifty" should not have to buy schooling for the "shiftless" and those morally and intellectually unfit for an education—mainly the poor.

One New York opponent of free school said that he "'would fill the belly' or 'cover the back' of a pauper, but he would never send him to school."
Ruskin Teeter, *The Opening Up of American Education: A Sampler* (New York: University Press of America, 1983), 59–60.

The schools were considered extensions of the community, unbureaucratic, and lacking a professional core of teachers. There was no oversight and the idea of a publically supported system of education was not universally accepted. Professional preparation was virtually nonexistent. The efforts to professionalize, homogenize, and organize common schooling threatened highly prized local control.

Furthermore, many parents were suspicious of what schools might have their children read. Community members exerted great control over their schools believing that the schools were theirs and not the property of professional teachers.[10]

Yet, while many reformers confronted these restraining social forces, the push for social change moved forward in an inexorable but at a sometimes slow pace. But, there was great hope for the republic and a fiery faith among school reformers "in the power and possibility of education."[11] The republic needed an intelligent and virtuous citizenry, thus public schools were crafted as an instrument of government serving as the lever for government policies, which addressed social, economic, and political problems. The rise of the common school was a response to three major problems facing American society: first, how to preserve the republican values; second, how to rid the urban centers of poverty and crime; and third, how to Americanize the waves of immigrants and the Native Americans.[12]

THE COMMON SCHOOL MOVEMENT RESPONSE TO EMERGING SOCIAL ISSUES: USING EDUCATION AS A LEVER FOR GOVERNMENT POLICY TO ADDRESS SOCIAL, ECONOMIC, AND POLITICAL ISSUES.

- *Provide a common educational experience for all students.*
  - *Educate students from different social backgrounds together.*
  - *Teach a common body of knowledge.*
- *State must provide clear-cut, stable financial support for public education.*
- *Education must be controlled by the state.*
  - *It was believed that education was too important to be left to the devices of parents and local communities.*
  - *"One might trust parental instinct to educate an individual child, but the state required homogeneity; the right of preservation of the body politic took precedence over all other rights." David B. Tyack,* The One Best System: A History of American Urban Education *(Cambridge, MA: Harvard University Press, 1974), 75.*
- *Professionalize teaching.*
  - *This was the linchpin of their modern system of public education.*
  - *Rise of normal schools for the training of elementary school teachers.*
- *Use education to fight poverty and crime.*
- *Americanize the immigrants and the Native Americans.*

The rise of the common school with its compulsory education brought more students into the educational system, thus adding more teachers to the male dominated workforce of the time—this would soon change. Concomitantly, the pressure to professionalize the teaching workforce impacted who taught. There were no widely available and recognized professional training programs; teaching did not have an evolving body of knowledge nor standards of practice and was, thus, adrift without these compass points to guide action.

Teachers in large part were transitory and did not identify with the profession of teaching. In too many cases, teaching was a way station for the more educated and ambitious male schoolmasters, who saw the classroom as the stepping-stone to their "real" careers in law or the church.[13] There was no profession of educators.

Both of these streams, the need for more teachers and the need to properly prepare them for the realities of the classroom, combined and had an impact on the rise of teacher unions. First, the need for more teachers brought women into the schools, which had previously been dominated by men. Women had few occupational options. Teaching became an avenue for semi-independence for women; it was a chance to earn a wage, and the opportunity to gain a sense of purpose outside the home. School boards seized the opportunity that an increased labor force of teachers was needed to educate all children in common, and they found the cheapest labor source available—women.

> God seems to have made women peculiarly suited to guide and develop the infant mind, and it seems . . . very poor policy to pay a man 20 or 22 dollars a month, for teaching children ABCs, when a female could do the work more successfully at one third the price.
> Littleton School Committee, Littleton, Massachusetts, 1849
> Public Broadcasting System, *Only a Teacher: Teaching Timeline* (n.d.). Site visited June 11, 2016, at http://www.pbs.org/onlyateacher/timeline .html.

Where moral superiority and nurturing of students were not valued in teachers during colonial times, they suddenly became prized attributes.[14] This coincided with the rise of the cult of domesticity in which women were cast in roles of the guardians of virtue. Teaching was an avenue in which women could work outside the home "while still being examples of purity and nurturance."[15] At the same time the push for universal schooling required more teachers for the increased number of students. By the 1850s the feminization of teaching had taken hold, especially in urban areas. "The image of the stern yet loving, young, single female schoolteacher was in place by the end of the 1800s."[16]

Women entered the teaching ranks in large numbers. Their numbers gave weight to the rise of unionization toward the end of the century through an alliance with blue-collar organized labor. Many of the early female teachers had not progressed much beyond their grammar school education and were, thus, unprepared for the challenges of teaching and instilling discipline. As a result, normal schools dedicated to preparing teachers soon arose. These schools sought to provide a "norm" for all teachers. Female teachers flocked to these normal schools, thus aiding to the eventual demise of the normal school and their incorporation into state colleges and universities.

At the turn of the twentieth century, compulsory education brought women into teaching. Their numbers and desire to learn helped to move the professional preparation of normal schools to the regular, typically state-supported colleges and universities. Inequalities between male teachers and female teachers became apparent. Organizing and political pressure, the arrows in the quiver of unions, were soon loosed in education.

Susan B. Anthony, in the summer of 1853, called for equal pay, professional recognition, and access to professional preparation at prestigious institutions, and deeper involvement of women in the union. Her speech prompted a resolution at the annual New York State Teachers' Association commitment "to remove the existing evil" of wage inequality.[17]

The role of women in education affected the development of the schools and the establishment of the role model status of teaching. Furthermore, "The earliest efforts by teachers to unionize in the late nineteenth century consciously embraced feminism and powerfully connected salaries and pensions for female teachers to tax collection and municipal budgets in cities like Chicago."[18] The stage was set for the emergence of teacher unions.

EDUCATION: A PEOPLE-INTENSIVE ENTERPRISE

Schooling is a social experience. A teacher's workspace is unique as is the work setting. It is far removed from the routinized, and in some cases robot dominated, factory floor and the workspace of other adults. Teachers have a large degree of autonomy within the confines of their classroom walls and primarily work with children. They are both isolated and protected from other educators and outside influences. Their work is delivered in an intensely personal environment. While teachers do not create the physical space, they are largely responsible for the creation of the environment in which instruction is delivered and learning takes place.

In fact, this is a recognized part of the teacher's professional responsibilities, the creation and maintenance of their classroom environment. The linchpin of our system of education is the teacher in his or her classroom exercising a large amount of discretion as to how that classroom is run and how knowledge is imparted and skills taught. In effect, teachers are decision makers and not just decision implementers.[19]

Teachers stand at the core of schooling. From this simple beginning the labor relations that take place in public schools are structured by the delivery system of labor, which is intensely personal. Students refer to "my" teacher and teachers discuss their class in terms of their students. It is within this personal setting where teachers are largely separated from other adults, and they, to borrow from Hiam Ginott, "create the weather"[20] in their classrooms in which their collectively bargained agreement plays out.

Susan Moore Johnson in her early study of teacher unions writes:

> It is individuals who strike bargains, make concessions, interpret language, advise strategies, and act on the basis of what they think others will do. Typically, personalities predominate over roles, rules and rituals. Collective bargaining is a people-centered process, just as schools are people-centered places.[21]

LABOR RELATIONS IN EDUCATION

The history of teacher unionism is rich, vibrant, and filled with numerous triumphs, tensions, and setbacks. For over a century, most education employees have been part of a public sector workforce that has been constrained by legal frameworks that assume that are not entitled to the same rights as private sector workers. Because they comprise the largest segment of public sector labor, the story of why and how teachers sought to organize helps us to understand many current debates surrounding education policies and the labor movement.

Adam Mertz, "A Century of Teacher Organizing: What Can We Learn?" *The Labor and Working Class History Association* (n.d.). Site visited June 10, 2016, at http://lawcha.org/wordpress/century-teaching-organizing/.

The term "labor relations" for many invoke an image of factory assembly lines, coalmines, longshoreman, and truckers. This is on the mark because the roots of the term "labor relations" are found in the relationship between unions and employers, and the early relations between employer and worker focused on these industrial work settings. Industrial relations systems consist of rules that govern work, the worker, and the workplace.[22]

Cresswell and Murphy consider labor relations as complex, because the "defining of employee-employer relations is continuous."[23] The relationship is always in process being formed and reformed building on the past by both parties—a reel of film being projected with the past connected to the projection and blank film to yet be recorded upon.

There are three classes of actors in industrial relations: the managers/administrators, the representatives who speak for labor (the union), and the third parties who establish and regulate the system (National Labor Relations Board for private sector and at the state level, for example, the Public Labor Relations Board in New Hampshire and the Public Employee Relations Board in California for public sector bargaining).[24] Individuals who work in the field of labor relations negotiate contracts, including compensation rates, benefits, working conditions, and rates of advancement, between workers and managers and manage those contracts.

Labor relations work is not just confined to the traditional private sector union workplace of the factory floor or the mine. Starting in the latter half of the twentieth century many public employees joined their unionized brethren who had made great strides in organizing starting in the 1960s. A boost was given to public employees when President John F. Kennedy signed Executive Order 10988 allowing federal public employees to bargain. Only Wisconsin had allowed its public employees to bargain when President Kennedy signed the order in 1962.[25] Public education became one of those unionized public work settings.

Another key event in the development of collective bargaining in public education was the New York teachers' strike of April 11, 1962, in which more than half of the teachers walked the picket line. Kerchner and Mitchell consider the outcome of the strike as causing "a permanent change in the relationship between teachers and their school district employers."[26] A profession used the hardball tactics of the industrial union to further the self-interests of its members. Teachers came together, took a stand, and changed the educational landscape.

Education today is a heavily unionized workforce, possibly the most heavily unionized in the nation. Consequently, "[t]eacher unions are major participants in American educational practice."[27] They have played a major role in the last half-century influencing policy and practice.[28]

The National Education Association (NEA), the nation's largest teachers union and the nation's largest union, has about 3 million members working in preschool settings to higher education.[29] The American Federation of Teachers (AFT), the second largest teachers union, has about 1 million members in 3,000 local chapters and is an affiliated international union of the AFL-CIO.[30] Rural, suburban, and urban schools have unionized faculty. Recently, a unionized faculty is arising in charter schools; a reform predicated upon reducing the hold of legal mechanisms including collective bargaining agreements.[31]

The NEA and AFT grew from different traditions, which initially shaped their approach to unionization and collective bargaining. In its early years, NEA was considered a professional organization and was not dominated by classroom teachers. Rather its leadership tended to be superintendents, college presidents, and college professors. In contrast, AFT, from its inception, has seen itself as a teachers' union. "It was organized by teachers, the membership was composed of teachers, and most important, the leadership came from classroom teachers."[32]

The focus of the AFT on the emerging collective bargaining rights of teachers in the 1960s forced NEA to shift its focus more strongly toward teachers' bread-and-butter interests. Today, differences between the nation's two largest unions have faded, and both AFT and NEA now clearly see themselves as advocates and representatives of classroom teachers. However, their convergence of goals does not obscure the fact that not all teachers are ardent supporters of the unionization of the profession.[33]

Some have argued that the NEA despite its early roots and the AFT because of its early roots, have embraced the tradition of the factory floor and the inferno like steel mills giving teachers the feel of the classic blue-collar worker "where winning workers big checks for the shortest possible hours has been the aim and quality of product is considered management's worry."[34] But, many teachers believe that their unions protect their interests. In a 2016 nationwide survey responding teachers, 76 percent believe that unions have a generally positive effect on education.[35]

In recent years, both major teachers unions have become powerful participants in the nation's educational policy debates where they make their voices heard regarding the interests of teachers and teachers' views about educational practice. They have a powerful voice in debates over educational policy and practice.

In some cases, the power of the union becomes part of the election in which one party candidate seeks their endorsement and another decries their endorsement and involvement in public affairs. Wirt and Kirst assert that no other group has had "increased influence on education policy in recent decades as much as have teachers. The timid rabbits of 30 years ago are today's ravening tigers in the jungle of school systems."[36]

For example, the general election in 2008 saw "teachers' unions around the country [shift] into high gear in the countdown to the presidential election."[37] Candidates often court individual teachers by separating them from their union; a common refrain is, "I support teachers, my concern is with the union which is hurting education." This occurs in public elections at the national, state, and local levels. Hess and Leal found that unions were the leading interest group in school board politics.[38]

Separating teachers from their union on the political stage also occurs over legislation. For example, the governor of Michigan was pushing for educational reform that impacted the union and its policy positions on education. The governor drew a distinction between teachers and their union. A member of the state board of education explained the strategy as avoiding the charge of teacher bashing and casting the political tensions as a struggle over power with the union concerned with promoting its political and economic power.[39] Attacking teachers as a profession has historically been a losing political strategy (but it may have changed since Wisconsin Governor Walker in 2011 sought to make the public sector unions irrelevant[40]), while portraying the union as protecting the status quo in the face of needed change often gains political capital for the politician with her/his constituents.

At the time that unions gained influence over public education, especially through collective bargaining, the education reform movement was growing and intensifying. Questions arise with regard to whether teachers unions can be effective promoters of educational reform while maintaining their traditional role as assertive advocates on the bread-and-butter issues important to their members.

Most school reforms implicate matters subject to bargaining, thus they must pass through the bargaining table. Commentators have characterized the relationship of bargaining differently. For example, Kerchner and Koppich assert that collective bargaining has evolved "as a principal tool to move districts and unions down a joint path of educational reform."[41] While other education labor relation commentators have asserted the collective bargaining has "held reform hostage."[42] DeMitchell and Carroll found in their 1999 five state exploratory study of superintendent perceptions of school reform and bargaining found that educational reform was on the bargaining table and could be bargained for, "but not necessarily with ease or with a strong sense of security that the reform will have an opportunity to work before it is watered down or eliminated in a new round of collective bargaining."[43] However, they also found that in a number of situations the bargaining table provided a venue for intense and quality dialogue about the reform.

The influence of unions and collective bargaining on the operations of school districts is demonstrated in a front-page, above-the-fold article in the *Boston Globe*, which reads, "City braces for a one-day school strike."[44] The newspaper provided a guide for parents in the event of a school strike. And, in Miami-Dade County, Florida, the United Teachers of Dade, an affiliate of the AFT, crafted an "unlikely" partnership with the private education firm Edison Schools Inc. to build and manage ten charter schools.[45] Unions, particularly teacher unions, exert influence over public education, which is an understudied topic of research.

Since collective bargaining affects the terms and conditions of employment—the work of teachers—what is bargained and how it is bargained is important. What happens at the bargaining table, how the participants treat each other, has consequences for the present and for the future of the schools and the educators who work in those schools.

Todd A. DeMitchell, *Educators at the Bargaining Table: Successfully Negotiating a Contract That Works for All* (Lanham, MD: Rowman & Littlefield 2018), 2.

Because of the influential role that unions play and the major activity of a union in collective bargaining, labor relations in education is an important part of a school leader's role. A majority of the states have public sector collective bargaining laws. Therefore, understanding unions and their work is important for effective school stewardship and union leadership. Knowledge of the dimensions of a contract, how to bargain it, and how to manage it enable educational leaders to lead and improve their organizations, schools and unions.

Negotiating the contract is a major part of labor relations. The other major part is managing the contract. While specialists, sometimes hired guns from the outside, are often tasked with negotiating the contract, all administrators in the school district are responsible for managing the contract. Labor relations are part of the larger human resource function. Young and Castetter write that the goals of human resources are to "attract, select, induct, develop, retain, and motivate personnel to achieve the system's mission; maximize career opportunities for employees; and coordinate organizational and individual objectives."[46] Negotiating and managing a contract impacts these human resource goals—quality labor relations attract and retain employees.

Almost sixty years of bargaining in the schools, and the rise of the two major teacher unions and their role as major policy actors, underscore the need for understanding labor relations in education. The following section will explore the work of unions and collective bargaining. But, first we begin with the role of people in education because it is unlike many industrial union workplaces in which technology is an extension of the worker. Education is work delivered individual-to-individual even in a virtual school.

WHAT DO UNIONS DO?

At the most fundamental level, collective bargaining pits teachers' demands for improved wages, hours, and conditions of employment against school boards' efforts to retain authority over educational policies and school operations.

Martha M. McCarthy, Nelda Cambron-McCabe, & Suzanne E. Eckes, *Public School Law: Teachers' and Students' Rights* (Boston: Pearson, 2014), 389.

What are unions? The National Labor Relations Act defines a labor organization as an entity in which "employees participate and which exists for the purpose, in whole or in part, of dealing with employers concerning grievances, labor disputes, wages, rates of pay, hours of employment, or conditions of work."[47] According to Tannenbaum, "unions are organizations designed to protect and enhance the social and economic welfare of their members."[48] A union is "a continuous association of wage earners for the purpose of maintaining or improving the conditions of their working lives."[49] Lieberman asserts that a union "exists in whole or in part to represent employees to their employers on their terms and conditions of employment."[50]

Unlike many unions throughout the world, American unionism has perceived its major task as the defense of their members' interests. This is in sharp contrast with unions in other countries, "many of which see themselves as defenders of the interests of the working class as a whole."[51] American unions focus on "bread-and-butter" issues, wages and benefits (business unionism), as opposed to viewing unionism as a vehicle for society-wide transformations that extend beyond the workplace.

McDonnell and Pascal posit that unions operate as political interest groups working to obtain benefits from the exterior environment. They have characterized the role of unions in the following manner: First, they operate as political interest groups, working to obtain benefits from the external environment. And, second they also function as voluntary organizations that must meet members' demands in the type and level of benefits they obtain and the services they provide. The challenge for the unions is to obtain sufficient benefits to maintain their membership, while also operating effectively in a world of political bargaining and compromise.[52]

Unions exist to represent the interests of the employees in the bargaining unit mainly through bargaining and implementing an enforceable employment contract. Bivens et al. assert, "'Collective bargaining' is how working people gain a voice at work and the power to shape their working lives."[53] Various state legislatures (for public employees) and the U.S. Congress (for private employees) found this to be legitimate through their passage of state and federal collective bargaining laws. These interests are wages, benefits, and terms and conditions of employment. These interests are pursued at the bargaining table and are bilaterally agreed upon with the representatives of government, which in education is the public school board.

In 1990, NEA's newly installed president stated, "As a union, we have to be in the forefront of the kinds of funding that are needed at the federal, state, and local levels."[54] Unions lobby and try to exert influence on political bodies to gain desired benefits or thwart perceived undesirable consequences to their institutional goals. In many ways they are just like other external educational special interest groups, such as school board associations, taxpayer watchdog groups, and fundamental Christian organizations that vie to have their ideas influence the public agenda. Thus, the union's voice is part of the cacophony of voices struggling to be heard by lawmakers. However, unions are also inside players (its membership are employees) as well as outside players in the school district's policy arena.

Teacher unions as political interest groups are visibile upon the national, regional, and local stages. They have an influential role as seen by the political candidates at all levels who either court their support or use the teacher unions as the whipping boy for the challenges public education faces and the failures it and its students have suffered. Education is an important activity, if not one of the most important activities, of the government.[55] The struggle over control over its curriculum and goals has long characterized America's system of public education.

Elections provide an opportunity for teacher unions and other interest groups to influence curriculum, assessment, and accountability. In the 2008 general election the federal, systems changing legislation No Child Left Behind (NCLB) became part of the policy debate. The NEA, highly critical of the federal law, at the national and state level backed candidates who held a similar position.[56] While the NEA tended to back Democrats who were critical of NCLB it also backed Republicans who supported other union positions such as teacher accountability through merit pay.[57]

As an organization, unions sell a service to specific groups of employees. Since unions can and must compete for membership, this is especially true in education, they must be able to demonstrate that its members receive a value for the dues they pay for the union to represent them. A major activity of unions is bargaining with management over the wages, benefits, terms, and conditions of employment and then managing the contract for consistent, uniform compliance across the school district. Their traditional duty is to meet members' demands in the type and level of benefits sought from the employer.

Potential consumers of union service judge the value received by what is secured through bargaining and other activities, which enhance the security and economic well-being of the employee. Essentially, unions try to get better wages, benefits, and working conditions for its members than they could get on their own. Unions speak for the employee to the employer on those three items. In addition, the union represents the employee's interests and rights regarding job security whether it involves discipline, layoffs, or dismissal. In fact, in most schools that have a collective bargaining agreement, a teacher has the right to have a union representative present in meeting with the school administrators in which discipline is a likely outcome.

Teachers join a union in order to secure more tangible benefits than they would without the union. If the union cannot secure an appropriate increase in wages, health care insurance, sick leave benefits, and other such benefits, why should the teacher pay money to join? The union must provide a service that the teachers believe they could not gain on their own. The union must deliver on bread-and-butter issues as well as providing job security. Otherwise, the union is nothing more than a social club, nice to join for the camaraderie and professional stimulation but not essential for the economic survival of its members.

At their core, unions pursue the self-interests of their members through collective action, primarily at the bargaining table. They provide or sell a service to the members of the bargaining unit through their dues, or a fee for nonmembers (however, see the discussion on the Janus decision in Chapter 7). They are spokespersons and advocates for those whom they represent. School districts speak for the students and the community and the union speaks for its employees at the bargaining table. Both parties, the union and the school board, represent their constituency, with neither party representing the legitimate interests of the other.

Once a union has been elected by a majority of the members who will form the bargaining unit with their community of interest in skills, duties, and working conditions,[58] the union becomes their exclusive representative. Only that union can speak for the members of the bargaining unit on issues germane to collective bargaining, which may be different from individual union members' views. Membership in the union is not required in order to be covered by the CBA. In fact, it is against the law to require that an employee, including teachers, to join a union.

The union and the school board sign a contract that has been negotiated. Because the union is the exclusive voice representing teachers', resolutions of grievances, overall enforcement of the contract, and any changes to the contract are done by the union. Individual teachers gave up their right to bargain for themselves over their wages, benefits, and terms and conditions of employment once an exclusive union representative was elected. In many ways, prior to collective bargaining management spoke for individual teachers. With collective bargaining the union speaks for individual teachers and the collective of teachers. However, teachers influence their union through the elections of union officers as well as through decertification rights in which the union can be replaced.

There is a trade-off for a union winning an election to be the exclusive representative of a recognized unit of employees. The union accepts the legal duty of fair representation of its members for the right to represent those members.[59] This duty is not confined to union members but extends to all members of the bargaining unit the union represents. Even though this duty is not always explicitly stated in statute, the courts have enforced it.[60]

The Supreme Court in *Steele v. Louisville & Nashville R.R.* (1944) first recognized the duty of fair representation when the union engaged in racial discrimination against Negro locomotive fireman.[61] However, this duty does not compel the union to agree to all requests made by a member of the union. For example, in *Vaca v. Sipes*, the Supreme Court decided whether an employee/union member could force the union to pursue a grievance to arbitration when the union believed it would be fruitless.[62] The Court upheld the union's decision not to arbitrate the grievance.

The Supreme Court in *Vaca* found that in exchange for surrendering individual rights and interests to the exclusive union representative the union accepts a duty of fair representation. This duty does not invest the member with veto rights over the union. It does, however, obligate the union to "serve the interests of all members without hostility or discrimination toward any, to exercise its discretion with complete good faith and honesty, and to avoid arbitrary conduct."[63]

As a practical matter, unions are rarely able to negotiate agreements that completely satisfy the desires of all members.
Bowerman v. UAW Local 12, 646 F.3d 360, 369 (6th Cir. 2011)

Inevitably differences arise in the manner and degree to which the terms of any negotiated agreement affect individual employees and classes of employees. The mere existence of such differences does not make them invalid.
Ford Motor Co. v. Huffman, 345 U.S. 330, 338 (1953)

In recent years, both major teachers unions have become powerful participants in the nation's educational policy debates, where they make their voices heard regarding the interests of teachers and teachers' views about educational practice. School leaders face the challenge of learning how to work effectively in a unionized environment in which teacher rights are codified in an enforceable contract. Teachers face the challenge of understanding how the contract affects their daily work. Union representatives face the challenge of shoring up support among their teachers for the work of the union:[64] "teachers may not see unions and collective bargaining as being related to activities that are at the core of teaching."[65] However, it is a foolish administrator who assumes that teachers will not publicly support their union. Horizontal pressure is powerful, at least as powerful as vertical pressure in many situations. A 2018 survey sample of 1,000 teachers found that 94 percent of unionized teachers and 74 percent of nonunionized teachers believe that teacher unions are absolutely essential or important but not essential.[66] Eighty-five percent of the total respondents strongly agree or agree with the statement that "without a union, teachers would be vulnerable to school politics or administrators who abuse their power."[67] A clear majority of the responding teachers want a union.

Diane Ravitch asserts that unions provide necessary protection against heavy-handed and arbitrary exercise of power by school administrators. Similar to the checks and balances between the three branches of government, society also needs a check and balance on our educational system. She writes that unions not only protect the rights of teachers but also "sound the alarm against unwise policies."[68] Essentially she asserts that teacher unions are a private benefit for the educators it represents, and it is public good, standing up to the power of public schools through its recognized representative voice of professional educators.

NOTES

1. Terry M. Moe, *Special Interest: Teachers Unions and America's Public Schools* (Washington, DC: Brookings Institution Press, 2011), 5–6 (emphasis in original).

2. Robert Pear, "Education Chief Calls Union 'Terrorist' Then Recants," *The New York Times* (February 25, 2004). Site visited July 9, 2017, at http://www.nyti mes.com/2004/02/24/us/education-chief-calls-union-terrorist-then-recants.html?_r =0. The secretary later apologized for his "poor choice of words." Ibid., No Child Left Behind (NCLB) was not renewed in 2007 when it was scheduled for rewriting. President Obama signed the replacement legislation, Every Student Succeeds Act in 2015. "The legislation eliminates the federal mandate[, NCLB,] that teacher evaluations be tied to student performance on statewide tests. Teachers' unions hated that idea, saying the high stakes associated with the tests were creating a culture of over-testing and detracting from the learning environment." Jennifer C. Kerr, "Obama Signs Education Law to Replace No Child Left Behind," *Boston Globe* (December 10, 2015). Site visited July 9, 2017, at https://www.bostonglobe.com/news/nation/2015/12/10/ obama-signs-education-law-replace-child-left-behind/zxpKsEZSfOF92M4qkDpfBN /story.html.

3. David Tyack and Larry Cuban, *Tinkering Toward Utopia: A Century of Public School Reform* (Cambridge, MA: Harvard University Press, 1995), 6.

4. Alan C. Ornstein and Daniel U. Levine, *Foundations of Education* (Boston: Houghton Mifflin Company, 2008), 123.

5. Author, "Massachusetts Bay School Law (1642)," *Constitution Society*. Site visited July 17, 2017, at http://www.constitution.org/primarysources/schoollaw164 2.html.

6. Ibid.

7. Ibid., As a consequence of "negligence" the "boyes" would be removed until they reached the age of twenty-one and girls until age eighteen and placed them with new masters. Ibid.

8. *Old Deluder Act (1647). Constitution Society*. Site visited July 18, 2017, at http://www.constitution.org/primarysources/deluder.html. The Act begins: "It being on chief project of that old deluder, Satan, to keep men from knowledge of the Scriptures. . . ." Ibid.

9. Ibid.

10. David B. Tyack, *The One Best System: A History of American Urban Education* (Cambridge, MA: Harvard University Press, 1974).

11. Lawrence A. Cremin, *American Education: The National Experience 1783–1876* (New York: Harper & Row Publishers, 1980), 5.

12. Todd A. DeMitchell, "Educating America: the Nineteenth-Century Common School Promise in the Twentieth Century, A Personal Essay," *International Journal of Educational Reform* 9 (2000): 79–88, 81.

13. Public Broadcasting System. *Only a Teacher: Teaching Timeline* (n.d.). Site visited June 11, 2016, available at http://www.pbs.org/onlyateacher/timeline.html. For example, Herman Melville taught during the winter in a remote and rural part of Massachusetts. He had thirty students of all ages crammed into a one-room schoolhouse with no supplies and tiny windows. He earned $11 a month, about the same salary as a farm laborer and boarded with a local family. Dana Goldstein, *The Teacher Wars: A History of America's Most Embattled Profession* (New York: Doubleday, 2014), 21.

14. Goldstein, *The Teacher Wars*, at 4, writing, "The nineteenth-century common school reformers depicted male teachers—90 percent of the classroom workforce in 1800—as sadistic, lash-wielding drunks, who ought to be replaced by kinder, purer (and cheaper) women."

15. Elizabeth Boyle, *Kempf Prize: The Feminization of Teaching in America.* MIT Program in Women's and Gender Studies (n.d.). Site visited July 18, 2017, at https://stuff.mit.edu/afs/athena.mit.edu/org/w/wgs/prize/eb04.html.

16. Boyle, *Kempf Prize*.

17. Goldstein, *The Teacher Wars,* at 36–37. *See also*, HistoryNet, *Susan B. Anthony*. Site visited June 12, 2016, at http://www.historynet.com/susan-b-anthony.

18. Jon Shelton, *Teacher Strike!: Public Education and the Making of a New American Public Order* (Urbana: University of Illinois, 2017), 18.

19. Samuel B. Bacharach, Joseph B. Shedd, and Sharon C. Conley, "School Management and Teacher Unions," *Teachers College Record* 91 (1989): 97–114, 101.

20. Hiam G. Ginott, *Teacher and Child: A Book for Parents & Teachers* (New York: Avon, 1972).

> I am the decisive element in the classroom. It is my personal approach that creates the climate. It is my daily mood that makes the weather. As a teacher I possess tremendous power to make a child's life miserable or joyous. I can be a tool of torture or an instrument of inspiration. I can humiliate or humor, hurt or heal. In all situations it is my response that decides whether a crisis will be escalated or de-escalated, and a child humanized or de-humanized. xii

21. Susan Moore Johnson, *Teachers Unions in Schools* (Philadelphia: Temple University Press, 1984), 167–168.

22. Charles J. Coleman, *Managing Labor Relations in the Public Sector* (San Francisco: Jossey-Bass Publishers, 1990), 15.

23. Anthony M. Cresswell and Michael J. Murphy, *Teachers, Unions, and Collective Bargaining in Public Education* (Berkeley, CA: McCutchan Publishing Corporation, 1980), 385.

24. Coleman, *Managing Labor Relations in the Public Sector*.

25. Carol Wright and David E. Gundersen, "Unions and Teachers: Differences in the State of the Nation," *Journal of Employment and Labor Law* 10 (2004): 1–12, 2.

Site visited August 16, 2008, at http://homepages.ius.edu/LCHRISTI/Journal%20o f%20emply/Teacher%20Unions-Gundersen.pdf.

26. Charles Taylor Kerchner and Douglas Mitchell, *The Changing Idea of a Teachers' Union* (New York: Falmer Press, 1988), 1–2.

27. Nina Bascia, *Unions in Teachers' Professional Lives: Social, Intellectual, and Practical* (New York: Teachers College Press, 1994), 1.

28. Guodong Liang, Ying Zhang, Haing Huang, and Zhaogang Qiao, "Teacher Incentive Pay Programs in the United States: Union Influence and District Characteristics," *International Journal of Education Policy & Leadership* 10(3) (2015): 4.

29. National Education Association. Site visited April 28, 2019, at https://ww w.nea.org/home/2580.htm?cpssessionid=SID-E2E8C039-B80517AA.

30. American Federation of Teachers. Site visited April 28, 2019, available at https://www.aft.org/about.

31. Stephen Sawchuck, "Unions Set Sights on High-Profile Charter-Network School," *Education Week* 1 (June 10, 2009): 14–15. Randi Weingarten, President of the AFT, argued "unionization is a necessity for charter schools' sustained success, once initial enthusiasm wanes and the hard work of educating students sets in." 14.

32. William A. Streshly and Todd A. DeMitchell, *Teacher Unions and TQE: Building Quality Labor Relations* (Thousand Oaks, CA: Corwin Press, Inc., 1994), 9.

33. Jeanne Ponessa, "Alternative Teachers' Groups Highlighted," *Education Week* (February 12, 1997): 36. A low-profile, but apparently growing, population of teachers who have declined membership in the country's two major teachers' unions have instead joined local teacher associations such as the Association of American Educators." Ibid.

34. Thomas Toch, "Why Teachers Don't Teach," *U.S. News & World Report* (February 26, 1996): 62–71, 64.

35. Michael B. Henderson, Martin R. West, Paul E. Peterson, and Samuel Barrows, "Ten-Year Trends in Public Opinion From the EdNext Poll," *EducationNext* (Winter 2017). Site visited July 4, 2017, at http://educationnext.org/ten-year-trends -in-public-opinion-from-ednext-poll-2016-survey/. This is an increase from 64% in 2013.

36. Frederick M. Wirt and Michael W. Kirst, *The Political Dynamics of American Education* (Berkeley, CA: McCuthchan, 1997), 181.

37. Vaishali Honawar, "Unions Battle For Democrats In Swing States," *Education Week* 1 (October 29, 2008): 14–15, 1. "By early October [2008], officials said the NEA and its affiliates had distributed more than 4.2 million pieces of mail, made more than 2.1 million phone calls, and sent more than 1.3 million emails to members in battleground states about the Nov. 4 presidential election." 14.

38. Frederick M. Hess and David L. Leal, "School House Politics: Expenditures, Interests, and Competition in School Board Elections," in *Beseiged: School Boards and the Future of Education Politics*, ed. William Howell (Washington, DC: Brookings Institution Press, 2005), 228–253.

39. William Lowe Boyd, David N. Plank, and Gary Sykes, "Teacher Unions in Hard Times," in *Conflicting Missions? Teacher Unions and Educational Reform*, ed. Tom Loveless (Washington, DC: Brookings Institution Press, 2000), 174–210, 181.

40. See Todd A. DeMitchell and Martha Parker-Magagna, "'A Law Too Far?' The Wisconsin Budget Repair Act: Point," *Education Law Reporter* 275 (2012): 1–15, 6–7.

41. Julie E. Koppich and Charles T. Kerchner, "Negotiating Reform: Preliminary Findings," in *Reforming Education: The Emerging Systemic Approach*, ed. Stephen L. Jacobson and Robert Berne (Thousand Oaks, CA: Corwin Press, Inc., 1993), 88.

42. Myron Lieberman, *The Teachers Unions: How the NEA and AFT Sabotage Reform and Hold Students, Parents, Teachers, and Taxpayers Hostage to Bureaucracy* (New York: Free Press, 1997).

43. Todd A. DeMitchell and Thomas Carroll, "Educational Reform On the Bargaining Table: Impact, Security, and Tradeoffs," *Education Law Reporter* 134 (1999): 675–693, 691.

44. Matt Viser, "City Braces For a One-Day School Strike," *Boston Globe* (February 13, 2007): A1–A7.

45. Mark Walsh, "Miami-Dade Teachers' Union Partners With Edison on Charter Plan," *Education Week* (September 20, 2000): 5.

46. I. Phillip Young and William B. Castetter, *The Human Resource Function in Educational Administration* (8th Ed.) (Upper Saddle River, NJ: Pearson, 2004), 4.

47. U.S. Code Title 29, Chapter 7, Subchapter II, Section 152: "National Labor Relations—Definitions." Site visited July 4, 2016, at http://www.law.cornell.edu/usc ode/text/29/152.

48. Arnold S. Tannenbaum, "Unions," in *Handbook of Organizations*, ed. James G. March (Chicago: Rand McNally and Co., 1965), 705–734, 705.

49. Sidney Webb and Beatrice Webb, *The History of Trade Unionism* (2nd ed.) (New York: Longmans, Green and Company, 1986), 1. Site visited February 19, 2008, at http://books.google.com/books?id=roAZAAAAMAAJ&dq=%22history+ of+trade+unionism%22&pg=PP1&ots=OsRvhvIr2l&sig=U94tPbgqs8XDiLOqKW iyLDEJej4&hl=en&prev=http://www.google.com/search?client=safari&rls=en-us&q =%22History+of+Trade+Unionism%22&ie=UTF-8&oe=UTF-8&sa=X&oi=print& ct=title&cad=one-book-with-thumbnail#PPR3,M1.

50. Myron Lieberman, *The Teacher Unions: How the NEA and the AFT Sabotage Reform and Hold Students, Parents, and Taxpayers Hostage to Bureaucracy* (New York: Free Press, 1997), 9.

51. Micah Uetricht, *Strike for America: Chicago Teachers Against Austerity* (London, UK: Verso, 2014), 110.

52. Lorraine M. McDonnell and Anthony Pascal, *Teacher Unions and Educational Reform* (Santa Monica, CA: RAND, 1988), VII.

53. Bivens, et al., "How Today's Unions Help Working People," *Economic Policy Institute* 1 (August 24, 2017): 1. Site visited January 14, 2018, at http://www.epi. org/files/pdf/133275.pdf. Citing to Article 23 of the Universal Declaration of Human Rights, note 1.

54. C. Herrington, "NEA's New President: Perspectives on the Union's Role for the Nineties," *Politics of Education Bulletin* 17 (Winter 1990–91): 2.

55. Today, education is perhaps the most important function of state and local governments. . . . In these days, it is doubtful that any child may reasonably be expected to succeed in life if he [or she] is denied the opportunity of an education. Such an

opportunity, where the state has undertaken to provide it, is a right, which must be made available to all on equal terms. *Brown v. Board of Education*, 347 U.S. 484, 491(1954)

56. Alyson Klein, "Races for Congress Have Sparse Debates on Education Issues," *Education Week* (October 29, 2008): 18–20.

57. Klein, "Races for Congress Have Sparse Debates on Education Issues." The NEA supported a Republican over a Democrat in a Congressional election in Washington. The Democrat supported merit pay and the Republican did not.

58. See, for example, *University System of New Hampshire v. State of New Hampshire*, 117 N.H. 96 (1977); *Lary v. Upper Valley Teachers' Association*, 3 VLRB 416 (1980); *San Francisco Classroom Teachers Association*, PERB Decision No. 444 (1985).

59. See National Labor Relations Board. "Right to Fair Representation" in which the union "has the duty to represent all employees—whether members of the union or not—fairly, in good faith, and without discrimination." Site visited July 4, 2017, at https://www.nlrb.gov/rights-we-protect/whats-law/employees/i-am-represented-unio n/right-fair-representation.

60. However, see California Educational Employment Relations Act, which provides an express provision for duty of fair representation. Government Code Section 3544.9 reads:

The employee organization recognized or certified as the exclusive representative for the purpose of meeting and negotiating shall fairly represent each and every employee in the unit.

61. *Steele v. Louisville & Nashville R.R.*, 323 U.S. 192, 202-03 (1944).

62. *Vaca v. Sipes*, 386 U.S. 171, 194-95 (1967) (writing, "the individual employee has no absolute right to have his grievance arbitrated under the collective bargaining agreement"). Ibid.

63. Ibid., 177.

64. For example, teachers appear to have a "limited level of engagement with their unions." Steve Farkas, Jean Johnson, and Ann Duffett, *Stand by Me: What Teachers Really Think About Unions. Merit Pay and Other Professional Matters* (Washington, DC: Public Agenda, 2003), 18.

65. Todd A. DeMitchell and Richard M. Barton, "Collective Bargaining and Its Impact on Local Educational Reform Efforts," *Educational Policy* 10 (1996): 366–378, 376.

66. Author, "Voices from the Classroom: A Survey of America's Educators," *Educators for Excellence* (2018), 1. Site visited August 17, 2019, at http://e4e.org/sites/ default/files/voices_from_the_classroom_preview.pdf.

67. Author, "Voices from the Classroom: A Survey of America's Educators," 3.

68. Diane Ravitch, "Why Teacher Unions Are Good for Teachers—and the Public," *American Educator* (Winter 2006–2007). Site visited July 3, 2016, at http://www .aft.org/periodical/american-educator/winter-2006-2007/why-teacher-unions-are-go od-teachers-and.

Chapter 3

The Rise of Teachers Unions

The Influence of the Law

[T]he interest of unions, as long as you have a factory model, is seeing to it that salaries are adequate and that they are not subject to some individual administrator who can use them politically or in a discriminatory way.[1]

[There are] inevitable tensions that exist between any employer and employee. That friction is not going to simply go away in states that abandon collective bargaining. Instead, disputes will just become harder to manage, harder to resolve, and ultimately more costly.[2]

A LEGAL FRAMEWORK FOR TEACHER UNIONS

Public sector bargaining is a creature of legal mechanisms. It is through individual state legislation built upon the foundation of federal legislation on private sector labor relations that public sector labor relations rests. Courts and public employee labor relations boards' decisions give substance to the law which guides labor relations in education and other public activities performed by a unionized workforce. Another important legal aspect of the legal framework for public sector collective bargaining is the U.S. Constitution.

The First Amendment right of association[3] allows employees to come together to pursue common interests.[4] The landmark case supporting the right of public employees to organize and join a union is *McLaughlin v. Tilendis*. First Amendment and the Fourteenth Amendment were used by the Seventh Circuit Court of Appeals in this case involving the teachers' right to strike: "Teachers have the right of free association and unjustified interference with teachers associational freedom violates the due process clause of the 14th

Amendment."[5] While the Constitution allows employees to organize it does not force employers to bargain with the union; enabling legislation precedes the right to bargain.

Federal legislation through the 1935 National Labor Relations Act (NLRA), commonly called the Wagner Act, established the right of employees in the private sector to organize and recognized their right to bargain with their employer. However, it "left states free to regulate labor relationships with their particular employees."[6] Most states followed the NLRA lead several decades later granting similar rights to their public employees.

The progress of securing bargaining rights for public employees proceeded at a slow pace. This occurred in large part because of the long-standing concern about the impact of public employees organizing on the ability of government to provide essential services and the use of private sector labor tactics such as a strike against the good of the public.

The watershed event, which focused public opinion on public sector labor relations, was the Boston police strike of 1919. Police officers walked off the job when the police commissioner suspended their union leaders. The walkout resulted in looting and violence. Calvin Coolidge's (a future U.S. president), the governor of Massachusetts, response to the strike captured the public's reaction: "there is no right to strike against the public safety by anybody, anywhere, anytime."[7]

This chapter starts with a discussion of the NLRA. This federal Act set the groundwork for public sector bargaining, which followed just over twenty-five years later. Next the history of the two teachers unions, the NEA and the AFT, will be explored. The chapter will conclude by reviewing the legal framework that gives structure to public sector collective bargaining.

NATIONAL LABOR RELATIONS ACT

The stock market crashed on October 24, 1929. Soon the Great Depression settled across the country bringing with it anxiety, loss of jobs and homes, and widespread, palpable fear. The economic hard times produced uncertainty resulting in a quest for security. There were more workers than jobs and workers that had jobs sought to protect them.

The New Deal legislation, 1933 National Industrial Recovery Act (NIRA), "encouraged and emboldened workers to form unions."[8] Strikes, lockouts, and violence marred labor relations. Employers disciplined, interrogated, blacklisted, and fired workers who joined unions. Workers and union leaders shut down factories and businesses. Stories of workers intent on clashing with their employers and their employers' private security forces, often backed by the police, who were equally intent on breaking the union, regularly filled newspapers with accounts of the violence. In 1933 and 1934 the nation was rocked by large-scale work stoppages, citywide strikes, and the occupation of factories as workers sought to organize.

For example, a strike over union recognition at an auto parts plant in Toledo resulted in an extended battle between workers and the Ohio National Guard.[9] In San Francisco the longshoreman went on strike to gain union recognition. The strike spread to include about 130,000 workers from different industries after the police and the National Guard were called in to break through the picket line.

Against this backdrop of deepening labor unrest and growing militant organizing, Senator Robert F. Wagner, a Democrat from New York, submitted a bill in 1933 entitled the NLRA.[10] The Secretary of Labor Frances Perkins backed the NLRA. The Act became known as the Wagner Act. On July 5, 1935, Congress enacted the NLRA; an Act some considered to be the *Magna Carta* of American Labor.

President Roosevelt signed the Act but he did not take part in developing it. The Act was designed to diminish labor disputes by protecting the rights of employees to organize and bargain collectively with their employer. The Act sought to safeguard "commerce from injury, impairment, or interruption, and promote the flow of commerce by removing certain recognized sources of industrial strife and unrest."[11]

The core of the Act is found in Section 7:

RIGHTS OF EMPLOYEES

Employees shall have the right to self-organization, to form, join, or assist labor organizations, to bargain collectively through representatives of their own choosing, and to engage in other concerted activities for the purpose of collective bargaining or other mutual aid or protection, and shall also have the right to refrain from any or all such activities except to the extent that such right may be affected by an agreement requiring membership in a labor organization as a condition of employment as authorized in section 8(a)(3) [section 158(a)(3) of this title].[12]

This section protects workers who seek to form and join unions through self-organizing efforts with the goal of selecting a representative of their choice. The employer, under the Act, must meet with the employee's exclusive representative to bargain in "good faith" the wages, benefits, and terms and conditions of employment. The Act "does not require agreement or specific outcomes."[13] The Act, in essence, altered the unilateral decision making that employers had enjoyed and replaced it with bilateral decision making on bargainable issues—wages, benefits, terms and conditions of employment.

Workers gained the full right of freedom of association and with it the protection to seek mutual aid and protection. Furthermore, the Act prohibited management from interfering with or restraining employees from exercising their right to organize and bargain or to dominate or influence a labor union. Thus, the NLRA posited a "fundamental dividing line between labor and management."[14] An *us* versus *them* mentality became codified in law. The NLRA posits in the unionized workplace, you are either labor or management—two separate and distinct categories. A dividing line between labor and management was drawn.[15] This separation becomes important once the collective bargaining rights of the NLRA are extended to public education.

The NLRA created the National Labor Relations Board, a quasi-judicial body, to administer the provisions of the Act. The board conducts elections for exclusive representatives, determines who is in the unit—through a process of deciding which employees have a "community of interest" in their positions—and investigates charges of unfair labor practices (violations of the Act). The board can issue "cease and desist" orders. While the board has no enforcement mechanism, it seeks enforcement of its orders in the U.S. Courts of Appeal. Similarly, parties to the board's decisions may seek relief through the courts as well. The board currently consists of five members and its General Counsel who is selected by the president of the United States and subject to approval by the Senate. Thirty-three regional directors assist the board.

Prior to the passage of the NLRA only about ten percent of the private sector workforce was organized. After the Act's passage there was a dramatic surge in union membership including both men and women. Industries such as automotive, manufacturing, steel, and rubber saw a significant increase in union membership. As their membership increased so did the political clout of the unions. Strikes over union recognition were reduced as the union movement's fight for recognition moved from the economic arena characterized by strikes, lockouts, and strife, to the political arena in which the rights of employees were resolved through a quasi-judicial process directed by the NLRB.

The NLRA faced a legal challenge but the Supreme Court upheld its constitutionality in *National Labor Relations Board v. Jones & Laughlin Steel Corp.* in 1937.[16] The NLRA survived the legal challenge but the Act was changed ten years later. The legislation responded to employers' and labor opponents' concern that the Act had gone too far in giving power to unions. Some asserted that the unions were corrupt and riddled with communists. Consequently, the Act needed to be rebalanced, the proponents argued.

In 1947, at the start of the Cold War, the Labor-Management Relations Act, commonly known as the Taft-Hartley Act, was passed. A Republican-controlled Congress passed the Act over the veto of President Truman. Opponents of the bill dubbed it the "slave labor bill," arguing that it would usher in an era of industrial slavery. Thus, the fulcrum for balance in their estimation had been reset in the wrong direction.

The NLRA only envisioned a restraint on management's action. There were no union activities that could be considered unfair labor practices. Taft-Hartley, it was asserted, leveled the playing field by adding prohibitions on labor while retaining the prohibitions on management. It classified such union acts as secondary boycotts, sympathy strikes, which antiunion groups called "blackmail strikes," and closed shops as unfair labor practices. Another course correction of Taft-Hartley was a move to an individualistic right and a diminishment of a group right. For example, the Taft-Hartley bill outlawed closed shops and protected employees from coercive and discriminatory acts committed by the union. It also compelled union officials to take an oath that they were not communists.

The NLRA followed by the Taft-Hartley Act pertains to the private sector. Neither extended the rights granted to private employees to government workers. "State employment was excluded because each state was viewed as a sovereign political entity not subject to Federal legislation."[17] However, starting in 1962 with President John F. Kennedy's Executive Order 10988, public sector bargaining gained a national audience. The resulting public sector collective bargaining laws were largely grafts from the NLRA and the Taft-Hartley Act. This "reliance on the NLRA as a model for state laws"[18] developed for the private sector, largely industrial union workplace has had and still has wide-reaching ramifications for teachers and school districts.

SIDEBAR: NLRB AND CHARTER SCHOOLS

Public schools fall under state public employee review boards where they exist, and charter schools have frequently been characterized as existing within public school systems, but three recent NLRB decisions question that assumption. As there appears to be a small but growing number of teachers in charter schools seeking union representation, the issue of jurisdiction is important. Establishing whether the federal NLRA or the state public sector bargaining law applies to a particular case is critical to determining which laws and precedents will structure the bargaining and resolution of conflicts between the union and the employer. Two cases involving charter schools in Pennsylvania and New York were heard as companion cases in 2016 before the NLRB.

The essential question in these cases is whether the employer/charter school is a political subdivision under *NLRB v. National Gas Utility District of Hawkins County*, 402 U.S. 600 (1971). If the charter school as the employer is a political subdivision, it is exempt under the NLRA. Thus, the teachers seeking exclusive representation by a union would fall under any applicable state labor law and its board.

Hawkins County serves as a benchmark for determination of whether or not an entity is an "employer" according to Sec 2.2 of the NLRA; if not, and the entity is a "political subdivision," the entity is exempt from NLRB jurisdiction. Since "political subdivision" is not explicitly defined in the NLRA, the NLRB provides a two-part test of the question. Under *Hawkins County the NLRA* "has limited the exemption for political subdivisions to entities that are either (1) created directly by the state, so as to constitute departments or administrative arms of the government, or (2) administered by individuals who are responsible to public officials or to the general electorate." At 604–605.

The first case is *Pennsylvania Virtual Charter School and PA Virtual Charter Education Association PSEA/NEA*, Case 04-RC-143831; 364 NLRB No.87 (2016). The board, in a split decision, did not find an exception under the two-part rule. The board wrote:

> Furthermore, even though charter schools may be subject to state and local regulatory oversight, we find that in many, if not most, respects, charter school cases are not much different from other Board cases involving government contractors.

> (p. 10)

Hyde Leadership Charter School–Brooklyn, Case 29-RM-126444; 364 NLRB No. 88 (2016) was heard as a companion case to *Pennsylvania*. The board submitted a split decision with the same board member (Miscimarra) writing the dissent in both cases. The majority wrote: "In sum, we find that *Hyde* does not satisfy the first prong of the *Hawkins County* test, because the School was not directly created by a New York government entity, special statute, legislation, or public official, but instead by private individuals as a nonprofit corporation" (p. 6). In other words, the Charter School's executive director and governing board created the charter and working documents and not the State. Thus, the Charter School was not created directly by the state (p. 5). Furthermore, it was found that no public official was involved in the selection or the removal of any member of the board of trustees.

While there are differences in the two cases, the board finds, in essence, that these charters operate as private companies contracted by the state but not as entities created by the states. The impact of charter schools operating with some independence from the state but still considered as a public school functioning under the NLRB as opposed to the state public employee relations board is unknown. In some ways, it may serve to highlight the crossover between federal law labor law governing private employers and state labor law. It is a development worth watching.

Jacob Bennett, M.F.A.
Graduate Assistant (Labor Relations)
Ph.D. candidate in Higher Education
Leadership & Policy Studies
University of New Hampshire

HISTORY OF TEACHERS UNIONS

During the early part of the nineteenth century, most Americans lived in dispersed farm communities or very small towns. The great majority of people lived in places with fewer than 25,000 inhabitants. The typical school was the district school, "organized and controlled by a small locality and financed by some combination of property taxes, fuel contributions, tuition payments, and state aid."[19] These one-room schools would often hold sixty to seventy students for six hours a day. The school reflected the community; it was the focus for people's lives outside of the home. The community members had little doubt that the school was theirs to control. Consequently, the degree of control that was exercised over the lives of teachers was pervasive.[20]

Teachers were dictated to in the classroom and scrutinized outside it. Because many teachers "boarded round" at the houses of pupils' parents, the pressure on teachers to conform to the mores of the community was great. From colonial days and clearly into the common public school movement, the public has been far more restrictive in its expectations for the conduct of teachers than for the conduct of the average citizen. This unique position has ultimately been translated into a legal concept termed "exemplar."

Teachers, as exemplars, are held to a higher standard of personal conduct than the average citizen. As education historian David Tyack notes: "With no bureaucracy to serve as a buffer between himself and the patrons, with little sense of being a part of a professional establishment, the teacher found himself subordinated to the community."[21] Because of their relationship to students they were, and still are, considered role models. Their actions away from school are judged as if their conduct would set an example for how students should act.

Teaching was without a professional anchor and the curriculum was neither articulated nor uniform. Teachers were largely transitory, using teaching as a way station to some other destination. With poor pay, teaching "was crowded with the very dregs, the down-and-outers of society."[22] Professor Carl Kaestle notes that in the South and in Pennsylvania teachers were often portrayed as "drunken, foreign, and ignorant."[23] The public did not hold teachers during colonial times through the War of 1812 in high esteem.

However, following the War of 1812 America saw the rise of new problems; immigration increased dramatically, urban centers grew with the attendant problems of crime and disease, and the start of the industrial revolution wrought changes in the economic and social fabric of America. In response, the "nation turned in large measure to education for the resolution of these social and economic problems."[24]

These unbureaucratized, unprofessional, inexpensive, locally dominated district schools became the target of reformers in the middle of the nineteenth century. This reform movement, called the common school movement, sought to bring the schools under state control, teaching a common body of knowledge in a common schoolhouse to students from different social and economic backgrounds. The drive was to professionalize the schools. In order to do this, the reformers wanted to replace the village forms of governance in which laymen participated in decentralized decision making with the new bureaucratic model in which "directives flowed from the top down, reports emanated from the bottom, and each step of the educational process was carefully prescribed by professional educators."[25]

Education became bureaucratized through the rise of the common school movement. Compulsory education joined the movement after the Civil War. It not only added more students, it required more teachers to handle the increased size of the student body. This resulted, in what has become characterized by several commentators, as the feminization of teaching. School boards and superintendents needed a cheap source of labor. Men moved into the higher paying roles of school administration leaving classrooms vacant.

This void was filled by women, who were just starting to emerge in growing numbers from the household into the workplace. The feminization of teaching, particularly elementary school teaching, came about not only because women could be hired more cheaply than men but also because society ascribed to women a more virtuous nature than that ascribed to men. "Deportment, moral character, social obedience, domestic virtue, and firm habits were virtues to teaching, whereas over exertion in academic subjects was sometimes actually frowned upon."[26]

The large-scale entry of women into teaching had major consequences for education and the wider suffrage movement. Women played a large role in the rise of the first teachers' union and formed the backbone of the suffrage movement. For example, Margaret Haley was the business representative for the Chicago Federation of Teachers, the forerunner of the AFT, was known, among other names, as the "lady labor slugger."[27] With her penetrating blue eyes and five-foot-tall stature, she did not shrink from knocking heads at city hall and the state capitol. Margaret Murphy, a labor historian, underscored this development writing, "The new teachers' unions were not just women-led; they were feminist."[28]

The stage was set for the emergence of the two major teacher unions—the AFT and the NEA. One emerged from one path and the other from a different path. However, the development of public sector collective bargaining in the 1960s brought them closer together. From divergent beginnings, convergence was achieved through the rise of public sector bargaining.

The AFT

One of the leaders of the nascent teachers' union movement was the daughter of a stonecutter who started working at age sixteen. Later in her life she would be given the sobriquet "fiend in petticoats" by the president of Harvard College. Her teaching career began in rural schools, but the twin magnets of higher salary and further education soon drew her to Chicago, where she taught sixth grade at the South Side Hendricks School. Her name was Margaret Haley, the lady labor slugger. She was the more colorful, flamboyant part of the team that took on the leadership of the Chicago Teachers Union.

The other team member, Catharine Goggin, was the strategist who alternately unleashed and reined in Margaret Haley. Goggin was one of five daughters, three of whom were schoolteachers. She was considered to be generous, often helping destitute teachers make it through difficult times. Together, Goggin and Haley were a formidable pair who worked tirelessly for the benefit of classroom teachers.

William Rainey, president of the University of Chicago, chaired the Chicago mayor's commission on centralizing the curriculum and the administrative structure of the school district. After having their salary frozen for 20 years at $825, a raise of $50 to their annual salary was passed. However, Rainey's commission sought to redirect the raise and use it to hire and promote male teachers. When a group of female teachers complained, he responded "that they should be happy they earned as much as his wife's maid." There is an old saying in labor relations—"Management always gets the union it deserves,"[29] and they got Margaret Haley and Catherine G.

Haley and Goggin were instrumental in the early formation of the Chicago Teachers' Federation (CTF), the forerunner of the AFT. The CTF was organized in 1897 by some 500 teachers formerly members of the NEA.[30] They had three major goals: to protect teacher pensions, to gain a pay raise, and to make the administration of the Chicago schools more democratic.[31] When it held its first meeting on March 16, 1897, over 2,500 teachers attended, about half of all of the Chicago elementary school teachers.[32]

Another rallying point was a reaction to the invasion of scientific management by administration conservatives, which engendered a feeling of powerlessness on the part of teachers. Teachers were caught in the Cult of Efficiency and became automatons, interchangeable parts that could be molded into efficient units.[33]

This nascent union movement clashed with the views held by a coalition of progressive reformers, school administrators, and business leaders. These elites believed that the inherent pursuit of self-interests of a union conflicted with the selfless ideology of professionalism espoused by the reformers. For example, in 1898, the *Chicago Times-Herald* commented in an editorial that the impetus for the formation of the CTF sprang from a "spirit not credible to the high standards of the profession."[34]

> The NEA was genteel. It conducted research on education and advocated politely for school funding. From the start, the Federation intended to be a totally different animal: a militant organization modeled after the male labor unions to which fathers and brothers of Chicago teachers belonged.
>
> Dana Goldstein, *The Teacher Wars: A History of America's Most Embattled Profession* (New York: Doubleday, 2014), 69.

From its beginnings the CFT signaled an ideological break with the larger NEA. It was founded by elementary school classroom teachers, from which it drew its leadership, and hence it was primarily a women's union. In 1902, the CTF formed a fateful alliance that would remain one of its defining differences with the NEA to the present day—it affiliated with the Chicago Federation of Labor. This move won it the enmity of the Chicago Board of Education as well as the NEA.

The CTF's early successes involved support for a number of social welfare causes, including the successful passage of the Illinois Child Labor Law of 1903. It also successfully litigated a case against several prominent Chicago companies, such as People's Gas, Light, and Coal Company, the Chicago Telephone Company, and the Edison Electric Light Company, which had failed to pay taxes due on their capital stock and franchises. The companies were ordered to pay nearly $600,000 in back taxes.[35] The Chicago Board of Education was anything but grateful for the union's efforts to fill the board's coffers. The board voted not to expend any of those funds on teacher salaries, and it carried its disapproval of the union further by voting in 1905 to condemn the CTF's affiliation with organized labor. In spite of this, the membership of the CTF grew.

In 1915, the board upped the ante by requiring all teachers to sign a yellow dog contract—a contract requiring employees to sign an instrument agreeing as a condition of employment that they will not join a union and that they understand they will be discharged if they do so; "only a yellow dog would sign such contracts." The yellow dog contract in Chicago was called the Loeb Rule. Jack Loeb, the president of the Chicago Board of Education, told stories throughout Chicago of innocent schoolteachers who were captured by the union and forced to conform to the dominance of the women leaders of the CTF. These radical union teachers, Loeb argued, were contemptuous and rebellious toward those in authority. The attack by the board was not only against unionism but also against female trade-union leadership. In 1916, thirty-five teachers, most of them CTF members, were dismissed under the Loeb Rule.[36] Haley quickly reorganized her own union, breaking her powerful ties with the Chicago Federation of Labor. The CTF never regained its former strength.

This was not the only battle the CTF was waging at the time. In 1895, Nicholas Murray Butler took the helm of the NEA. He brought to the association a sense that teaching was a service akin to a religious vocation. He wedded this vision of commitment to a modern notion of professionalism that encompassed educational training and scientific inquiry. The first clash between Butler and the CTF took place at the July 1899 convention, which was held in Los Angeles.

A group of 800 teachers from Chicago boarded a train hired by the CTF bound for the summer convention in Los Angeles. The CTF had decided to launch its campaign to organize a national teachers' federation at the annual NEA meeting, because that provided the greatest concentration of teachers. The CTF did not receive a warm reception from the NEA leadership. The elements in control of the NEA labeled the Chicago teachers "revolutionists." A coalition of high school and college teachers (dominated by males) took a critical stance toward the CTF (dominated by females).

The attack reached a crescendo when Butler prepared a report from the Resolutions Committee deliberations and delivered it during the last general session. Butler's report condemned the CTF for using political influence and protecting incompetents—a charge against teacher unions that would recur over the decades from various quarters. Butler called the Chicago teachers "insurrectionists" and "union labor grade teachers," whose "pernicious activities were offensive to the teaching profession."[37]

The new national teachers' organization was officially censured before it even got organized. (It is interesting to note that the strongest union members were elementary school teachers, not high school teachers. And more women were militant than men.) The *Chicago Times-Heralds* editorial (1898) on the formation of the Chicago Teachers Federation charged that the CTF sprang from a "spirit not credible to the high standards of professional ethics."[38]

Rebuffed by the NEA and outmaneuvered legally by the Chicago Board of Education, the CTF lost its voice for speaking out on matters of concern to teachers. The path that the CTF was clearing was soon used by a new entity after the CTF was reorganized. In April 1916, representatives from four unions met in South Chicago to organize a national federation of teachers. This new union, the AFT, turned away from Margaret Haley and elected Charles Stillman of the Chicago Federation of Men Teachers as its first president.

In choosing Stillman, members remarked that they needed strong leadership in times of crisis, insinuating that male leadership would provide greater strength. With this election, the union became primarily a high school teachers' union. Growth of AFT locals in the elementary schools up to the Second World War was minimal. However, the rise of public sector bargaining in the early 1960s changed the fortunes of the AFT.

The NEA

In 1857,[39] forty-three teachers from ten state teacher associations met, with the objective of upgrading teaching to a profession, elevating it above an ordinary vocation.[40] The assembled group called the new organization the National Teachers' Association. Years later, when it merged with the National Association of School Superintendents, the two organizations took the name NEA. At first, the teachers, even though they constituted the majority, had difficulty gaining power within the NEA; a classroom teacher was not elected president of that body until 1928. Through 1945, only three classroom teachers had served as president.

The NEA was an association dominated by superintendents and college professors. Control of policy and control of the occupation of education rested firmly in the hands of administrators. Administration domination was evidenced in its response to a growing labor movement at the turn of the century. In the 1903 NEA convention, Margaret Haley, the leader of the Chicago Teachers Federation, critiqued capitalism and its impact on education. She also argued for the need to improve the lot of teachers. The NEA's focus was on influencing policies that affected public education. Following Haley's comments the NEA created a national committee to work on improving teacher salaries, pensions, and their tenure. Four years later Ella Flagg Young became the NEA's first female president. She argued against the isolation of teachers from the administration of the school and asserted that teachers must have a stronger hand in planning.[41]

The split between a focus on "professionalism" and a push for improving the working conditions and salaries arose. The AFT was decried as a "special interest" that made "excessive demands" while the NEA emphasized the progressive "public good" and the "common interest."[42] Aaron Gove, the superintendent of the Denver School District, captured the tension asserting that teachers' involvement in the conflict between labor and capital invited the "sordidness of our personal life" where "selfishness and acquisitiveness" dominate.[43]

The issue was compounded by prevailing gender norms. The majority of teachers were female, thus the push to improve teachers' working conditions was a push to improve the lives of females. Consequently, "most other citizens viewed their participation in unions or demonstrations as inappropriate, since these were considered 'manly' behaviors."[44]

This signature of administration domination and reaction to unionism's perceived inherent conflict with professionalism would remain etched on the parchment of the NEA through the 1960s, as it fended off competition from the AFT and came to grips with collective bargaining and its attendant union bread-and-butter issues.

From 1917 to 1920, NEA membership increased significantly. The campaign to attract new members was built around improving teacher salaries, gaining greater support for the schools, and securing greater participation of teachers in the administration of the schools. Ironically, as teacher membership increased, what power teachers did have was virtually eliminated for almost fifty years by a reorganization of the association.

Prior to NEA reorganization in 1920, the association's conventions were conducted much as New England town meetings, with each member in attendance allowed one vote. Thus, wherever the convention was held, the teachers from that city could attend en masse and outvote other delegations. This reorganization was important because the leadership of the NEA, made up primarily of administrators and college professors, wanted to move to a representative form of governance in which each state association would elect delegates to the convention, thus breaking the hold of teachers.

Prior to 1920, activists could pack the convention with local teachers. These tactics were defeated when the convention was held in Salt Lake City, Utah. "In a conservative state like Utah, teachers listened to their administrators and bowed to their authority. At the convention, teachers voted in town-meeting style to eliminate that voting format in favor of voting for delegates."[45] Administrators dominated the NEA, with little power left over for teachers.

An example of the impact of this shift is provided by Wayne Urban, who notes that of the 167 voting delegates from Illinois in the 1920s, 135 were administrators or college professors, and of the remaining thirty-two delegates, only fourteen were elementary school teachers.[46] This increased tension between teachers and school administrators lasted until the 1970s, when the NEA transformed itself into a militant teachers' union in response to the spread of public sector bargaining and competition from the AFT to represent teachers.

COLLECTIVE BARGAINING IN THE PUBLIC SCHOOLS

The AFT, from its inception, was a union of teachers. It was organized by teachers, the membership was composed of teachers, and, most important, the leadership came from classroom teachers. In contrast, the NEA's early leadership came from individuals who held such positions as superintendent and college president or college professor. The AFT differentiated itself from the NEA by defining itself as the people's union rather than as a professional association.

"The AFT leadership did not believe that professionalism had benefited the majority of teachers."[47] Following this theme of separate NEA and AFT visions of their organization's purposes, Theodore Martin, the NEA director of membership, proclaimed just prior to the advent of public sector collective bargaining:

> Unionism lowers the ideals of teaching, by emphasizing the selfish, though necessary economic needs of teachers—salary, hours, tenure, retirement—unionism misses altogether the finer ideals of teaching and the rich compensations that do not appear in the salary envelopes.[48]

Prior to 1962 only Wisconsin allowed state employees, including teachers, to collectively bargain. Teachers were largely powerless on their own to improve their working conditions or their economic status. Salaries, benefits, hours of employment, class sizes, and assignment and transfer procedures were set by school boards and enforced by administrators. However, a nationwide movement gained momentum, not so much from Wisconsin's lead but from President John F. Kennedy's signing of Executive Order 10988, which gave collective bargaining rights to federal employees. States in the industrial north with a history of private sector unionism, soon passed legislation for public sector bargaining. However, the south, which did not have such a history and viewed unions with unfamiliarity and suspicion, did not.[49]

When public sector collective bargaining started its march across the educational landscape in Wisconsin in 1959, the NEA thought it would destroy professionalism and erode the teacher's status in the community. In contrast, the AFT embraced collective bargaining arguing that teachers would gain respect because their salaries would finally be commensurate with their preparation.

In the 1960s, when public sector collective bargaining emerged in many states, the NEA's long-cherished concept of professionalism was being seriously challenged. Teachers wanted higher salaries and better benefits, not necessarily a higher standard of respect. Yet, the NEA in 1960 failed to pass a resolution, by a sound majority, that stated that collective bargaining is "compatible with the ethics and dignity of the teaching profession."[50] Soon afterward, the NEA reversed not just its course but also its essential, long-held core philosophy.

The NEA, like the AFT, is a business, even though it is nonprofit. Both sell a product, protecting and securing the self-interests of its members. The success of the AFT in the nascent stage of public sector collective bargaining, especially in urban centers awakened the NEA and led them to question whether can they remain relevant and keep their share of representation of the nation's school districts. In some ways, the shift for the NEA may be characterized as a realization that bread-and-butter and not professionalism through a top-down organization attracts teachers.

In order to remain competitive with the AFT, the NEA changed its philosophy and tactics, which it did several years later after the success of strikes in New York City (1962), Detroit (1964), and Philadelphia (1965) approving its first official policy supporting teachers' right to "insist" on the right to negotiate with their school board and to strike (1969).[51] The NEA came to look and act more like the AFT. Lieberman asserted that in order to "survive the challenge from the AFT, the NEA had to become a union."[52] The professional association became the union it had denigrated for decades.

Frederick Wirt and Michael Kirst, two educational policy professors, wrote in 1997 of the AFT and the NEA, no other group has had an "increased influence on education policy in recent decades as much as have teachers. The timid rabbits of 30 years ago are today's ravening tigers in the jungle of school systems."

Frederich M. Wirt & Michael W. Kirst, *The Political Dynamics of American Education* (Berkeley, CA: McCutchan, 1997), 181.

Reflecting on this sea change by the NEA in the 1960s, Bob Chase, the current president of the NEA, stated, "we took a rather quiet, genteel professional association of educators, and we reinvented it as an assertive—and, when necessary, militant—labor union."[53] Survival often dictates change, and the NEA found itself in a fight and on grounds it did not chose.

The emergence of AFT as a collective bargaining force, particularly in urban centers, in the 1960s forced the NEA to shift its focus more strongly toward teachers' self-interests.[54] The AFT and the NEA, with their different roots, came to resemble each other with the advent of public sector collective bargaining. Today, differences between the nation's two largest unions have largely, but not completely, faded, and both AFT and NEA now clearly see themselves as advocates and representatives of classroom teachers and as unions. Both pursue their advocacy through politics and the policies of the collectively bargained contract.

PUBLIC SECTOR LABOR LAWS

Teachers began to organize well before the rise of public sector collective bargaining. However, it was the advent of public sector bargaining laws that provided the fuel for the rise of teacher unions on the public school stage. As discussed earlier, private sector bargaining is structured by federal law, the NLRA, but public sector bargaining is the province of the various states. This creates a hodgepodge of laws with no one unifying piece of legislation or enforcement that explains all public sector bargaining.[55]

The touchstone for understanding public sector collective bargaining is to explore the common organizing legal structures of collective bargaining laws. Collective bargaining is a creature of the law: created by law, changed by law, and eliminated by law. Five states, as of 2014 (Georgia, North Carolina, South Carolina, Texas, and Virginia), prohibit bargaining with public school teachers. Arizona has no statute authorizing or prohibiting bargaining, thus it is essentially left to local laws.[56] When comparing firefighters and police, there are only two states that prohibit bargaining for all three categories of public employees, North Carolina and South Carolina.[57]

However, one state, Colorado, secured public sector collective bargaining via case law. Thirty-eight of Colorado's 181 school districts voluntarily entered into negotiations with teachers and agreed upon a contract. This was done in the absence of authorizing legislation, but there was no prohibiting legislation either. The Littleton Education Association had successfully bargained two contracts starting in 1967. In 1973, upon the expiration of the contract (December 31, 1973), no successor agreement had been ratified. The school board adopted a salary schedule that it implemented. On January 3, 1974, the teachers went on a two-week strike arguing "no contract, no work."[58]

The strike ended when the school sought and received a preliminary injunction. A salary schedule was agreed upon. However, the school district sent out individual contracts for the teachers to sign. Failure to sign the contract and return it within a month would be considered an abandonment of the teaching position. The union went to court alleging that individual contracts were inconsistent with the terms of the agreement. The trial court found the agreement to be unenforceable, in part, because there was no authorizing legislation for a collectively bargained contract.[59]

The Colorado Supreme Court disagreed with the trial court. It held that the school board's "participation in collective bargaining is not per se an unlawful delegation of its authority."[60] The court further held that the agreement cannot conflict with existing statutes and that the ruling does not compel school boards to enter into collective bargaining.

Setting aside the *Littleton* case, states typically fashion their public sector collective bargaining statute with several components: enforcement of the law, who is the representative, what must the representative provide to the members it represents, and work stoppages. Each will be briefly addressed next.

ENFORCING THE LAW: STATE PUBLIC SECTOR LABOR BOARDS

The states that choose to allow their public employees to bargain collectively over their wages, benefits, and terms and conditions of employment codify the processes and procedures for bargaining into law. Some also state the purpose for the law. For example, in my state, New Hampshire, the Legislature's Statement of Policy reads, "It is the policy of the state to foster harmonious and cooperative relations between public employers and their employees and to protect the public by encouraging the orderly and uninterrupted operation of government."[61] Alaska state law reads, "The legislature declares that it is the public policy of the state to promote harmonious and cooperative relations between government and its employees and to protect the public by assuring effective and orderly operations of government."[62] The similarity of the two statutes is striking.

Similar to the NLRA, which establishes a board to administrator the law, public sector laws also establish such boards. These boards are quasi-judicial administrative state agencies tasked with administering and enforcing the law. In California it is called the Public Employment Board and consists of five members drawn from the public and private sectors.[63] The Florida Public Employees Relations Commission, similar to many state employment boards, conducts elections for representation, resolves disputes about the composition of bargaining units, and decides cases of an unfair labor practice—a violation of the labor law.[64]

These state labor relations agencies interpret, implement, and enforce the law. The decisions of the labor board have consequences beyond the parties to a dispute. Because the board/commission has quasi-judicial responsibilities, their interpretation of the collective bargaining law provides precedent for future similar fact-based issues, much like court cases provide precedent with their decisions.

One of the major responsibilities of labor relations' board is the election and designation of the exclusive representative for a unit of employees. An exclusive representative is the elected representative for a unit of employees—a group of employees who have a community of interest that allows for an efficiency for bargaining.

As an exclusive representative it must represent all members of the bargaining unit without regard as to whether they are a member of the union or not. The union owes a duty of fair representation (see chapter 2). Failure to fairly represent a member of the unit may result in filing an unfair labor practice by the unit member against the union.

An unfair labor practice is one of the responsibilities of a labor board that most resembles a court case.[65] There are two parties to the dispute, evidence is gathered, and a hearing is held before a neutral tribunal with authority in the matter. An unfair labor practice is an allegation that one party, either labor or management, with the exception of the duty of fair representation which will be discussed below, has violated the state labor relations law. It is typically not an allegation of a violation, misinterpretation, or misapplication of the collective bargaining agreement.

An example of unfair labor practices from Pennsylvania follows:

MY RIGHTS: UNFAIR LABOR PRACTICES

Pennsylvania's Public Employee Relations Act, or Act 195, governs relationships between public sector employers and employee organizations.

Act 195 states that public employers, their agents or representatives are prohibited from engaging in "unfair labor practices."

Act 195 defines unfair employer practices as:

(1) Interfering, restraining or coercing employees in the exercise of the rights under Act 195.
(2) Dominating or interfering with the formation, existence or administration of an employee organization.
(3) Discriminating in regard to hire or tenure of employment or any term or condition of employment to encourage or discourage membership in any employee organization.
(4) Discharging or otherwise discriminating against an employee because he has signed or filed an affidavit, petition or complaint or given any information or testimony under this Act.
(5) Refusing to bargain collectively in good faith with an employee representative, which is the exclusive representative of employees in an appropriate unit, including but not limited to the discussing of grievances with the exclusive representative.

(6) Refusing to reduce a collective bargaining agreement to writing and sign such agreement.
(7) Violating any of the rules and regulations established by the board regulating the conduct of representation elections.
(8) Refusing to comply with the provisions of a binding arbitration award.
(9) Refusing to comply with the requirements of "meet and discuss."

Examples of unfair labor practices by an employer include the following actions:

- Unilaterally declaring a position to be out of the bargaining unit
- Discriminating or retaliating against anyone on the basis of the person's protected union activity
- Unilaterally diverting bargaining unit work to non-bargaining unit personnel, whether through subcontracting, asking for volunteers from the community, or assigning people from other bargaining units to perform the work of the unit at issue
- Unilaterally changing a term and condition of employment.[66]

State labor relations boards essentially enforce the laws that created public sector bargaining. They are basically analogous to the National Labor Relations Board. They are quasi-judicial in that they adjudicate disputes (unfair labor practices). The certification and the decertification of public sector unions in their state are part of their portfolio. And they oversee bargaining in the state. These boards are critical to the overall functioning of state-level labor relations. Who is appointed and the process for appointment consequently are important.

NOTES

1. Albert Shanker, "Al Shanker Speaks on Unions and Collective Bargaining," *Education Week* (May 14, 1997): 35–36.

2. David Well, "The Short-sighted Attack on Collective Bargaining," *Boston Globe* (May 28, 2011). Site visited June 22, 2019, at http://www.boston.com/bostongl obe/editorial_opinion/blogs/the_angle/2011/05/collective_barg.html.

3. Freedom of Association as a Constitutional concept grew out of a series of cases in the 1950s and 1960s in which some states sought to curb the activities of the National Association for the Advancement of Colored People. It has been asserted that the Right of Association, while not explicitly stated in the First Amendment, is derived from the rights of assembly, petition, and speech. Site visited January 8, 2008, at http://supreme.lp.findlaw.com/constitution/amendment01/12.html#f194.

4. It is beyond debate that freedom to engage in association for the advancement of beliefs and ideas is an inseparable aspect of the 'liberty' assured by the Due Process Clause of the Fourteenth Amendment, which embraces freedom of speech. . . . Of course, it is immaterial whether the beliefs sought to be advanced by association pertain to political, economic, religious or cultural matters, and state action which may have the effect of curtailing the freedom to associate is subject to the closest scrutiny. *NAACP v. Alabama ex rel. Patterson*, 357 U.S. 449, 460–61 (1958)

5. *McLaughlin v. Tilendis*, 398 F.2d 287, 288 (7th Cir. 1968). For an application of state law to this proposition see *Central School District 13J v. Central Education Association*, 962 P.2d 763 (Or. Ct. App. 1998), in which the court held that a teacher could not be discharged for engaging in the right of association under state law.

6. Robert C. Cloud, "*Davenport v. Washington Education Ass'n*: Agency Shop & First Amendment Revisited," *Education Law Reporter* 224 (2007): 617–627, 619.

7. Francis Russell, *A City in Terror: 1919, the Boston Police Strike* (New York: Viking, 1975), 191.

8. John W. Budd, *Labor Relations: Striking a Balance* (Boston: McGraw-Hill, 2005), 123.

9. See Philip A. Korth and Margaret R. Beegle, *I Remember It Like Today: The Auto-Lite Strike of 1934* (East Lansing: Michigan State University Press, 1988).

10. 29 U.S.C. §§ 151–169.

11. Section 1 [§ 151].

12. Section 7. [§ 157].

13. Budd, *Labor Relations*, 157.

14. Charles Taylor Kerchner and Julia Koppich, "Organizing Around Quality: The Struggle to Organize Mind Workers," in *Teacher Unions and Education Policy: Retrenchment or Reform?* ed. Ronald D. Henderson, Wayne J. Urban, and Paul Wolman (Amsterdam: Elsevier, 2004), 205.

15. Kerchner and Koppich, "Organizing Around Quality."

16. *National Labor Relations Board v. Jones & Laughlin Steel Corp*, 301 U.S. 1 (1937). The United States Supreme Court held that the Act was based on the Commerce Clause because labor-management disputes were directly related to interstate commerce. Unregulated industrial activities, the High Court reasoned, had the potential to disrupt and restrict interstate commerce.

17. Carol Wright and David E. Gundersen, "Unions and Teachers: Differences in the State of the Nation," *ASLB Journal of Employment and Labor Law* 2 (2004): 1–12, 2.

18. Susan Moore Johnson, "Paralysis or Possibility: What Do Teacher Unions and Collective Bargaining Bring?" in *Teacher Unions and Education Policy: Retrenchment or Reform?* ed. Ronald D. Henderson, Wayne J. Urban, and Paul Wolman (Amsterdam: Elsevier, 2004), 33–50, 47. See also, Harry Edwards, "The Emerging Duty to Bargain in the Public Sector," *Michigan Law Review* 71 (1973): 885–934, 932 (noting "accelerating" trend among states toward using "private sector principles to guide the development of labor relations in the public sector").

19. Carl F. Kaestle, *Pillars of the Republic: Common Schools and American Society, 1780–1860* (New York: Hill & Wang, 1983), 13.

20. For a discussion of how the community controlled the private lives of teachers, see Todd A. DeMitchell, "Private Lives: Community Control vs. Professional

Autonomy," *Education Law Reporter* 78 (1993): 187–197; John E. Rumel, "Beyond Nexus: A Framework for Evaluating K–12 Teacher Off-Duty Conduct and Speech in Adverse Employment and Licensure Proceedings," *University of Cincinnati Law Review* 83 (2015): 685–746.

21. David B. Tyack, *The One Best System: A History of American Urban Education* (Cambridge, MA: Harvard University Press, 1974), 19.

22. Ruskin Teeter, *The Opening Up of American Education: A Sampler* (New York: University Press of America, 1983), 50.

23. Kaestle, *Pillars of the Republic*, p. 20.

24. Todd A. DeMitchell, "Educating America: The Nineteenth-Century Common School Promise in the Twentieth Century, A Personal Essay," *International Journal of Educational Reform* 9 (2000): 79–86, 80.

25. Teeter, *The Opening Up of American Education*, 40.

26. Tyack, *The One Best System*, 61.

27. Dana Goldstein, *The Teacher Wars: A History of America's Most Embattled Profession* (New York: Doubleday, 2014), 70.

28. Marjorie Murphy, *Blackboard Unions: The AFT and NEA, 1900–1980* (Ithaca, NY: Cornell University Press, 1990), 12.

29. Goldstein, *The Teacher Wars*, 69.

30. Charles J. Coleman, *Managing Labor Relations in the Public Sector* (San Francisco: Jossey-Bass Publishers, 1990), 40.

31. Murphy, *Blackboard Unions*, 62.

32. Goldstein, *The Teacher Wars*, 69.

33. *See* Raymond E. Callahan, *Education and the Cult of Efficiency* (Chicago: University of Chicago Press, 1962).

34. Charles T. Kerchner and Douglas E. Mitchell, *The Changing Idea of a Teachers' Union* (Philadelphia: Falmer Press, 1988), 56.

35. Anthony M. Cresswell and Michael J. Murphy, with Charles T. Kerchner, *Teachers, Unions, and Collective Bargaining in Public Education* (Berkeley, CA: McCutchan Publishing Company, 1980), 71.

36. Murphy, *Blackboard Unions*, 83.

37. Ibid., 54.

38. Kerchner and Mitchell, *The Changing Idea of a Teachers' Union*, 56.

39. The earliest educational association was the American Institute of Instruction. Charles J. Coleman, *Managing Labor Relations in the Public Sector* (San Francisco: Jossey-Bass Publishers, 1990), 35.

40. Cresswell and Murphy, *Teachers, Unions, and Collective Bargaining in Public Education*, 59.

41. Sabrina Holcomb, "Answering the Call: The History of NEA, Part 2," *National Education Association* (February 21, 2006). Site visited August 18, 2019, at http://www.nea.org/archive/12172.htm.

42. Adam Mertz, "A Century of Teacher Organizing: What Can We Learn?" The Labor and Working Class History Association (LAWCHA) (n.d.). Site visited August 18, 2019, at https://www.lawcha.org/century-teaching-organizing/.

43. Murphy, *Blackboard Unions*, 59.

44. Mertz, "A Century of Teacher Organizing."

45. Joel Spring, *The American School 1642–1990* (2nd ed.) (New York: Longman, 1990), 272.

46. Wayne Urban, *Why Teachers Organize* (Detroit: Wayne State University Press, 1982), 127.

47. Dan Goldhaber, "Are Teacher Unions Good for Students?" in *Collective Bargaining in Education*, ed. Jane Hannaway and Andrew J. Rotherham (Cambridge, MA: Harvard Education Press, 2006), 143.

48. Kerchner and Mitchell, *The Changing Idea of a Teachers' Union*, 57.

49. Carol Wright and David E. Gundersen, "Unions and Teachers: Differences in the State of the Nation," *ALSB Journal of Employment and Labor Law* 10 (2004): 1–12, 2.

50. L. Dean Webb and M. Scott Norton, *Human Resources Administration: Personnel Issues and Needs in Education* (5th ed.) (Upper Saddle River, NJ: Merrill Prentice Hall, 2009), 261.

51. Webb and Norton, *Human Resources Administration*, 263.

52. Myron Lieberman, *The Teacher Unions: How the NEA and AFT Sabotage Reform and Hold Students, Parents, Teachers, and Taxpayers Hostage to Bureaucracy* (New York: The Free Press, 1997), 26.

53. Bob Chase, "The New NEA: Reinventing Teacher Unions for a New Era," Remarks Before the National Press Club (Washington, DC: February 7, 1997). Site visited January 6, 1998, at www.nea.org, 2.

54. Terry M. Moe, "A Union by Any Other Name," *EducationNext* (2001). Site visited December 4, 2004, at http://www.educationnext.org/20013/3/38moe.htm.

55. Milla Sanes and John Schmitt, *Regulation of Public Sector Collective Bargaining in the States* (Washington, DC: Center for Economic and Policy Research, March 2014), 3. Site visited April 15, 2014, at http://cepr.net/documents/state-public-cb-2014-03.pdf.

56. Sanes and John Schmitt, *Regulation of Public Sector Collective Bargaining in the States*, 5.

57. Ibid.

58. *Littleton Education Association v. Arapahoe County School District*, 553 P.2d 793, 795 (1976).

59. Ibid.

60. Ibid., 797.

61. N.H. Rev. Stat. Ann. § 273-A. Site visited January 23, 2015, at http://www.nh.gov/pelrb/index.htm.

62. Alaska Stat. Ann. § 23.40.070. Illinois also states that harmonious relationships between educational employees and their employers are necessary, IL St, CH 115 5/1.

63. Public Employment Relations Board, *The Board and Its Duties* site visited June 21, 2016, at http://www.perb.ca.gov/duties.aspx. The Illinois Educational Labor Relations Act (1984) purpose is "to promote orderly and constructive relationships between educational employees and their employers, recognizing that harmonious relationships are required between educational employees and their employers." State of Illinois Educational Labor Relations Board, Welcome site visited June 21, 2016, at http://www.illinois.gov/elrb/Pages/default.aspx.

64. Public Employees Relations Commission, site visited June 21, 2016, at http://perc.myflorida.com/.

65. An unfair labor practice is different than a grievance. As stated earlier in the chapter, an unfair labor practice is an allegation of a violation of the state collective bargaining law by either management or the union. A grievance is an allegation of a violation, misinterpretation, or misapplication of the collective bargaining agreement by either party. While the administration must follow the contract, so must the union, and the employees covered by the contract. For example, see *Provens v. Stark Cty. Bd. of Mental Retardation & Developmental Disabilities* (1992), 64 Ohio St.3d 252, 262 (Douglas, J., concurring), in which Judge Douglas in a concurring opinion wrote, "An employee has no more right to ignore a collective bargaining agreement than does an employer."

For a discussion of grievances, see Todd A. DeMitchell, *Educators at the Bargaining Table: Successfully Negotiating a Contract That Works for All* (Lanham, MD: Rowman & Littlefield), 12–14.

66. Pennsylvania State Education Association, "My Rights: Unfair Labor Practices." Site visited June 21, 2016, at https://www.psea.org/general.aspx?id=6979.

Chapter 4

The Industrial Union Legacy

Industrial bargaining was good for setting rules and dividing resources but of little use in addressing the many educational challenges that educators faced, such as reorganizing schools schedules, supporting interdisciplinary teaching, effectively integrating students with special needs into regular classrooms, or engaging parents more actively in the education of their children.[1]

Bob Chase, president of the National Education Association, speaking about teacher contracts, stated in 1997: "The procedures for conflict resolution and the definition of management, and their respective rights were all borrowed, in many cases word for word, from the private labor sector which embraced the industrial model."[2]

LABOR, NOT CRAFT, ART, OR PROFESSION: THE ORGANIZING MODEL

Starting with the first public sector bargaining law in Wisconsin in 1959, state legislatures had to decide what model they would use for their emerging labor relations law. Charles T. Kerchner and Douglas E. Mitchell[3] note that there were four existing models that legislators could have selected. The four constructions of work are labor, craft workers, professionals, and artisans. The following are some of the characteristics they ascribe to the four constructions.[4]

Laborers

- Preplanned tasks.
- Close supervision; insubordination is a concern.

61

- Personal loyalty expected because personal responsibility for the purposes (policy) of their efforts.
- "Laborers are told what to do, when they are told to do it. If the result is inadequate, the fault lies with the manager, not the worker."[5] They do not have control over the product of their work; policy regarding the product is the domain of management.
- Labor bargains over wages, benefits, terms and conditions of employment.

Craft Workers

- Organizes its workers through task definition and apprenticeships.
- While laborers are expected to follow directions, craft workers are judged on how adequately they perform their tasks.
- "Craft workers follow standard procedures because they are technically correct."[6]

Professional Workers

- Accepts personal responsibility for the outcome of the service/work, thus malpractice is the accepted accountability mechanism.
- A professional not only knows how to perform a task but whether the task should be performed. They are flexible and adaptive.
- Professionals develop standards of practice.
- Professions certify practitioners and define their work through public policy and client treatment.

Artistic Work

- Granted considerable autonomy in the exercise of artistic creativity.
- Often artists "are expected to rise above the limits of specific technique or established conventions and to develop novel, unconventional, or unexpected techniques."[7]

The work of teachers involves elements of all four dimensions of work. Their work is preplanned through the adopted curriculum. They demonstrate the craft of teaching as handed down from other teachers—the wisdom of practice. They are professionals in that they translate policy into practice based on the application of standards with consideration for the context of their classroom and school. And, they are creative artisans transforming sterile classrooms into places of vibrancy unleashing their creativity and the creativity of their students.

For purposes of the emerging labor relations legislation, teacher's work was considered labor rather than a craft, a profession, or an art. Legislators chose the industrial labor model of the National Labor Relations Act as the organizing structure for public sector labor law. This decision has had consequences for education and educators.

FROM THE ASSEMBLY LINE TO THE CLASSROOM

Private sector labor law provided the foundation for public sector bargaining, which includes public school teachers.[8] "By the time teachers entered into collective bargaining in the 1960s and 1970s the word unionism largely meant industrial union."[9] This legacy from the industrial unions presents a challenge that teacher unions and school districts continue to face decades later. For example, a lead 1997 editorial in the *Boston Globe* offered the opinion that "continuing efforts at school reform in Boston are being hampered by a factory-style approach to collective bargaining."[10] Bread-and-butter, hardball negotiations and strikes, activities associated with the industrial union, for many, became descriptors of the emerging public sector teacher unions.

Johnson and Kardos assert that the states modeled their public sector collective bargaining laws directly on the National Labor Relations Act of 1935 discussed earlier.[11] The home page for the Massachusetts Labor Relations Commission underscores the historical link to the NLRA. It writes on its first page that its commission is the "counterpart to the National Labor Relations Board."[12] "This initial choice of models to use for the public sector has had major consequences for education, given the uniqueness of public schools and a workforce that struggles with the issue of professionalism."[13] The procedures for conflict resolution, the definition of management and labor, and their respective rights were all borrowed, in many cases word for word, from the private labor sector, which embraced the industrial model.

As discussed in chapter 2, unions exist to protect and enhance the social economic welfare of their members. This truism applies to teacher unions—the union advances the interests of their members chiefly through collective bargaining.

Consequently, unions in the private and public sectors strive to protect the worker from the "whims" of management through a collectively bargained, legally enforceable contract that defines the terms and conditions of employment in addition to setting the wages and benefits associated with the job.

This creates a system with two distinct parties. A "consequence of applying the factory model to education is the creation of an atmosphere of antagonism between school districts and employee unions."[14] Therefore, "industrial unionism assumes permanent adversaries. It organizes around vigorous representation of the differences between teachers and managers."[15] An us and them mentality is fostered. "Industrial-style unionism is organized around anger"[16] which all too often colors the working relationship.

Consequently, a great premium is placed on conflict management. This is so fundamental that the absence of conflict actually "arouses anxiety and uncertainty among both union leaders and school managers who fear that they will be seen as having 'gone soft.'"[17] If teachers and administrators get along too easily, is a union needed to provide protection? A relationship predicated on conflict and adversity has consequences for the long-term goals of the school when collaboration between teachers and administration is considered important, if not necessary.

Linda Kaboolian writes of this consequence, "adversarial relationships between teachers and school management significantly impede change efforts required to improve student achievement."[18] An outcome of collective bargaining, conflict between educators, is in opposition to the need for collaboration among educators. How to move from the "them" of bargaining to the "us" for educating students is a challenge.

Teaching has been characterized as a lonely profession when the classroom door closes. However, teachers are not solo practitioners. There is a social, collegial, and collaborative aspect to teaching. The classroom is not an island unconnected to or independent of the school and fellow school members. The knowledge and skills that a student brings to her/his new class at the start of the school year is largely dependent on their previous knowledge and skills learned last year. This in turn provides the foundation for the current year's instruction. Teachers are not solo practitioners. Their professional practice takes place within a community of practitioners including the administration who are not faceless bureaucrats, but rather they are colleagues who also serve within the same learning environment, walk the same hallways, and work with the same students and parents.

A study of teachers' perceptions of the compatibility of being a union member and a professional, a section of the survey instrument explored the issue of us and them as an outcome of the industrial union model as applied to education.

The subset on us and them asked three questions using five-point Likert style question format. Respondents selected from one of the following five points and applied to a position statement. Point 1 is Strongly Disagree, the second is Disagree, the third point is Neutral, the fourth point is Agree, and the last point on the scale is Strongly Disagree. The following chart collapses Strongly Disagree and Disagree into one statistic and Agree and Strongly Agree into another. The following lists the question, the mean, the disagree, neutral, and agree combination[19] (table 4.1).

Teachers in this study believe, by almost three to one, that their professional activities are enhanced through collegial relations with school administrators. The difference is almost three-to-one in favor of agreeing with the importance of the relationship. The belief that unionization does not create conflict (45.8%

Table 4.1 Us and Them Questions

Questions	Mean (s.d.)	Strongly Disagree/ Disagree (%)	Neutral (%)	Agree/Strongly Agree (%)
My professional activities are enhanced through collegial relationships with administrators.	3.52 (1.068)	22	14	64
Unionization institutionalizes conflicts between teachers and school administrators.	2.73 (9.46)	45.8	29.2	25
The contract separates educators into us (teachers) and them (administrators).	3.18 (1.094)	30.4	22.6	47.0

to 25%) fits the narrative that the teachers' and administrators' relationship is important for professional action and therefore institutional conflict may interfere with the relationship. However, by a margin of almost two-and one-half to one (19.4% to 47%), the responding teachers believe that the contract does separate the educators into us and them. The respondents' view of the us and them relationship in a unionized environment is certainly tangled.

The respondents assert that collegial relations with administrators are important. Unions do not institutionalize conflict. However, the contract does create an us and them relationship. The teachers may believe that conflict may be a two-way street in which both administrators and unions cause conflict.

Industrial organization, strictly interpreted would hold teachers responsible only for the faithful reproduction of lesson plans and classroom routines developed elsewhere. It would not require, expect, or sometimes even tolerate invention, creativity, and spontaneity on the part of teachers.
Charles Taylor Kerchner & Julia Koppich, "Organizing Around Quality: The Struggle to Organize Mind Workers," in Ronald D. Henderson, Wayne J. Urban, & Paul Wolman (eds.), *Teacher Unions and Education Policy: Retrenchment or Reform?* (Amsterdam: Elsevier, 2004), 187–221, 188–189

When the industrial labor model is applied to education teachers become labor and administrators become management, creating a professional chasm between teachers and administrators. Lawrence Cremin points out that "even after teacher education . . . had been dramatically upgraded in the 1960s, teachers . . . still articulating the rhetoric of professionalism, joined the union movement in large numbers and related to school administration . . . through collective bargaining rather than professional colleagueship."[20]

The fact that both groups are educators with common goals and values is lost in this model. The separateness of some work activities performed by the teachers and the administrators are emphasized, and not the commonality of purpose, roots, interests, or overlapping functions. Us under the industrial labor is no longer inclusive; it is exclusive by defining the them.

Consequently, the emphasis on separateness places a great premium on conflict management within the labor relations and the contract. Keane likens traditional industrial union based bargaining to a game of marbles. The Board has all the marbles and the union's job is to take them away; a zero-sum game. When I win, you lose.[21] Victory under this model is too often defined by vanquishing the other.

This focus on conflict management is further enhanced because collective bargaining is a system for creating agreement when trust is low and the union members believe that they must be protected by a legally binding instrument that spells out in some, and at times excruciating, detail the terms and conditions of their work. Earlier researchers of collective bargaining in education wrote, "contracts must be legally explicit, anticipate contingencies, and provide for policing and enforcement. Such a system may well exaggerate the differences and diminish trust between parties."[22] The relationship becomes formal, standard, and enforced through a centralization of decision-making (see chapter 5 for a more in-depth discussion). It becomes bureaucratic through a web of rules.

Agreements that are too easily reached engender suspicion that the union has been co-opted by management, and that if the union leaders had just held out longer and fought harder the membership would have "won" more from management, or so the argument goes. If there are no battles to be won by the union, why should union members continue to shell out some of their hard-earned wages to pay union dues? If there is no conflict of interest, there is nothing to bargain and, consequently the need for a union is called into question.

The ability to secure the interests of their members is what unions do and sell to potential members. "[I]t is bread-and-butter issues—securing money and benefits—that have a lot to do with why unions enjoy teacher loyalty. Teachers simply believe their unions protect their interests."[23] The brand name of the union must be protected by its vigorous actions to protect its members from administrators.

Workers relinquished control over the outcomes of the product of their work with the advent of industrial unionism. Decisions about what is produced and how it is produced passed from the worker into the hands of management. Workers were divorced from the formation of policy; all they can do is implement it and not develop it. For example, in several states, public employee collective bargaining law prohibits management from bargaining over matters of policy.

The court in *Ridgefield Park Education Association v. Ridgefield Park Board of Education* buttressed this idea of union separation from public policy formation when it asserted:

> There would be little room for community involvement if agreements concerning educational policy matters could be negotiated behind closed doors . . . . However, the very foundation of representative democracy would be endangered if decisions of significant matters of governmental policy were left to the process of collective negotiations, where citizen participation is precluded. Matters of public policy are properly decided, not by negotiation and arbitration, but by the political process. This involves the panoply of democratic institutions and practices, including public debate, lobbying, legislation and administration.[24]

Similarly, a later New Jersey court stated, "Matters of public policy are properly decided, not by negotiation and arbitration, but by the political process."[25] Clyde Summers, a leading scholar in labor law, posits that a subject of bargaining removes the decision-making from the normal open public forum to a closed forum when the union speaks for all employees.[26]

Furthermore, Kerchner, Koppich, and Weeres note, "collective bargaining invests in the union the obligation to enhance and protect the rights of its members. It implicitly invests in management the responsibility for the health of the educational enterprise."[27] Under the industrial union model, teachers, like factory line workers, are only supposed to perform a labor function; they are not supposed to influence the outcome of the product. Uniform rules and procedures standardizing work may work well on the factory floor but not in the classroom where flexibility to address changing conditions an context is a valued professional attribute.

This is not the reality of teaching. Classroom teachers' daily work with students is a translation and reconfiguring of policy to meet the highly individualized contexts of their classroom. Educators do not turn out mass-produced students; teaching is a highly complex process calling for the use of judgment in nonroutine situations. "The problem, of course, is that schools are utterly dependent on teachers not acting like industrial workers. Real teaching is a mixture of imperatives drawn from craft, artistic, professional, and industrial routines."[28] Classroom teachers make and adapt policy with the myriad decisions they make daily.[29] Teachers are not divorced from policy as the industrial union labor model would have us believe.

> Call it the industrial-factory model: power resides at the top, with state and district officials setting goals, providing money and holding teachers accountable for realizing predetermined ends. While rational on its face, in practice this system does not work well because teaching is a complex activity that is hard to direct and improve from afar. The factory model is appropriate to simple work that is easy to standardize; it is ill suited to disciplines like teaching that require considerable skill and discretion.
>
> Jal Mehta, "Teachers: Will They Ever Learn?" *New York Times* (April 12, 2013). Site visited June 29, 2019, available at https://www.nytimes.com/2013/04/13/opinion/teachers-will-we-ever-learn.html?pagewanted=all.

Another problem created by the importation of the industrial labor model into education is the inherent proposition that teaching is labor: teachers labor but they are not laborers. This viewpoint seeks to standardize labor so that the work of the member of the bargaining unit so that it can be reduced to a common language, thus making enforcement of the CBA more uniform and efficient. Thus, the rich texture and nuanced actions combining the professional and artistic elements of teachers in preparing and presenting lessons are often distorted and contorted into a meaninglessness mélange to fit into contract language. Harvard professor Susan Moore Johnson captures this outcome asserting that collegiality and pedagogical technique do not easily bend to the cast-like form of contract language.[30]

The industrial labor union model ill-serves a profession that thrives on the collegial relations of educators: teachers and principals working in concert at the school level. La Rae Munk asserts that the factory model of labor relations "does not work well for individual professionals working in an educational setting. Teachers are not assembly line workers and their 'product' is not mass produced and interchangeable widgets, but individual educated children."[31] Like students, teachers are more than interchangeable labor parts.[32]

The industrial union paradigm fits uncomfortably on the shoulders of educators. Susan Moore Johnson and Susan M. Kardos note the challenges of this paradigm for the realities of professional educators. They write:

> Industrial bargaining was good for setting rules and dividing resources, but of little use in addressing the many educational challenges that educators faced,

such as reorganizing school schedules, supporting interdisciplinary teaching, effectively integrating students with special needs into regular classrooms, or engaging parents more actively in the education of their children.[33]

Harvard education professor Susan Moore Johnson notes this limitation referring to the standardizing effect of collective bargaining asserting that the industrial model "prizes uniformity not variety."[34] This works in opposition to schools and classrooms that need flexibility and responsiveness to the changing and challenging needs of the student population. While professionalism looks to standards of practice that inform and define the standard of care that the professional must exercise, underlying that standard of care is the exercise of professional judgment based on a literature that informs that standard of care.

The standardization and uniformity found in industrial style bargaining often, too often, results in narrow and highly detailed descriptions of rights of teachers and responsibilities of administrators. An example can be found in restrictions that define how many staff meetings can be held and how long to the minute they can be held. It is as if the expected collegiality and policy discussions that create a professional flexible school environment must fit neatly into prescribed time slots without regard for complexity. These types of provisions create "new professional roles for teacher or eliminate the deliberate divide between labor and management."[35]

Collegiality and contextualized decision-making, critical aspects of professional educational practice, do not fit neatly into a system that is standardized and centralized. As Amy Gutman writes:

> If the democratic ideal of professionalism suggests that school boards and principals treat teachers as partners in determining school policy, then it also suggests that unions demand fewer fixed policies regarding curriculum, discipline, and work schedules, and more participatory structures within which teachers can join administrators and members of school boards in shaping these policies.[36]

STRIKES AND WORK-TO-RULE

Industrial unions have used external strategies (strikes)[37] and in-plant strategies (work-to-rule) to bring pressure to bear on the employer to meet their demands that they may not be achieving at the bargaining table. Teacher unions have adopted these tactics to varying degrees. Strikes have greater public visibility and result in greater disruption of the school, and the lives of parents as well as students. Work-to-rule (WTR) is not as obvious in that many of the pressure points used occur inside the school, before, during, and after the school day.

A strike is a "work stoppage; a concerted refusal of employees to perform work that their employer has assigned to them in order to force the employer to grant certain demanded concessions"[38] that the union has not gained at the bargaining table. Its purpose is to "coerce" the employer to accede to their demand "by preventing the conduct of [the employer's] business until [there is] compliance with the demand."[39] The work stoppage in education and coercion to meet the demands is stopping, or at least interrupting the education of the children of the community. Strikes in private business are aimed at the business's bottom line. The coercive harm is the loss of profits.

"Unlike a strike in the private sector, a strike in the public sector is not an economic instrument operating through the market. It is primarily a political instrument working through the political process."[40] In education, the harm is aimed at the education of students. A student's education is the bottom line.

The target of a strike is the business of the employer and any potential harm or discomfiture to the public can be mitigated by the going to another place of business to purchase the desired goods. The potential customers lost through the strike will eventually return, so the argument goes, and business will continue. The irony is that working with students in meaningful ways is what brings the great majority of teachers into teaching. Yet, in order to respond to bargaining challenges, teachers and their union sometimes turn to those students and withhold those services that sustain and define educators as professionals arguing that it is ultimately in their best interests that they strike and withhold important services. Some may argue that striking runs counter to the interests of the teacher.

Arguments for the right of teachers to strike include this is the counterbalance to the power of the school board. Another is that it is only through a strike that appropriate public funds will be allocated for the schools. Fiscal crisis and less than supportive state legislators have a devastating effect on public schools. The union could lobby for more funds, but often they were just one of many special interest groups. From the early 1970s, strikes often responded to drastic cuts to education, which negatively impacted wages and benefits as well working conditions for teachers. The Philadelphia strike of 1972–1973 and New York's 1975 strike over pensions were precipitated by such financial crises.[41]

Similarly in the Chicago strike of 2016, teachers stated that it is not just about step and lane, pay raises, and pensions.[42] The strike also purported to address the following:

Over the years, we have witnessed cut after cut after cut to our student's education. We watch as programs are slashed and budgets are reduced and we see firsthand how this affects our students and how it affects are ability to do our jobs, to teach. We have watched as schools are closed, class sizes increases, special education budgets are slashed, and wrap around services (such as social workers, counselors, psychologists, and nurses) are stripped to the bare bone for our students. We have worked in schools that have become increasingly filthy and not allowed our students to drink from the drinking fountains because of the lead in the water.[43]

Other arguments assert that any harm to students from a strike is transitory. The students are typically statutorily entitled to a set number of days of instruction. Therefore, when the strike is over the students will get the days of instruction they are entitled to receive. Schools do not go out of business in a prolonged strike, which often serves on a brake on private sector strikes. Teachers will get paid for the days they teach even if the employment occurs during the summer to make up for the strike days.

The Ocean Hill-Brownsville Strike

While most teacher strikes involved wages and benefits, one major strike and seemed more in line with larger policy issues. This was the 1968 Ocean Hill-Brownsville strike in New York City, also referred to as the Ocean Hill-Brownsville crisis.[44] The Ocean Hill-Brownsville neighborhood schools served a predominantly black and Latino/Latina students while two-thirds of the teachers were white. In 1968 there was a push for greater community influence and control over public schools. Three districts, including Ocean Hill-Brownsville were given local control over schools through local boards.

The local school board clashed with the largely white union, the United Federation of Teachers, whose president was Albert Shanker. The local school board received a report from a hall monitor in which he observed and intervened in an art class in Junior High School 271 in Brooklyn. The students were shouting and flinging paint at one another while the teacher stood by "helplessly."

Several days later the local school board and the principal dismissed the art teacher and eighteen other white teachers and administrators. There was no due process given prior to the dismissals, several were called out of their classrooms and given a telegram informing them of the dismissal from the school. This set the stage for the conflict between the union and the school board.

The local board could not dismiss the teachers and administrators from employment in the New York School District. Its action, instead, barred the educators from working in the Ocean Hill-Brownsville schools. Albert Shanker ordered the dismissed teachers to report to their teaching assignments asserting that they had not received any due process before their discipline. This sparked a standoff between union members and activists, causing a riff between the union, the community, and many liberal groups. In many ways it was a conflict between local control and teacher rights.

Shanker's position was that the summary dismissals violated a bedrock principle of teacher unionism. The union stood solidly for the proposition that teachers cannot be fired "because of their political leanings, gender, race, religious beliefs, pregnancy or opposition to administrative—all once-common practices."[45] When the educators were barred from entering their schools 350 UFT teachers went on strike. The strike morphed into three strikes involving almost 58,000 teachers affecting about one million students.

However, 60 percent of the Ocean Hill-Brownsville students continued to attend classes. Students entered their school through police barricades separating the picketing teachers from community-control activists. Police in riot gear were stationed on rooftops of schools with police helicopters circling overhead.

The strike lasted thirty-six days. It ended in November of 1968 when the New York State Board of Regents transferred three principals and reinstated the fired teachers. Following the end of the strike at a lecture at Oberlin College, Shanker responded to a question whether he worried about the strikes affecting children stating, "Listen, I don't represent children. I represent the teachers."[46]

THE OCEAN HILL-BROWNSVILLE STRIKE

On one side, community-control advocates argued that the education of poor black and brown children was too urgent a matter to bother with labor protections, bureaucratic protocol or even basic politesse—much the same argument we hear from opponents of teacher tenure today. On the other side, the UFT worried that allowing parents and noneducator activists to essentially fire teachers they didn't approve of would devalue the professionalism of educators and return them to a climate of constant job insecurity.

Dana Goldstein, "The Tough Lessons of the 1968 Teacher Strikes" *The Nation* (October 13, 2014). Site visited July 29, 2017, available at https://www.thenation.com/article/tough-lessons-1968-teacher-strikes/.

A strike is part of the tangled relationship discussed by DeMitchell and Cobb about simultaneously being a professional with an ethic of service to the other (the other) and the legitimacy of being represented by a union with a requirement to serve the interests of the unit members. Their exploratory study asked, "Hardball labor tactics such as work-to-rule or strikes associated with industrial unions conflicts with my sense of professionalism?" Fifty-six percent agreed or strongly agreed with this question, while 32 percent strongly disagree or disagree.[47] Yet, teachers will be moved to strike by circumstances in their workplace.

Focusing on the legitimate self-interest of teachers is the question striking teachers must confront, "Are you better off for having gone out on strike?" "Is the school better off for having gone out on strike?" Focusing on the recipient of the service asks, "Are my students better off for me going out on strike? Does it matter if the answer is, in the short-term, no, but in the long-term yes?"

Work-to-Rule: Just Follow the Rules

Work-to-rule (WTR) is a tactic that is used by unions to force the administration/management to accede to their bargaining demands. It is not a strike, which withholds all work and the employee removes herself/himself from the workplace. But it is a similar pressure tactic in which the employee reports to work and only does the work that is explicitly required—strictly complying with the rules, including the CBA and no more but no less.[48]

In WTR in the schools, teachers show up, offer instruction during the allotted time, teach, and nothing more. For example, in Hawaii in 2012, teachers only performed, under the contract, their duties from 8:00 AM to 3:00 PM. School meetings, meetings with parents, IEP meetings for example which may be held after 3:00 PM may not be attended. In 2013, the Harford County Education Association (Maryland) issued guidelines to their teachers regarding a WTR action taken in response to stalled negotiations over several years that was set to take place at the start of the next school year. The guidance stated in part:

- DON'T call or email parents outside of the duty day.
- DON'T purchase any materials for your classroom. . . . Request all materials for your classroom which you normally purchase on your own from your principal. If your principal cannot provide needed materials through their normal budget, simply do not use them.
- Consider resigning from coaching and other extra-curricular activities.
- Notify your principal that you will no longer be performing the voluntary activities that you normally do. These include but are not limited to [School Improvement] Team, Social Functions, Clubs, Dances, etc.
- Meet at the lobby at the prescribed end of the teacher day. Walk out together. Take nothing home with you.[49]

The Maryland State Education Association described WTR in the following manner:

As educators our time is valuable. Sometimes it is necessary to pull back and remind administrators and supervisors how valuable we really are. Collective action, like working to rule, can be a powerful tool for your negotiations team at the bargaining table. It's amazing to see the change of attitude of board negotiators when confronted with an active, aware, involved group of educators willing to take action to protect their careers, students, and schools.[50]

Impasse was reached in Northhampton, Massachusetts, in May of 2019. The union and the school board had been negotiating since February of 2019. A negotiating team member stated after the decision to go to WTR, "We're not going to be working for free—we're not going to be doing things outside of our contract."[51] Andrea Egitto, the bargaining team member, stated clearly laying the blame for the actions on the school committee: "It's not something we want to do," she said. "Every single person I've spoken to today feels sad. We all feel really sad and disappointed in our school committee and our city."[52]

Strikes and WTR actions in education are borrowed from the industrial unions. Whether in the public schools or in a private business, the pressure tactics of a strike or a WTR are designed to force management to accede to the demands of the union. If we exert enough pressure that management is no longer willing to accept the harm to their bottom line (a cost-benefit analysis, at least in the short term) they will settle. For private business the bottom line is clear, return on investment. For public education the bottom line is not clear, it is not found on the ledger but in the future lives of students.

If the long-term bottom lines of education are both the private benefit of an education which can positively impact life's opportunities for the individual and the public benefit of support of the citizen to actively support the society, is the impact of such power tactics supported by a profession? Can public education continue to adhere to and follow the template of the organizing principle of the industrial union? I answer no, we must resist the effort to turn the public education into a market model and must instead adhere to the principles of education as a fundamental interest of our society.

> The American people have always regarded education and the acquisition of knowledge as matters of extreme importance. We have recognized the public schools as a most vital civic institution for the preservation of a democratic system of government and as the primary vehicle for transmitting the values on which our society rests.
> *Plyler v. Doe*, 457 U.S. 202, 221 (1982).

NOTES

1. Susan Moore Johnson and Susan M. Kardos, "Reform Bargaining and Its Promise for School Improvement," in *Conflicting Missions? Teachers Unions and Educational Reform*, ed. Tom Loveless (Washington, DC: Brookings Institution Press, 2000), 19.

2. Bob Chase, *The New NEA: Reinventing Teacher Unions for a New Era*. Remarks Before the National Press Club (February 1997) at 2. Site visited August 9, 1997, at http://www.nea.org.

3. Charles T. Kerchner and Douglas E. Mitchell, *The Changing Idea of a Teachers Union* (New York: The Falmer Press, 1988).

4. Kerchner and Mitchell, *The Changing Idea of a Teachers Union*, 206–212.

5. Ibid., 208.

6. Ibid., 209.

7. Ibid., 210.

8. The exception to the NLRA as the touchstone for public sector bargaining is the Lloyd-LaFollette Act guaranteeing federal workers the right to organize—postal workers in 1863 formed the first federal employee organization—and to petition Congress regarding grievances. William L. Sharp, *Winning at Collective Bargaining: Strategies Everyone Can Live With* (Lanham, MD: The Scarecrow Press, Inc., 2003), 1–2.

9. Charles Taylor Kerchner and Julia E. Koppich, "Organizing Around Quality: Examples and Policy Options from the Frontiers of Teacher Unionism," Site visited February 9, 2003, at http://63.197.216/crcl/mindworkers/udpages/fulldoc.htm.

10. Author, "Time for Teaching," *The Boston Globe* (September 8 1997): A14.

11. Susan Moore Johnson and Susan M. Kardos, "Reform Bargaining and Its Promise for School Improvement," in *Conflicting Missions? Teachers Unions and Educational Reform*, ed. Tom Loveless (Washington, DC: Brookings Institution Press, 2000), 7–46, 8.

12. http://www.mass.gov/lrc/. Site visited January 26, 2008.

13. Todd A. DeMitchell, "A Reinvented Union: A Concern for Teaching, Not Just Teachers," *Journal of Personnel Evaluation in Education* 11 (1998): 255–268, 257.

14. La Rae G. Munk, *Collective Bargaining: Bringing Education to the Table* (Midland, MI: Mackinac Center for Public Policy, 1998), 16.

15. Charles Taylor Kerchner and Krista D. Caufman, "Building the Airplane While It's Rolling Down the Runway," in *A Union of Professionals: Labor Relations and Educational Reform*, ed. Charles Taylor Kerchner and Julia E. Koppich (New York: Teachers College Press, 1993), 1–24, 15.

16. Julie E. Koppich, "Getting Started: A Primer on Professional Unionism," in *A Union of Professionals: Labor Relations and Educational Reform*, ed. Charles T. Kerchner and Julie E. Koppich (New York: Teachers College Press, 1993), 194–204, 200.

17. Kerchner and Mitchell, *The Changing Idea of a Teachers Union*, 237.

18. Linda Kaboolian, *Win-Win Labor Management Collaboration in Education: Breakthrough Practices to benefit Students, Teachers, and Administrators* (Mt. Morris, IL: Education Week Press, 2005), 24.

19. Todd A. DeMitchell and Casey D. Cobb, "Teachers: Their Union and Their Profession. A Tangled Relationship," *Education Law Reporter*, 212 (2006): 1–20, 15.

20. Lawrence A. Cremin, *American Education: The Metropolitan Experience 1876–1980* (New York: Harper & Row Publishers, 1988), 500. The original quote included nursing education, nurses, and hospital administrators parallel to teachers.

21. William G. Keane, *Win Win or Else: Collective Bargaining in an Age of Public Discontent* (Thousand Oaks, CA: Corwin Press, Inc., 1996), 11. Keane states that the focus of our concern must move from "How much can we get (union) or keep (management/Board)?' to 'How can we fairly (to students, staff, and community) and wisely use the resources available to us?"

22. Anthony M. Cresswell and Michael J. Murphy, with Charles T. Kerchner, *Teachers, Unions, and Collective Bargaining in Public Education* (Berkeley, CA: McCutchan Publishing Company, 1980), 479.

23. Steve Farkas, Jean Johnson, and Ann Duffett, *Stand by Me: What Teachers Really Think about Unions, Merit Pay and Other Professional Matters* (Washington, DC: Public Agenda, 2003), 17.

24. *Ridgefield Park Education Association v. Ridgefield Park Board of Education*, 393 A.2d 278 (N.J. 1978), 287.

25. *Local 195, IFPTE, AFL-CIO v. State of New Jersey*, 443 A.2d 187, 191 (N.J. 1982).

26. Clyde Summers, "Public Sector Bargaining: A Different Animal," *University of Pennsylvania Journal of Labor and Employment Law* 5 (2003): 441–452, 448, writing, "Designating a subject as bargainable means that the decision-making process has moved from the open public forum of normal political processes to a closed forum where the union speaks for all employees."

27. Charles Taylor Kerchner, Julia E. Koppich, and Joseph G. Weeres, *United Mind Workers: Unions and Teaching in the Knowledge Society* (San Francisco: Jossey-Bass Publishers, 1997), 137.

28. Charles Taylor Kerchner and Julia E. Koppich, "Organizing Around Quality," in *Conflicting Missions? Teachers Unions and Educational Reform*, ed. Tom Loveless (Washington, DC: Brookings Institution Press, 2000), 284 (emphasis in original).

29. See Michael J. Lipsky, *Street-Level Bureaucrats: Dilemmas of the Individual in Public Services* (New York: Russell Sage Foundation Publications, 1983) for a discussion of how teachers and other street-level bureaucrats while not making policy for an organization adapt and implement policies within the confines of the classroom to better render their service to the public.

30. Susan Moore Johnson, "Can Schools Be Reformed at the Bargaining Table?" *Teachers College Record* 89 (1987): 269–279.

31. La Rae G. Munk, *Collective Bargaining: Bringing Education to the Table* (Midland, MI: Mackinac Center for Public Policy, 1998), 16.

32. Johnson and Kardos, "Reform Bargaining and Its Promise for School Improvement," 10, state that industrial unionism assumes that "similarly skilled workers are interchangeable and should be treated alike."

33. Ibid., 19.

34. Susan Moore Johnson, "Paralysis or Possibility: What Do Teacher Unions and Collective Bargaining Bring?" in *Teacher Unions and Education Policy: Retrenchment or Reform?* ed. Ronald D. Henderson, Wayne J. Urban, and Paul Wolman (Amsterdam: Elsevier, 2004), 33–50, 40.

35. Johnson, "Paralysis or Possibility," 44.

36. Amy Gutman, *Democratic Education* (Princeton, NJ: Princeton University Press, 1987), 83–84.

37. An interesting study found a relationship between the experience of the negotiators and a reduced likelihood of a strike. They postulated that increased experience allowed the negotiators to better judge the "true concession curve" and thus were less likely to be involved in negotiations that end in a strike. Their study of public school

bargaining "supports the hypothesis that bargainers' experience is an important determinant of the incidence and duration of strikes." Edward Montgomery and Mary Ellen Benedict, "The Impact of Bargainer Experience on Teacher Strikes," *Industrial and Labor Relations Review* 42 (1989): 380–392, 391.

38. Legal Dictionary: The Free Dictionary, "Strike." Site visited July 27, 2017, at http://legal-dictionary.thefreedictionary.com/strike.

39. Henry Campbell Black, *Black's Law Dictionary: With Pronunciations* (5th ed.) (St. Paul, MN: West Publishing Company, 1979), 1275.

40. Summers, "Public Sector Bargaining," 452.

41. John Shelton, *Teacher Strike!: Public Education and the Making of a New American Political Order* (Urbana: University of Illinois, 2017), 8.

42. DNAinfo Staff, "It's Not Just the Money: Chicago Teachers Explain Why They Might Strike," DNAinfo (October 10, 2016). Site visited July 27, 2017, at https://www.dnainfo.com/chicago/20161010/downtown/ctu-teachers-strike-class -sizes-support-staff-classroom-crowding.

43. DNAinfo Staff, "It's Not Just the Money."

44. D.L. Chandler, "Little Known Black History Fact: Ocean Hill Brownsville Conflict," (2017). BlackAmericaweb.com. Site visited July 28, 2017, at https://bl ackamericaweb.com/2014/05/12/little-known-black-history-fact-ocean-hill-brownsvi lle-school-conflict/. See also Jerald E. Podair, *The Strike that Changed New York: Blacks, Whites, and the Ocean Hill-Brownsville Crisis* (New Haven, CT: Yale University Press, 2004).

45. Dana Goldstein, "The Tough Lessons of the 1968 Teacher Strikes," *The Nation* (October 13, 2014). Site visited July 29, 2017, at https://www.thenation.com/ article/tough-lessons-1968-teacher-strikes/.

46. Ibid.

47. DeMitchell and Cobb, "Teachers," 13.

48. John W. Budd, *Labor Relations: Striking a Balance* (Boston: McGraw-Hill, 2005), 300.

49. Cindy Mumby, "Harford County Education Association Outlines 'Do's and Don'ts' of Work-to-Rule," *Dagger: Local News with An Edge* (July 17, 2013). Site visited April 16, 2019, at http://www.daggerpress.com/2013/07/17/harford-county-ed ucation-association-outlines-dos-and-donts-of-work-to-rule/. (emphasize in original).

50. Author, "Work to Rule," *Maryland State Education Association* (n.d.). Site visited June 25, 2019 at https://www.marylandeducators.org/work-rule.

51. Greta Jochem, "Northampton Teachers Announce Work-to-rule Over Stalled Contract Talks," *Daily Hampshire Gazette* (May 15, 2019). Site visited June 10, 2019, at https://www.gazettenet.com/Northampton-teachers-and-staff-announce-wor k-to-rule-25570247.

52. Jochem, "Northampton Teachers Announce Work-to-rule Over Stalled Contract Talks."

Section 2

TRANSITIONS

THE IMPACT OF UNIONIZATION

Chapter 5

Transitions

Formalize, Standardize, and Centralize Relationships

Conflict arises when policies and procedures are formalized and standardized, one of the key results of collective bargaining.[1]

The union as an organization must be prepared to "let go" of standardized and centralized work rules.[2]

COLLECTIVE BARGAINING AND RELATIONSHIPS

When a group of workers, whether it is a group of teachers or administrative staff or school administrators, seeks to unionize, relationships between the employees and the employer change. A written contract is inserted between the teacher and her/his administrator and adds to the web of rules that define the teachers' and the administrators' working conditions. This move to reduce the working relationship to an enforceable written contract that seeks to define the working relation has consequences.

Uniformity is sought across the school district impacting all teachers alike. For many, this uniformity through formalization, standardization, and centralization of relationships results in lack of flexibility, or nimbleness to respond to changing conditions and the differing contexts of schools and classrooms. Collective bargaining has three results that impact labor relations in a school district.

First, a collective bargaining agreement (CBA) is a formal document that establishes an enforceable agreement between the union and the school district. It is a promise to do something (e.g., teach, serve the interests of students) in return for a valuable benefit (e.g., wages). In public sector education, the contract establishes the relationship between teachers and the school board regarding wages, benefits, and terms and conditions of employment. The CBA

81

is a written document that replaces informal understandings, unilateral control by the school district over specific activities, and conflicting school board policies with explicit statements defining expectations and responsibilities between members of the bargaining unit and the school district.

Second, it standardizes teachers' work because the contract defines the working conditions for all teachers who serve under the contract. And, third, it centralizes relationships in that standardization is best assured when the two parties to the contract collaborate to ensure that the contract is applied equitably to all members of the unit and across all schools. Collective bargaining is a rule-making activity. The duty of the enforcement of the rules belongs to both management and the union, thus centralizing decision-making.

Formalization, standardization, and centralization typically occur because, as a matter of public policy, collective bargaining is designed to achieve labor peace. Labor peace is more easily maintained and managed if it is controlled. Formalizing, standardizing, and centralizing relationships are means that are used to attain labor peace, manage conflict, and maintain stable operations. Each of these three effects on labor relations in education resulting from collective bargaining will be discussed here (figure 5.1).

Formalize Relationships

Prior to collective bargaining relations between teachers and principals could be informal. With the advent of collective bargaining the relationship

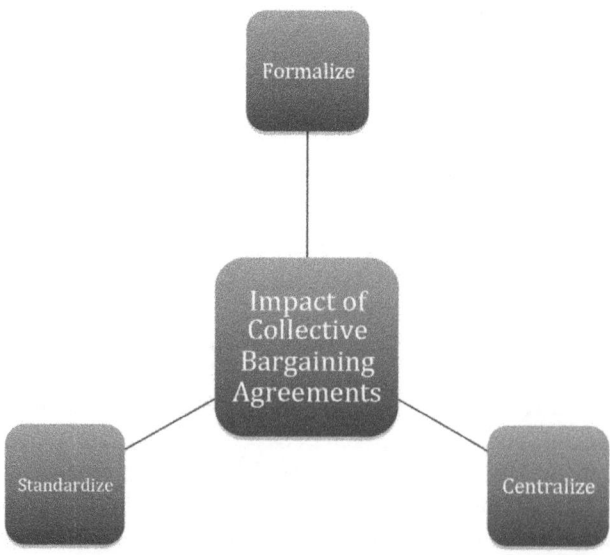

Figure 5.1   Relations in Education in Response to Collective Bargaining: Formalization, Standardization, and Centralization. *Source*: Created by Author.

between employee and supervisory, teacher and principal, is no longer just between those two. Their interaction is now connected to others in a larger mosaic.

Reducing the relationship to a written contract (that in many school districts is literally reduced to a size that could fit in a pocket) helped to formalize the relationships. Comments such as "I have to check on the contract before we proceed further" catch educators in a web of rules. The contract becomes a mediating force between teacher and principal. Individual responses to specific needs are often replaced with a response that fits within the contract. A tug on one strand of the web of rules can be felt throughout the web. What happens between one teacher and principal can affect all.

This is not to say that collective bargaining does not allow for the give-and-take that characterizes a good workplace or a good school. Those informal relationships still exist. But, lurking behind the space for informal, collegial relationships carved out from the *us* and *them* industrial union mind-set is the knowledge that informality will give way to formality if the contract is threatened. Adam Urbanski, a nationally known union leader, writes, "Central to any specific efforts to improve our urban schools, is the relationship between school managers and teachers' unions. Without labor management collaboration, even the best efforts of management are tantamount to one hand clapping."[3]

It can be argued that a more formal relationship grounded in the bilateral contract establishes a more professional relationship, one not based on personal relationships conjuring up the specter of favoritism. However, formalization is also associated with efficiency, which leads to predictions of increased bureaucratic control as well as due process guarantees.[4] A formal relationship better characterizes the hierarchical reality of large school districts, some could argue.

Standardize Relationships

A collectively bargained contract covers all members of the bargaining unit. Because the CBA applies equally to all teachers in all schools within the school district, contracts tend to "produce more standardized work environments."[5]

The standardized work environment envisioned in a contract fails to capture the ethos of the education profession, the complexity of teaching, or the need for some autonomy in the classroom in order to effectively respond to the needs of students. Cooper and Liotta describe teaching as "highly interpersonal, individualistic, and human."[6] These are not the attributes/activities that are easily standardized so as to enhance control and enforcement.

Standardization is not the same as professional standards developed through rigorous examination of practice, which comports with the accepted literature and research that forms the core knowledge of the profession. A basic tenet of collective bargaining and unionization is that the negotiated contract must apply uniformly and equally to all teachers covered by the contract. How the contract is interpreted and applied in one school must be consistent with how it is interpreted and applied in all schools in the school district.

A uniform contract calls for standard application irrespective of differing conditions and needs at the various schools. "Under conventional labor relations, unions negotiate for an entire district but pay little heed to the needs of individual schools."[7] Standard cookie cutter responses replace handcrafted responses in a uniform contract. This standardization and resulting uniformity do not fit easily into a profession that requires flexibility of response to context. The predictability of the factory line arguably does not capture the richness, autonomy, and interdependence of the classroom.

Collegiality and pedagogical technique necessary to education do not bend easily into the structures of contract language.[8] Normative descriptions of professional work do not easily translate into the legal descriptions of a contract.

Professional teaching practice calls for diagnosis of the situational factors of the class and its individual students and an adaptation of teaching strategies. Professional practice demands flexibility and differential action based on the context of the learning situation. In addition, Johnson and Kardos note that teacher collective bargaining has "meant more standardized schools, leaving principals with less latitude to run their schools."[9] Unfortunately, the standard union work rules found in contracts too often contribute to an inflexible environment.

Karl E. Weick has characterized schools as loosely coupled organizations.[10] Loosely coupled organizations are characterized as largely self-functioning subsystems. They often have a lack of coordination. For example, prior to No Child Left Behind (NCLB), if one asked a teacher where the school district curriculum guide was located, the query may be met with a blank stare because teachers sought autonomy once their classroom door was closed. A more tightly coupled structure, a top-down structure, is a result of NCLB. Now teachers not only know where the district's curriculum guide is located but they often refer to it as well as the state grade-level expectations and benchmarks. The adopted curriculum is becoming the taught curriculum.

A trade-off with a more tightly coupled system is that a loosely coupled system is a good system for localized adaptation. Local groups can adapt to their part of the environment without changing the entire system. The opposite, standardization, may be too restrictive. Standardization leads to a more tightly coupled system with a resulting greater control and command over activities. Standardization leads to less flexibility. Since the standardization of a contract impacts teachers and principals primarily, it leads to less flexibility, less ability to adapt quickly to unique conditions and changes in the work environment and new pressures from the external environment.

A quick look at the Detroit teachers' strike in September of 1992 reinforces this conclusion that standardization leads to less flexibility at the school site level. In 1992, the Detroit teachers went on strike. The Detroit strike, in part, was over the school board's conception of restructuring schools so as to give the schools greater autonomy and flexibility to respond to their unique circumstances. "Under the school board proposal at issue in the Detroit strike, a school could become 'empowered' if it's principal, 75 percent of its teachers, and its parent council agreed."[11]

An empowered school would be free to operate as it wished, as long it met the achievement standards for Detroit students and it balanced its budget. An empowered school, according to the school board proposal could waive provisions of the teaching contract after a two-week notice to the union of the waiver request. This two-week notice would give union leaders time to discuss the issue with the teachers and to possibly convince them to vote against the measure thus preserving the contract for all.

In response to the school board's plan to decentralize and restructure decision-making in the school district, John Elliott, the teachers' union president, argued that "Detroit teachers prefer a centralized school system with the same work rules and procedures for everyone."[12] A school board member countered the union's insistence that the same work rules must apply to every teacher that it was to him "the antithesis of professionalism."[13]

Randall Eberts et al. draw an interesting intersection between the standardizing effect of the negotiated contract with student outcomes and dropout rates. They cite studies that found modestly positive effects of teacher unions for average students but negative effects for atypical students.[14] They posit that part of the answer is the "standardizing effect of teacher unions on schools."[15] Their explanation for this phenomenon is that unionized schools rely more heavily on traditional instruction, which benefits the average student, rather than on differentiated instruction, which benefits the atypical student.

DeMitchell and Cobb, in their study of teacher perceptions of professionalism and unionism, offer another view of the role of the standardizing effect of the contract on teaching. They asked whether quality teaching could be standardized into a contract. The responding teachers cast doubt on the relationship. On a Likert type scale of one, Strongly Disagree, to five, Strongly Agree, the teachers had a mean of 2.45 tending to the "Disagree" (point 2 on the scale) that quality teaching can be standardized into a contract. Only 16.7 percent of the responding teachers "Agreed" or "Strongly Agreed" with the proposition, whereas, 62.8 percent "Disagreed" or "Strongly Disagreed" with whether quality teaching can be standardized into a contract.[16]

The core professional activity of teachers, teaching, according to these respondents, cannot be successfully implented into a contract. The contract, with its standardizing effect, cannot easily capture the uniqueness of teaching with its differing contexts and the need for differential instruction given the makeup schools and classrooms. Reflecting back on chapter 4 and the discussion of four dimensions of work, the artistic portion of teaching is not easily cataloged and assigned to a section of the CBA.

The Mayor of Boston commissioned a report on the implementation of school-based management reform. School-based management requires a decentralization of authority. This reform strategy was designed to give teachers and principals more authority to run their individual schools. In return for increased authority and increased salaries, teachers promised to become more accountable for educational results.

Fossey and Miles concluded in their report to Mayor "that school-based management had little impact on the quality of education in Boston."[17] The study identified two major reasons why school-based management had so little effect on school performance. First, the School Committee and the administrators lacked commitment to the reform as evidenced by their reluctance to grant waivers and a seeming unwillingness to cede authority to individual schools. The second reason, and most important one for this study, was the relationship between the union and the administration reflected in the union contract, grievances, and arbitration decisions.

Specifically, the study pointed to contract rules that contributed to an inflexible environment for managing schools, an emphasis on seniority, and an industrial model of labor relations that "discouraged innovation by requiring that all changes in working conditions be submitted to the union for negotiation prior to implementation."[18] These were rules that valued standardization throughout the school district in contradiction to the tenets of school-based management that decentralized important decisions.

In other words, the reform of decentralization to move decisions closer to the place where they are enacted conflicted with the standardization required by a CBA. The conundrum of the reform of the decentralization of school-based management in a collective bargaining environment is underscored in that the schools could seek a waiver of the CBA. The standardizing effect of the contract required a waiver for the reform to work.

Stanford professor Terry M. Moe, an opponent of teacher unions, asserts that the specificity of CBA rules on such activities as how many minutes must be spent in the classroom, how much time can be spent in work activities outside the classroom, and how much time on campus are not supportive of professionalism. He writes, "This is an industrial approach characteristic of what blue-collar unions insist upon for unskilled workers."[19]

Centralization for Uniformity

This need for standardization leads to centralization since the contract must be administered uniformly. The contract is between the union and the school board, therefore both parties are charged with its uniform application. Uniformity is enforced at the central office by both union and school district officials through the formal grievance process and the informal and sometimes guarded relationship that often develops between union officials and district-level administrators. Both parties to the contract seek uniform application of the contract; otherwise, instability might ensue, thus endangering the labor peace achieved by the contract. "Both the union and the district office administrators seek to centralize and standardize behavior through consistent rule interpretation, scrutiny, and enforcement."[20]

When I served as the Director of Personnel and Labor Relations for a California school district, we started each administrative leadership team meeting with the question, "What grievances have been filed or may be filed?" This question was designed to centralize the enforcement and implementation of the CBA. This agenda item was designed to make sure our responses to grievances and contract issues were consistent and standard.

On the rare occasion that a principal wanted to take a position that was contrary to the central view that the school district held on a specific contract section, I would inform the principal that I would not support her/his position and that I would overturn it at the next grievance level. This is fairly regular practice and one that reinforces the centralization of the contract so as to achieve a standard interpretation of the CBA. It is an aspect of centralization so as to achieve the standardization of the CBA across the school district. While formalizing relationships so that they can be standardized and enforced centrally provide a rational model for adherence to a collectively bargained contract, it does little to support proper activities and responses to the context of schools and its students.

TRANSITIONS

As discussed earlier, collective bargaining moves relationships from the informal to the formal, from greater individualization of local needs to the one-size-fits-all standardization of responses that contracts require for the uniformity of the contract, and the need for centralization at the district level to enforce uniformity between schools and teachers. Collective bargaining impacts the relationship between teachers and administrators as well between the union and the school district. The union and the administration must work in tandem to formalize, standardize, and centralize relationships.

The sidebar here explores another transition, a more personal transition. Nathan Fellman explores the transition he experienced as he moved from union leadership to school leadership—moving from us to them. His discussion of his transition underscores the personal nature of changing perceptions. Administrators who have moved from the classroom to the front office will likely identify with the challenges they faced from all fronts.

SIDEBAR: TRANSITION: UNION PRESIDENT TO ADMINISTRATOR

Nathan Fellman, M.Ed., Ed.S. (Ph.D. Student, Leadership & Policy Studies, University of New Hampshire)

Assistant Principal

Ross A. Lurgio Middle School

Bedford, New Hampshire

In the spring of 2013, I accepted a position as assistant principal in the middle school where I had been teaching for the previous five years. This otherwise fairly routine transition occurred in my second year in the role of union president. Prior to serving as the president, I worked as a negotiator on the union's bargaining team since 2009. Needless to say, those early years of the Great Recession were difficult and tense times for labor relations in public education across the country, and our district was no different. Where once, I sat across the table from the administrators, I now sit with them as peers working through the implementation issues from a management perspective that I bargained as a union negotiator.

Despite the pay increase and job title, stepping into an administrative role was in some ways a demotion. As union president, I was directly involved with negotiations of salary, benefits, and working conditions of the over 360 professional staff members in the district. I met with the superintendent on a regular basis and discussed district policies and practices. But more interestingly, as union president I was able to be a leader in unique ways. I expressed and promoted my ideals of professionalism, collaboration and student success that I truly believe make education a great profession. My peers accepted them. As a school administrator, using those same lofty ideals somehow became interpreted as petty management directives. The same words and concepts were perceived very differently. Where I soared on lofty rhetoric previously, I am now weighed by the pull of gravity in my new position.

Transitioning from a union president to a school administrator in the same district provided me with some insights into the roles of district leaders, both in the union and in administration, that I doubt I would understand in the same way had I not made the transition within the same district. I imagine that I would have dismissed some of the changes in how people perceived me as having changed rather than a change in the perceptions about my new leadership roles.

This change in perception came not just from teachers but also from other administrators in the district. I'll never forget how the superintendent introduced me to the leadership team during my first leadership retreat in the summer of 2013. There were some other new faces around the table at the retreat, so the superintendent went around introducing the new administrators. But my face was not new to the group, so when he finally came to me, he made the very kind and strategic remark: "So as you can see, for the first time ever, I've decided to invite the association to the leadership retreat." Everyone laughed—genuine laughter—and a tension I had not yet realized was there was broken; my new peers accepted me.

That initial tension at that leadership table is important to note because it represents unease that was apparent among my former colleague teachers and my new colleague administrators alike as I transitioned from one leadership role to another. That it was so quickly broken is also important because it demonstrates the power of collaboration and trust between teachers and administrators, between the union and the district.

As I grow in my role as an assistant principal, I am learning how to balance my new responsibility as a manager with my old ideas on leadership. I am building trust with teachers as their assistant principal the same way I helped build trust as their union president. Because of the nature of the work that educators do, there is far more in common between teachers and administrators, between the union and the district, than many people often acknowledge. Certainly, there will always be areas of tension but also there are wide fields of common ground in which to plant the seeds of trust and collaboration that can overcome that tension.

Role change is not always easy. Allowing people to change roles is not always straightforward; transitions are hard. Individuals carry their perceptions of colleagues, which may not change as their colleagues change their classroom for an office. Just as the relationship between individuals changes when collective bargaining is introduced, relations and expectations change for those who move from the classroom to the Patience, understanding, and communications focusing on those shared commitments may reduce some of the "them" and build more of "us."

Formalization, standardization, and centralization as a by-product of collective bargaining may not well serve education. Susan Moore Johnson in her early and seminal study of the impact of unions in schools wrote, "[t]he increased centralization of the school district is thought by others to have excessively and unwisely formalized, standardized, and rationalized school operations."[21] It is no coincidence that some reforms, such as restructuring schools require a suspension of some of the more inflexible articles in a CBA.[22]

Uniqueness or context of teaching environments is typically not accommodated in CBAs. Normative descriptions of professional work do not easily translate into the legal descriptions and standardizing language of a contract. Collegiality and contextualized decision-making, important aspects of professional educational practice, do not fit neatly into a system that is formalized, standardized, and centralized.[23]

NOTES

1. Daniel J. Julius and Nicholas DiGiovanni, Jr., "What's Ahead in Faculty Collective Bargaining? The New and the Déjà vu," *Journal of Collective Bargaining in the Academy* 4 (2013): 26.

2. Julie E. Koppich, "Getting Started: A Primer on Professional Unionism," in *A Union of Professionals: Labor Relations and Educational Reform*, ed. Charles T. Kerchner and Julie E. Koppich (New York: Teachers College Press, 1993), 202.

3. Adam Urbanski, "Improving Student Achievement Through Labor-Management Collaboration in Urban School Districts," *Educational Policy* 17 (2003): 503–518, 503–504.

4. William P. Bridges and Wayne J. Villemez, *The Employment Relationship: Causes and Consequences of Modern Personnel Administration* (New York: Plenum Press, 1994), 104.

5. Robert M. Carini, "Teacher Unions and Student Achievement," in *Reform Proposals: The Research* Evidence, ed. Alex Molnar. Education Policy Research Unit, Arizona State University (Tempe: AZ, 2002) Site visited June 4, 2016, at http://nepc.colorado.edu/files/Chapter10-Carini-Final.pdf, 10.12

6. Bruce S. Cooper and Marie-Elena Liotta, "Urban Teachers Unions Face Their Future: The Dilemmas of Organizational Maturity," *Education and Urban Society* 34 (2001): 101–118, 109.

7. Charles Taylor Kerchner, Julia E. Koppich, and Joseph G. Weeres, *Taking Charge of Quality. How Teachers and Unions Can Revitalize Schools* (San Francisco: Jossey-Bass Publishers, 1998), 14.

8. Susan Moore Johnson, "Can Schools be Reformed at the Bargaining Table?" *Teachers College Record,* 89 (1987): 269–280, 269.

9. Susan Moore Johnson and Susan M. Kardos, "Reform Bargaining and its Promise for School Improvement," in *Conflicting Missions? Teachers Unions and Educational* Reform, ed. Tom Loveless (Washington, DC: Brookings Institution Press, 2000), 18.

10. Kenneth E. Weick, "Educational Organizations as Loosely Coupled Systems," *Administrative Science Quarterly* 21 (1976): 1–19.

11. Ann Bradley, "Teachers in Detroit Strike Over Proposal for Flexible Schools," *Education Week* (September 9, 1992): 21.

12. Bradley, "Teachers in Detroit Strike Over Proposal for Flexible Schools."

13. Ibid.

14. Randall W. Eberts, Kevin Hollenbeck, and Joe A. Stone, "Teacher Unions: Outcomes and Reform Initiatives," in *Teacher Unions and Education Policy: Retrenchment or Reform?* ed. Ronald D. Henderson, Wayne J. Urban, and Paul Wolman (Amsterdam: Elsevier, 2004), 51–79, 56.

15. Eberts, Hollenbeck, and Stone, "Teacher Unions."

16. Todd A. DeMitchell and Casey D. Cobb, "Teachers: Their Union and Their Profession. A Tangled Relationship," *Education Law Reporter*, 212 (2006): 1–20, 18.

17. Richard Fossey and Karen Miles, *School-Based Management in the Boston Public Schools: Why Isn't It Working?* Unpublished Report Commissioned by the Mayor of Boston (1991). A copy of this report was furnished by Richard Fossey.

18. Fossey and Miles, *School-Based Management in the Boston Public Schools*, 9.

19. Terry M. Moe, *Teachers Unions and America's Public Schools* (Washington, DC: Brookings Institution Press, 2011), 205.

20. Todd A. DeMitchell, "Collective Bargaining, Professionalism, and Restructuring," *International Journal of Educational Reform* 2 (1993): 77–81, 79.

21. Susan Moore Johnson, *Teachers Unions in Schools* (Philadelphia: Temple University Press, 1984), 5.

22. See Todd A. DeMitchell and Thomas Carroll, "Educational Reform on the Bargaining Table: Impact, Security, and Tradeoffs," *Education Law Reporter*, 134 (1999): 675–693, 691, conclude in their study of superintendents' perception of reform and bargaining, "Educational reform can be bargained but not necessarily with ease or with a strong sense of security that the reform will have an opportunity to work before it is watered down or eliminated in a new round of collective bargaining."

23. Some union officials and school administrators have recognized the potential negative impact of these outcomes by recommending that "thin contracts" be negotiated alongside of, and not as exceptions, to the comprehensive, one-size-fits-all CBA. While standardized conditions across the school district are formalized and centrally controlled to ensure standardization, thin contracts focus on the site level where education is delivered and the contract is implemented. It recognizes the differences among schools and seeks flexibility for meeting the differing needs of students and the community. Sensitivity and responsiveness to local needs drive thin contracts.

While not widespread, it has surfaced in certain specific situations. For example, consider Howard Blume's 2011 comments in *The Los Angeles Times*:

"Some union activists say thin contracts diminish both employee rights and the union's legitimate influence over school operations. Other teachers defend the thin contracts, saying they provide needed flexibility at schools and potentially give teachers more meaningful input."

Howard Blume, "'Thin Contracts' Will Be Required for Groups Bidding to Take Over L.A. Schools," *The Los Angeles Times*, L.A. Now (May 10, 2011). Site visited June 6, 2016, at http://latimesblogs.latimes.com/lanow/2011/05/thin-contracts-will-be-required-for-groups-bidding-to-take-over-schools.html.

Chapter 6

The Union Member and the Professional

A Tangled Fit

Could unionized teachers simultaneously fight for their own interests as workers and for the educational interests of the city's children? Or were those two priorities at odds?[1]

Only professionals are *expected* to act in the public interest, to create a calculus that balances self- and civic interest.[2]

Unionism is predicated upon serving the needs of those employees it represents at the bargaining table and through enforcement of the collectively bargained agreement. Professionalism, broadly speaking, is predicated upon rendering a service to another, someone in need of their service. Unions serve the needs of its members; professions serve the broader needs of society and the specific needs of patients and clients. Both roles of union member whose interests are being served by a union and a professional who serves the needs of others are legitimate and both may be contradictory at times.

For some, the words "professional" and "union member" do not fit easily together. Tina Maragou Hovekamp sums up the conundrum in her article on unions and professional librarians. She notes that librarians, through their professional associations, focus on the autonomy and independence of the job. However, it is often assumed that unions are "mainly interested in the membership's private benefits, mainly economic, and perpetuate an impression for professional employees as dependent workers with limited control over their jobs."[3] How to resolve these two is a challenge. This chapter explores this challenge.

Professionals tend to work in complex and sometimes ambiguous settings and exercise judgment informed by the accepted practices of the profession. Some have considered this to the essentially description of teaching in a classroom filled with students. "Education researchers often focus on the nature of teaching as ambiguous, complicated work, requiring judgment, action, and the continuous ability to reflect and revise decisions on the basis of one's observations and insights."[4]

Another education commentator wrote, "To some extent teaching can be described as floating and full of surprises."[5] Teachers' work is not rote, mechanical, nor capable of being reduced to a recipe of ingredients. Normative descriptions of professional work do not easily translate into the legal descriptions of a labor contract. Teachers use the craft knowledge of teaching handed down from teacher to teacher as the wisdom of practice as well as developing creative and artistic teaching strategies, however, it is, or it should be, essentially a profession whose members are bound by expert research based shared knowledge; a degree of autonomy to adjust accepted practices of the practitioners based on the research of the field to meet the context of the classroom; and a deep commitment to align decisions with the best interests of their students, rigid work rules tend to serve standardization and individual defined professional practice do not reflect the expectations of fellow professionals. Shared knowledge, practices, and commitment to students reflect professional practice.

Teachers consider themselves to be professionals,[6] and public education is the most heavily unionized occupation in the United States.[7] Teacher unionism and professionalism have had a peculiar and tenuous relationship. David Schuman writes the following of this conundrum: "Teachers want to be respected, want to be thought of as professionals, yet are members of strong labor unions."[8]

For the great majority of teachers, the crush of the workday in the classroom consumes their time and energy. For most teachers, the reality of the classroom forces the role of professional front and center. Comments such as "I am a professional, this is my professional judgment, and I need to be treated as a professional" are heard more often in schools than the comment "I am a union member." Teachers seek to present themselves to the public and to each other as professionals.

While they consider themselves professionals, they want the protection that comes from being a member of a union. How the tenets of unionization and professional notions of teaching coexist is an issue with which many educators as well as teacher unions have struggled. "Historically, professionalism has been defined in ways that are detrimental to union organization."[9]

The influence of collective bargaining and unions and their impact on teachers and schools is salient in a time of high stakes accountability and policy making. Too little is known about the impact of these two forces on public education.[10] DeMitchell and Barton in their study of principals', teachers', and union building representatives' perceptions of reform and collective bargaining posed the following tentative conclusion: "Although the rise of unions and collective bargaining was built on a foundation of self-interest, that self-interest may not extend to professional activities. . . . Teachers may not see unions as being related to activities that are at the core teaching."[11]

The concern about the impact of the industrial labor model on teaching leads to the issue—does collective bargaining, the work of unions, promote "a conception of teaching as labor rather than as professional work."[12] How do teachers reconcile the seemingly disparate, even contradictory roles of member of a learned profession and union member?

Professor Poole describes the challenge in the following way: On the one hand, there are members of the organization who identify with a professional image and who strive to create a teacher organization that will affirm this professional image. On the other hand there are members whose desire to perceive themselves, and to be perceived by others, as professionals is less of an imperative.[13]

For the great majority of teachers, the crush of the workday in the classroom consumes their time and energy. According to Cooper and Liotta the conundrum is that while "teachers in many communities are union members, they still see themselves and their work as primarily professional—helping children to learn. They identify with their students and the needs of their students."[14]

For most teachers, the reality of the classroom forces the role of professional front and center. Comments such as "I am a professional, this is my professional judgment, and I need to be treated as a professional" are heard more often in schools than the comment "I am a union member." Teachers seek to present themselves to the public as professionals.

THE CONUNDRUM: THE UNION MEMBER

Unionism is predicated upon serving the needs of its members. Teachers under collective bargaining moved from being spoken for by school administrators and board of education to having their interests represented through an exclusive representative—the union. Those needs, commonly called bread-and-butter, are wages, benefits, terms and conditions of employment including security. At the advent of collective bargaining "[t]eachers wanted higher salaries and better benefits, not necessarily a higher standard of respect."[15] The job of the union is to "get" those things for its members. "Unions provide a collective voice that seeks to enhance and secure the social and economic wellbeing of its members."[16]

However, as Kerchner and Mitchell note, the legitimization of unions pursuing teacher economic interests through collective bargaining "has aroused public suspicion that teachers no longer speak for the public interest of schools or represent the real needs of children."[17] If teachers don't, which professional does? The daily work in the nation's classrooms evince teachers addressing the needs of their students.

Teachers look to their union for protection from those outside their classroom, primarily administrators and to some degree parents. A 2011 survey of teachers found that 81 percent of the respondents strongly or somewhat agreed with the following statement: "Without a union, teachers would be vulnerable to school politics or administrators who abuse their power." Furthermore, 77 percent strongly or somewhat agreed with the statement: "Teachers facing unfair charges from parents or students would have nowhere to turn without a union."[18]

There is an old saying in labor relations that, "administrators always get the union they deserve." In other words, if administrators are excessively intrusive, arbitrary, and/or capricious in their decision-making, employees will feel the need for the protection a union provides.

The findings of the DeMitchell and Cobb study underscore this point. Teachers who responded to their survey question, "without a union school administrators would diminish my professional decision making," agreed or strongly agreed with this statement by a margin of 55.3 percent to 30.1 percent strongly disagreeing or disagreeing with it.[19] Teachers in this study believe they need to be protected from administrators. Yet, 64 percent of these respondents believe that their professional activities are enhanced through collegial relationships with administrators.[20]

Similarly, more respondents in the study agreed or strongly agreed (81.4% versus 9.8% who strongly disagreed or disagreed), "I am better off as a professional with a union contract than without a union contract." However, it is interesting to note that union leaders and rank-and-file members significantly disagreed on the question with union leaders more strongly agreeing than the rank-and-file members.[21]

Teachers in this study believe that a union protects them from administrators, and that they are better off with a contract, yet believe that their professional activities are enhanced through collegial relations with these same administrators. As the title of the DeMitchell and Cobb study states, the relationship between union and profession is tangled.

In her study of union leaders, Poole, discusses what she calls the "paradox" of self-interest and educational interest. She writes, "Union leaders have a belief system that values quality public education for its own sake because it is right for children and right for society; however, they also support quality public education because it provides the means to support the union and its members."[22] A union leader in her study melded the pursuit of the economic welfare of its members with educational quality in the following way:

> The union can create a good environment for children by after and protecting the teachers. And I guess that boils down to [economic welfare]. . . . That trickles down to children. Because if your teachers are hurting, then your children are going to hurt. If you have teachers who are happy and are satisfied with their union, and have a reasonable wage to live comfortably, and don't have to worry about whether their job is going to be there next year or not, then I think you're going to have a better educational environment for the children.[23]

In other words, what is good for teachers is good for children, and it is best to take care of teachers first, which will in turn take care of children. This view places teachers at the core of education. Student wellbeing flows from teacher wellbeing, ostensibly secured through bargaining. Is this position akin to saying that what is best for physicians "trickles down" to what is best for patients? What is best for students is what is best for students. This should be the touchstone for the profession.

The union's function is legally and psychologically distanced from the responsibility for the institution of education[24] Even though both the NEA and the AFT have stressed that teaching is a profession, their emphasis has been on attaining material benefits such as higher wages and better health insurance. The importance of this central function of the union cannot be understated.

The Rand study conducted by McDonnell and Pascal found that "union efforts to obtain status benefits such as increased participation in school-site decision making often engenders teacher suspicion and a feeling that the union is 'falling down on the job.'"[25] And, that until a "union obtains these bread-and-butter items, movement toward greater professionalism is not likely."[26] Clearly, teachers expect their union to take care of business first, and the first business of a union is to secure the material benefits of their employment. Professionalism may ride in the backseat with bread-and-butter riding up front.

DeMitchell and Cobb's research underscores this point. They posed the following statement: "Unions pursue the bread and butter issues of wages, benefits, and security over professional issues." Sixty-seven percent of the respondents agree or strongly agree with the proposition. Only 2.9 percent strongly disagree.[27] The researchers write, "This is not surprising because this is what unions do in the collective bargaining process—pursue the self-interests of the members. It also underscores the tension between the work of unions and the goals of professionals."[28]

But, interestingly, the response to another question on self- interest and professional interests points to the tangled view that teachers have regarding the two roles. Just over 38 percent (38.4%) agree or strongly agree with the statement "If I had to choose, I would prefer that the contract protect my self-interest (e.g., salary) over my professional interests (e.g., pedagogy)." Almost a third (32.7%) sought the safe harbor of Neutral while just under 29 percent (28.7%) strongly disagree or disagree with the statement.[29] Does the large neutral response reflect a tension between the preferred response—protect my professional interests—and the reality-based response—protect my self-interests?

Bob Chase, the former president of the NEA, pursued a policy of reinventing the union. Speaking to the local NEA leadership in Florida about the union's role in achieving school quality, one union member stated, "Your job isn't to look out for the children; your job is to look out for me!"[30] This succinct statement captures the basic role of a union—to look out for the welfare of its members. Unions protect the legitimate interests and represent their members.

This perception appears to state that one can either be a union member pursuing collective self-interests or one can be a professional who pursues the interests of patients, clients, or students. However, Urbanski finds the dichotomy to be false writing, "to achieve a more genuine profession, teachers themselves will have to reject the phony choices between compensation and dedication, between unionism and professionalism, and between equity and excellence."[31]

DeMitchell and Cobb are not so sure that this dichotomy is so easily resolved. Susan Moore Johnson captured this position of tension some two decades earlier to the DeMitchell and Cobb study writing, "The school site is a place where teachers' values rather than union values prevail."[32] Teachers take pride in their work. Professor Johnson writes, "For most teachers, being part of a good school took precedence over union membership."[33]

The table is set. On one side is the union member pursuing his or her self-interest through a collectively bargained contract. On the other side of the table is the professional educator who serves the best interests of the students. Or, do they sit on the same side of the table?

But with today's protests, public school teachers are pushing back harder than ever against rigid definitions of professionalism. Instead, they are offering their own student-centered approach, combining training, context, flexibility, and a lifelong commitment to children and society.

Robert Bruno, "When Did the U.S. Stop Seeing Teachers as Professionals?" *Harvard Business Review* (June 20, 2018). Site visited June 26, 2019, available at https://hbr.org/2018/06/when-did-the-u-s-stop-seeing-teachers-as-professionals.

Most teachers probably are content to stay in the role of professional and only leave it in times of stress when their security is threatened. It could reasonably be asserted that this is the way teachers untangle the two roles; I am a professional by choice and preparation and a union member by circumstance. The roles are tangled but will they become less tangled in the future? Whatever the answer, there is a tension of roles that is worth exploring.

The DeMitchell and Cobb studies (2006 & 2007) will be reviewed after the discussion on professionalism to gain a perspective on how teachers may be reconciling or attempting to reconcile these two roles.

THE CONUNDRUM: THE ROLE
OF THE PROFESSIONAL

What does it mean to be a professional? Casey states that professionalism is essentially a "contested concept."[34] The term is used loosely in everyday life. Helterbran notes that the general practice is to use the term "professional" "as both a position for which someone is paid and the quality of the performance of one's job."[35] George Strauss identified three main categories for organizing organizations that include professionals:

(1) *Professional Societies*, concerned with the advancement of knowledge and/or professional interests.
(2) *Quasi-unions*, associations with a professional base and job-oriented interests.
(3) *Unions*, which concentrate on the economic situation of their members.[36]

Where does the teacher reside in these three categories? Are they members of a learned profession with a strong research base to guide accepted standards of practice aimed at the best interests of the student. Are they semi-union members?[37] Or are they full fledged union members?

This chapter focuses on neither of those conceptions of professionals—the professional athlete versus the amateur athlete or the cab driver who treats you in a professional manner and gets you directly to your destination quickly and in one piece. Instead, this chapter will focus on the member of a learned profession.

Professional educators should obviously be paid as opposed to volunteering their services, they should treat students, parents, and fellow educators, including administrators in a respectful professional manner, and they should act with integrity;[38] they should also strive for the higher standard of a member of a learned profession which holds service to the other—the individual or individuals dependent upon the service being rendered—as the highest ideal. This chapter will use the term "professional" to mean a member of a learned profession.

Professionalism is built around expert knowledge, usually gained through extensive education and training.[39] Professional work is complex and non-routine. It involves a standard of practice recognized and adhered to by the practitioners but applied in varying contexts. The standards are enforced by the professional organization, typically through an internal code of ethics.[40] Professionals exercise judgment within the accepted standards in the best interest of the client or others. Because judgment must be used in applying professional knowledge to meet client's needs, that knowledge cannot be easily reduced to rules or prescriptions.

Further divorcing industrial unionism from professional practice is the understanding and accepted notion that it is exercised for the good of the public, whereas, unionism protects the self-interest of its members. "Professionals are obligated to do whatever is best for the client, not what is easiest. Most expedient, or even what the client himself or herself might want."[41] Similarly, William J. Goode argued that one of the two core principles of professionalism is a "service orientation."[42] The second is a specialized body of knowledge gained through extended study.

Specific to education and professionalism, the National Board for Professional Teaching Standards has identified five core propositions: (1) teachers are committed to students and their learning, (2) teachers know the subjects they teach and how to teach those subjects to students, (3) teachers are responsible for managing and monitoring student learning, (4) teachers think systematically about their practice and learn from experience, and (5) teachers are members of learning communities.[43] These five propositions are supported by the assumptions that professionalism is predicated upon the following:

> [A] body of specialized, expert knowledge together with a code of ethics emphasizing service to clients. The knowledge base typically provides substantial, but not complete, guidance for professional practice. Professionals possess expert knowledge, but often confront unique, problematic situations that do not lend themselves to formulaic solutions. Professionals must cultivate the ability to cope with the unexpected and act wisely in the face of uncertainty. . . . [P]rofessionals . . . pursue an ethic of service and . . . employ special knowledge and expertise in the interests of their clients.[44]

Echoing the National Board, Linda Darling-Hammond offered the following three principles of professionalism:

1. Knowledge is the basis for permission to practice and for decisions that are made with respect to the unique needs of clients.
2. The practitioner pledges his first concern of welfare to the client.
3. The profession assumes collective responsibility for the definition, transmittal, and enforcement of professional standards of practice and ethics.[45]

Professionalism holds a special place for teachers. For example, in a follow-up study on teachers' perceptions of their academic freedom,[46] Fries, Connelly, and DeMitchell conducted focus group research with public school teachers.[47] The participants were given a scenario on academic freedom that served as a springboard for the discussion. Higher education considers academic freedom to be a constitutionally based freedom. The teachers in this qualitative study did not adopt that legal foundation for academic freedom. Instead, the first theme that emerged from the data was professionalism defines academic freedom.

The teacher participants consistently referred to professionalism when discussing the contours of their academic freedom. Professionalism to them was less of a right and more of a responsibility. The teachers couched their analysis of academic freedom in terms of their professional relationship to the students and not in terms of a constitutional right to free speech.

The term "professional" is not one that is associated with jurisprudence on academic freedom in either higher education or academic freedom in the public schools. Professionalism is a wider concept than free speech in the schools. "Free speech as the touchstone for academic freedom focuses on the rights of the teacher/professor, whereas academic freedom based on professionalism is based on the responsibilities owed to the recipient of the professional activity (e.g., instruction)."[48] It is noteworthy that these teachers grounded their sense of academic freedom on the bedrock of the professional responsibility that they owe their students.

THE FIT IN TWO PARTS

As stated earlier, DeMitchell and Cobb conducted a single study on the fit between union membership and a member of a profession but reported their findings in two articles. The two studies will be reviewed. The overarching question was, "Is teacher unions and collective bargaining compatible with teacher perceptions of professionalism?"[49] The following specific questions focused the research:

1. Do union activities support the professionalism of its members?
2. Does a collectively bargained contract support the professional activities of teachers?
3. Is there a difference between the union leaders' perceptions and the perceptions of the rank-and-file members with regard to professionalism?

The survey included twenty-four Likert-style items that asked respondents their level of agreement with a variety of statements relative to their perceptions of the teaching profession and teacher unions.[50] The items were developed to discern respondents' understanding of how they reconcile the apparent contradiction of the role of unions predicated on furthering their self-interest and their role as a professional grounded in service to the student (e.g., *professionalism is compatible with union activity*).

In particular, items were constructed around seven categories: (1) the intersection of professionalism and unionism, (2) the legacy of the industrial union, (3) the tension between self-interest and professional interests which focus on an ethic of care to one whom receives the professional service, (4) the separation of educators into us and them, (5) the elements of professional work, (6) the intersection of teaching and the contract, and (7) serving the professional needs of teachers.

The surveys were sent to randomly selected schools in states that have public sector collective bargaining laws. One hundred and three teachers responded.

The second part of the research asks teachers to respond to two prompts.[51] These prompts seek to gather more in-depth knowledge about teachers' perceptions of professionalism and the role of the union by asking whether unions support or harm professionalism. This part is an extension of the quantitative method of the first part of the study utilizing a quasi-quantitative method designed to gain greater depth of understanding of the data. While it uses qualitative analytical tools, it is not, strictly speaking, a qualitative design. The two prompts were: *Unions support professionalism in the following ways* and *Unions harm professionalism in the following ways.*

The respondents were given the following definition of professionalism in an effort to provide clarity and consistency in responses.

"For purposes of this survey, please use the following definition of professionalism or professional work:

- Professionalism involves the use of expert knowledge gained through extended study.
- Professionalism involves the use of expert knowledge in unique and problematic situations.
- Professionalism is bounded by a code of ethics that emphasizes service to a client/student.
- Professional work is essentially intellectual and varied.
- Professional work requires the autonomy to control's one work.
- Professional work is not routine work."[52]

Only a few of the more salient findings for this chapter will be reported here leaving the reader to go to the original if greater depth of understanding is warranted.

- The teachers consider their union to be a professional organization rather than a traditional industrial union ($M = 3.80$).[53] However, almost one-third (32.3%) disagree/strongly disagree that hardball labor tactics like strikes conflict with their sense of professionalism.[54] In other words, the teachers belong to a professional association not a labor union but almost one-third saw no conflict when this professional association acts like an industrial union.
- Unions are predicated upon serving the self-interests of its members. Yet, less than half of the respondents in this research (42.5%) agree or strongly agree

with the proposition *(M* = 3.10). Why would teachers not acknowledge this essential truth – unions exist to serve the self-interests of its members?

The respondents seemed similarly conflicted about the role of the union protecting the interests of the students (*M* = 3.15) and the interests of the public (*M* = 3.01).[55] These latter two statements are more consistent with the role of professionalism, protecting the "other" over self. In an interesting twist, elementary school teachers' responses were significantly different than middle and high school teachers. The elementary school teachers had a mean of 2.63 disagreeing with the statement that unions protect the interests of the public while middle (*M* = 3.21) and high school teachers (*M* = 3.32) agree with the statement. Elementary school teachers, on this question, appear to hold the more traditional view that a union is not created to further the public good.

This question tends to lay bare the issue of unionism versus professionalism. If unions do not protect the public's interests, can teachers lay legitimate claim to being part of a true profession since teachers tend to find unionism and professionalism to be compatible? Does the teachers' apparent conflicted responses reflect this tension between legitimate roles, union member and professional, without finding a satisfactory resolution?

- The section of the instrument on Teaching and the Contract goes to the heart of professionalism and unionism. Five questions sought to understand how the contract supports or inhibits teaching, the core professional activity. Teachers believe that the contract protects their professional activities (*M* = 3.77) but the mean response to the statement that the contract fosters quality teaching is on the other side of neutral (*M* = 2.72).[56] Only 21.8 percent agree or strongly agree with the statement. However, almost one-third (31.8%) take refuge in the neutral response. Does this mean that they do not know what impact the contract has on their teaching or are they uncomfortable with their conclusion?

While the teachers believe that the contract supports their ability to make independent decisions regarding their teaching (*M* = 3.50), they also believe that the artistic/creative elements of teaching (*M* = 2.66) cannot be addressed in the contract nor can quality teaching be standardized into a contract (*M* = 2.45).[57] "Teachers in this study perceive that teaching may be too complex to fit neatly into the strictures of collective bargaining."[58] The responses to this section underscore how tangled the relationship is between union member and member of a learned profession. The contract, according to the responding teachers, supports professional decision-making but it does not seem to support quality teaching.

DeMitchell and Cobb conclude:

Teachers are professionals. How their professionalism meshes with union membership and bargained contracts is tangled. The contract protects their professionalism in the abstract but may not protect it in concrete ways. They want the union and the contract to fit into their professional lives but may have not buffed those edges or possibly figured out a way to buff those ragged edges that allow for a neat fit between professional activity and union membership. Could it be that unions and contracts protect teachers' sense of professionalism but other mechanisms enhance and support the professional activities of teaching?[59]

Short Answer

A total of seventy-seven teachers responded to the prompts of harm and support.[60] Most responded to both prompts but not all did. All responses were transcribed and an iterative process of reviewing each response was conducted. Categories of responses were developed and then refined several times. Three themes emerged from the support prompt and four themes emerged from the harm prompt. The theme of protection was found in both prompts but with opposite meanings.

Unions support professionalism in the following ways:

A total of seventy-one teachers responded to this prompt. There was a strong sense in some of the responses of harbored past wrongs. Specific resentments were directed at administrators, whether past or present administrators is unknown. For example, an elementary school teacher wrote, "*Provide support to abused teachers (those unfairly reprimanded),*" and a high school teacher stated, "*They protect my legal right from being trampled.*"[61]

DeMitchell & Cobb also found that a second use of language in this prompt that stands out is the unilateral power of the union and the checking power of the union on administrative action. Power words describing unions include: protect, secure, support, provide, ensure, and guarantee. At times the impression from the response is that the union is exercising unilateral power. For example, an elementary school teacher states that the union "*provides days for inservice and professional development.*"[62] Obviously, unions cannot provide inservice and professional development days unilaterally. The workdays are not theirs to give. However, for these teachers, including past and present union leaders, these conditions of employment would not be possible without the union. In other words, these teachers may question whether the school district would support these activities.

However, in their first study, DeMitchell and Cobb posed this question to the same respondents, "I look to the union and not to the school district to meet my professional inservice needs." Eighty-three percent (83.5%)

strongly disagree or disagree with the statement. Only four respondents agree or strongly agree with the statement.[63] Once again, the roles of the professional and the union member are tangled. For professional issues teachers looked to the district for support and not to the union. Was their union relegated to a position outside the classroom door, while the school administration was invited inside?

Three themes emerged from the data: protection, advocacy, and support.

PROTECTION

The major thrust of this theme is that teachers would be in deep trouble without the union protecting them from administrators who are often characterized as mean, venal, and petty. For example, teachers write:

- *"I feel that teachers would be taken advantage of by administrators in their district if not protected by our union"* (elementary school teacher, union officeholder).
- *"Protect you from inept administrators and Protect teachers from the whims of administrators"* (elementary school teacher).
- *"The best teachers are often a threat"* (middle school teacher).
- *"Protection from arbitrary actions by incompetent administrators who stifle the creative professionalism possible in our career"* (high school teacher, union officeholder).[64]

These written responses are consistent with the responses to a question in the section The Profession and the Union ("Without a union school administrators would diminish my professional decision making"). The mean was 3.49 with 55.3 percent agreeing or strongly agreeing that the union protects teachers from administrators.[65]

ADVOCACY

The theme of advocacy includes how the contract attracts, retains, and frees up teachers. "A number of these comments describe a powerful union that 'assures' and 'allows' teachers to perform their professional duties without interference from administrators. The comments tend to give the impression that the union is not just a restraint on administrative action but that it may compel administrative action. These comments describe a proactive union and not a reactive union."[66] These elements focus on one of the major duties of the union, bargaining.

Another related concept is that unions enhance teaching through their advocacy that teaching is a profession. The comments on the contract as advocate include: *"bargains for teachers to be paid like they are professionals"* (elementary school); *"guarantees competitive wages, etc. to keep good individuals in this profession"* (middle school teacher, emphasis in original, union officeholder); *"Union contract speaks to a variety of important conditions that make professionalism prosper"* (high school teacher, union officeholder); and a middle school teacher provides a good summary, *"Allow[s] teachers to pursue their profession with less concern for contractual issues, which they would otherwise dedicate valuable time pursing if they negotiated individually."*[67]

The concept of enhancing teaching within the advocacy theme includes such comments as: *"In this era of 'scripted teaching,' I am assured my right to teach students in creative & effective ways"* (elementary school, union officeholder) and *"My union allows me to try things without long term censure from my administrators"* (middle school teacher, union officeholder).[68]

This subtheme appears to reconcile the two roles of professional and union member because it is the union that supports the professional work of the teacher. However, if the major work of unions is the bargaining and management of the contract, how is the following statement from the quantitative portion reconciled with this subtheme? The statement reads, "The artistic/creative elements of teaching can be addressed in a contract." The mean is 2.66 (disagreeing) with only 26.8 percent agreeing or strongly agreeing with the statement.[69] Furthermore, just over 61 percent of the respondents strongly disagreed or disagreed with the following proposition, "If I had a professional issue/question, unrelated to the contract, I would first turn to the union for assistance."[70]

The findings of the two parts of the study are tangled and not straightforward. Is advocacy for an external audience while the search for support for professional practice turns inward to the school and administrators?

SUPPORT

The last theme concerns inservice days and professional development. The respondents credit the union with securing time for these important pursuits. There are a total of fourteen (eight elementary school teachers, four middle school teachers, and two high school teachers) responses constituting 20 percent of the total written comments. Offering workshops, peer collaboration, promoting activities to support best practices, encouraging professional development, and *"require[ing] professional development as part of the contract"* (high school teacher) are cited as examples of how unions support professionalism.[71]

The teachers who responded to this prompt of support, believe that not only is union membership compatible with professionalism but that it is associated with providing a professional service to students.[72] The responses comprising these three themes reflect the quantitative responses that the teachers need the protection of the union and that they are better off working under a union contract than working without a contract.

Unions harm professionalism in the following ways:

A total of twenty-three (seven union officeholders) elementary school teachers, twenty-three middle school teachers (four union officeholders), and fifteen high school teachers (five union officeholders) responded to this prompt. The views expressed are not as hard-edged as some of the comments cited earlier. While there are some frustrated commentators, the comments, by-and-large, do not contain the same emotional content of personal wrongs. The comments appear to be more disagreements with and lamentations about the current state of affairs. However, one middle school teacher's comments may have captured the tone of the most strident criticisms of unions and summed up for many their concerns about unions. The middle school teacher wrote in the prompt for how unions support professionalism, *"Unions are the antithesis of professionalism!"*[73]

Four themes emerge from the analysis of harm—blind protection, the work of unions, divisiveness, and the union label.

Blind Protection

The issue of protection was the strongest theme of how unions support professionalism.[74] It is also the strongest theme of how unions harm professionalism. Clearly the issue of union protection is a central concern for many teachers and it is also a cause of great concern for many other teachers. Protection appears to be a double-edged sword: the union provides needed protection from the powerful and sometimes less than professional administrators versus protection of incompetent teachers, which demeans the profession.[75] Protection of the least capable teacher is a challenge for unions because most teachers are "troubled by the presence of incompetent teachers in their school building."[76]

For some, union protection is almost an unthinking genuflection of protection of the least worthy, while for others the protection of a union member is important for all teachers regardless of the fitness of the individual. One high school union leader wrote of this conundrum for unions, *"Sometimes we have to support people who we think are poor teachers."* An elementary school teacher and union officeholder stated, *"Automatically defending teachers whether they are right or wrong."* However, one high school teacher placed the blame on administrators for the retention of incompetent teachers writing, *"If administrators would do their jobs there has always been ways provided in contracts to help these teachers or eventually remove them."*[77] Should the protection of the least effective to the incompetent be the function of the union if there is a professional responsibility of its membership to serve the public?

WORK OF THE UNION

Two sub-themes comprise this theme: union activities (*"Unions focus on money, making teachers seem self-serving and unprofessional"*)[78] and pressure to conform (*"Also, if the union member does not wish to participate in certain activities, such as refusing to do activities after the school day, other staff members will sometimes try to apply pressure to conform"*).[79] The larger connection of the two sub-themes is found in an elementary school teacher's response: *"[The union] totally disregards the* work ethic *teachers choose to put into their job and instead places trivial issues at the forefront of their day-to-day business."*[80] This comment incorporates the pressure to conform—the disregard of the effort teachers put into their job—and what the teacher chooses is immaterial if it does not fit the viewpoint of the union on what should be done as part of the work. It also includes union activities, although not specified, that supersede what teachers want to do. This is opposite of the positive theme of advocacy discussed earlier.

DIVISIVENESS

Some of the comments are purely descriptive—*"Creates a 'them' and 'us' atmosphere"* (middle school teacher), while some respondents see conflict in the divisiveness—*"Often promotes an antagonistic relationship between teachers and administrators and school board"* (middle school teacher) and *"Interfere w/ positive interactions between admin & teachers: Create adversarial atmosphere"* (high school teacher, union officeholder).[81] Koppich notes this outcome when she writes, "[o]n the one hand, industrial-style collective bargaining gave teachers a voice and influence when they had none. . . . On the other hand, industrial unionism circumscribed teaching and created a kind of professional chasm between teachers and administrators."[82]

Interestingly, the responses to the survey instrument paint a different picture. The responses to the statement "Unionization institutionalizes conflict between teachers and school administrators" can be separated in the following manner: 45.8 percent (strongly disagree/disagree), 29.2 percent (neutral), and 25 percent (agree/strongly disagree). And, the same analysis can be applied to "The contract separates educators into us (teachers) and them (administrators): 30.4 percent (strongly disagree/disagree), 22.5 percent (neutral), and

47 percent (agree/strongly agree)."[83] The respondents establishing this theme clearly must be in the minority of the total respondents. However, it is striking that there are large neutral responses.

The responses to these two questions are consistent with the other in this subset of Us and Them. Sixty-four percent of the respondents agreed or strongly agreed that their professional activities are enhanced through collegial relationships with administrators.[84]

THE UNION LABEL

The union label theme refers to a belief that association with a union harms professionalism in the eyes of teachers and possibly more importantly in the eyes of the public. One elementary school teacher stated, *"just the paradigm of 'union' causes hostility."* A middle school teacher wrote, *"Unions harm professionalism in the negative feelings/opinions that some have of unions."* Another elementary school teacher may have summed up this theme with the comment, *"I don't hold banners/pickets . . . it's not what I do if it's for self-interest."*[85]

If the union label means the teacher association acts like its predecessor the industrial union, the response to the following statement supports this theme of harm, "Hardball labor tactics, such as work-to-rule or strikes, associated with industrial unions conflict with my sense of professionalism." Just over half of the respondents (56.2%) agreed or strongly agreed with the statement.[86] Union leaders and rank-and-file members had a significant difference on this question ($p = 0.002$) with union leaders having a mean of 2.83 meaning that hardball tactics do not conflict with their sense of professionalism and non-leaders having a mean on the other side of neutral of 3.61.[87] Nonunion leaders believe that hardball tactics conflict with their sense of professionalism, while union leaders hold an opposite viewpoint.

The teachers in this study are not monolithic in their understanding and approach to this potential conflict. Teachers want the protection of a union and a collectively bargained contract. They, however, note that there are limits to what the contract and the union can do to support their professional activities, especially when it comes to bargaining the professional contours of teaching. Union leaders and non-leaders differ significantly on several specific issues. However, they appear to be united as to whether they are better off with a union and a contract. "While their responses as to how unionism and professionalism fit together may be tangled, they are clear that ambiguity is preferable to working without a union and a collective bargaining contract."[88]

Teachers struggle for ways to find a fit between their union membership with its emphasis on pursing self-interest with their possibly greater identification as a professional providing a service in the best interests of the other, their students. In an essay critical of unions and professional responsibilities, Terry Moe concludes, "The education system is not a jobs program. It does not exist for the benefit of the adults who run it. It exists to educate children."[89]

BREAD-AND-BUTTER AND/OR PROFESSIONALISM

Today's teachers want more than just bread and butter basics from their unions. They expect that unions will not only protect them, but also will engage in some of the reforms aimed at transforming their profession.

Sarah Rosenberg & Elena Silva, *Trending Toward Reform: Teachers Speak on Unions and Future of the Profession* (Washington, DC: Education Sector, 2012), 3.

Unions and their members face the challenge of how to emphasize teacher professional responsibilities to students without predicating those responsibilities on securing their self-interests first. The old adage of what is best for teachers is best for students must be discarded. What is best for students is what is best for students; that is our professional obligation. A community of professional educators cannot easily thrive within the confines of standardized, central work rules, like those found in industrial union labor contracts.

Do teachers want their union to focus on professional issues or on the traditional bread-and-butter issues of higher wages, expanded benefits, better working conditions, and security? Just over twenty years ago the Seattle Education Association successfully negotiated a contract aimed at decentralizing the school system by guaranteeing teachers a say in their school's budgets, academic direction, staff development, and hiring. This move emphasizing school improvement has "raised fears among some of the rank and file that the union leaders have abandoned their traditional mission of protecting their members."[90] Twenty years later would those same fears be raised?

Ronald Henderson, the Director of the Research Department at the NEA underscores this point. He writes, "Collective bargaining has been too weak and too narrow to change the basic conditions that prevent teaching from becoming a profession on par with other vital functions in society."[91] If not through collective bargaining, the major work of a union, what can the union do to secure, maintain, and augment their member's professional work and professional standing? Or, is the union inherently constrained by its central role of protecting the self-interests of the unit of employees it was elected to represent?

While this remains a conundrum, it cannot be allowed to be further entrenched by administrators and teachers, unions and school boards, and legislators and citizens. The tangled fit must be untangled.

"One thing I said was teachers shouldn't have to make the choice between making a difference and making a living."—Jonathan Yuan, Ed.M.

Lory Hough, "Show Me the Money" (The Teacher Issue: A Special Report) *Ed.* (Harvard Graduate School of Education), 163 (Summer 2019): 40–44, 43.

NOTES

1. Dana Goldstein, *The Teacher Wars: A History of America's Most Embattled Profession* (New York: Doubleday, 2014), 74.

2. Charles T. Kerchner and Douglas E. Mitchell, *The Changing Idea of a Teachers' Union* (Philadelphia: Falmer Press, 1988), 227.

3. Tina Maragou Hovekamp, "Professional Associations or Unions? A Comparative Look," *Library Trends* 46 (1997): 232–244, 236.

4. American Federation of Teachers, *Building a Profession: Strengthening Teacher Preparation and Induction. Report of the K-16 Education Task Force* (American Federation of Teachers, 2000), 22.

5. Glenn Hultman, "Ambiguity as Work: Teachers' Knowledge Creation in Classrooms," *New Zealand Journal of Teachers' Work* 5 (2008): 21–35, 26.

6. Todd A. DeMitchell and Casey D. Cobb, "Teachers: Their Union and Their Profession. A Tangled Relationship," *Education Law Reporter* 212 (2006): 1–20, 11. On a five-point Likert type scale (1 = strongly disagree to 5 = strongly agree) teachers had a mean of 4.91 on the question "Teaching is a profession."

7. Terry M. Moe writes, "the largest, most powerful union in the country is not the Teamsters or the United Auto Workers, but the National Education Association." *A Union by Any Other Name* (2001), Education Next. Site visited June 15, 2007, at www.educationnext.org/20013/38moe.html.

8. David Schuman, *American Schools, American Teachers: Issues and Perspectives* (Boston: Pearson, 2004): 89.

9. Charles Taylor Kerchner, and Krista D. Caufman, "Lurching Toward Professionalism: The Saga of Teacher Unionism," *The Elementary School Journal* 96 (1995): 107–122, 110.

10. Michael Kirst likened our understanding of the role unions in policy making as a "dark continent" (Ann Bradley, "Education's 'Dark Continent,'" *Education Week*

(December 4, 1996): 25; Charles Taylor Kerchner, Julia E. Koppich, and Joseph G. Weeres, *United Mind Workers: Unions and Teaching In the Knowledge Society* (San Francisco: Jossey-Bass Publishers, 1997), xi, referred to unions as "the blind spot on the radar scope of educational reform"; Jane Hannaway and Andrew J. Rotherham, *Collective Bargaining in Education: Negotiating Change in Today's Schools* (Cambridge, MA: Harvard Education Press, 2006), 1, states there is a "profound lack of relevant data, research, and analysis" on the role of collective bargaining and reform.

11. Todd A. DeMitchell and Richard W. Barton, "Collective Bargaining and Its Impact on Local Educational Reform Efforts," *Educational Policy* 10 (1996): 366–378, 375.

12. Nina Bascia, *Unions in Teachers' Professional Lives: Social, Intellectual, and Practical Concerns* (New York: Teachers College Press, 1994), 3.

13. Wendy L. Poole, "The Construction of Teachers' Paradoxical Interests by Teacher Union Leaders," *American Educational Research Journal* 37 (2000): 93–119, 101–102.

14. Bruce S. Cooper and Marie-Elena Liotta, "Urban Teachers Unions Face Their Future: The Dilemmas of Organizational Maturity," *Education and Urban Society* 34 (2001): 101–118, 109.

15. William A. Streshly and Todd A. DeMitchell, *Teacher Unions and TQE: Building Quality Labor Relations* (Thousand Oaks, CA: Corwin Press, Inc., 1994), 10.

16. Todd A. DeMitchell and Casey D. Cobb, Commentary "The Professional and the Union Member: A Tangled Fit." *Teachers College Record*, December 12, 2007, http://www.trecord.org/content.asp?ContentId=14854ID14854.

17. Kerchner and Mitchell, *The Changing Idea of a Teachers' Union*, p. 239.

18. Sarah Rosenberg and Elena Silva, *Trending Toward Reform: Teachers Speak on Unions and the Future of the Profession* (Washington, DC: Education Sector, 2012).

19. DeMitchell and Cobb, "Teachers: Their Union and Their Profession," 11. There is a significant difference between the responses of union leaders and members. Union officers had a mean of 4.21, above 4.00 agree while non-officers had a mean of 3.08 just above neutral.

20. Ibid., 15.

21. Ibid., 18.

22. Poole, *supra* note 13, 117.

23. Ibid., 107–108.

24. Kerchner and Mitchell, *The Changing Idea of a Teachers' Union*.

25. Lorraine M. McDonnell and Anthony Pascal, *Teacher Unions and Educational Reform* (Santa Monica, CA: Rand, April 1988), 53.

26. McDonnell and Pascal, *Teacher Unions and Educational Reform*.

27. DeMitchell and Cobb, "Teachers: Their Union and Their Profession," 16.

28. Ibid.

29. Ibid., 13.

30. Bob Chase, "The New NEA: Reinventing Teacher Unions for a New Era," Remarks before the National Press Club. Washington, DC (February 7, 1997). Site accessed August 9, 1997 available at http://www.nea.org.

31. Adam Urbanski, "Improving Student Achievement Through Labor-Management Collaboration in Urban School Districts," *Education Policy* 17 (2003): 503–518, 507.

32. Susan Moore Johnson, "Teacher Unions in Schools: Authority and Accommodation," *Harvard Educational Review* 53 (1983): 309–325, 325.

33. Susan Moore Johnson, *Teacher Unions in Schools* (Philadelphia: Temple University Press, 1984), 163.

34. Leo Casey, "The Educational Value of Democratic Voice: A Defense of Collective Bargaining in American Education," in *Collective Bargaining in Education: Negotiating Change in Today's Schools*, ed. Jane Hannaway and Andrew J. Rotherham (Cambridge, MA: Harvard Education Press, 2006), 181–201, 189.

35. Valeri R. Helterbran, "Professionalism: Teachers Taking the Reins," *The Clearing House* 81 (2008): 123–127, 124.

36. George Strauss, "Professionalism and Occupational Associations," *Industrial Relations: A Journal of Economy and Society* 2 (1963): 7–31, 27. Cited in Gail Ann Schlachter, "Professionalism and Unionism," *Library Trends* 25 (1976): 451–473, 451.

37. Amitai Etzioni, *The Semi-Professions and Their Organization: Teachers, Nurses, Social Workers* (New York: Free Press, 1969).

38. Helterbran, in "Professionalism," writes that anecdotal responses to her query about what contributes to teacher professionalism, received some of the following responses; "doing my job, loving to be around children, dressing well. Doing my own lesson plans, not calling in sick on professional development days, and providing fun, engaging activities for my students." 124.

39. Eliot Freidson, *Profession of Medicine* (Chicago: University of Chicago Press, 1988).

40. Bernard Barber, "Some Problems in the Sociology of Professions," *Daedalus* 92 (1963): 669–688.

41. Linda Darling-Hammond, "Accountability for Professional Practice," *Teachers College Record* 91 (1989): 59–80, 67.

42. William J. Goode, "Encroachment, Charlatanism, and the Emerging Profession: Psychology, Medicine, and Sociology," *American Sociological Review* 25 (1960): 902–914, 903.

43. National Board of Professional Teaching Standards, "What Teachers Should Know and Be Able To Do: The Five Core Propositions of the National Board." Site visited November 2, 2003, at www.nbts.org/about/coreprops.cfm#introfcp, 3–4.

44. Ibid., 6.

45. Darling-Hammond, "Accountability for Professional Practice," 67.

46. Todd A. DeMitchell and Vincent J. Connelly, "Academic Freedom and the Public School Teacher: An Exploratory Study of Perceptions, Policy and the Law," *Brigham Young University Education and Law Journal* 2007 (2007): 83–117.

47. Kim Fries, Vincent J. Connelly, and Todd A. DeMitchell, "Academic Freedom in the Public K-12 Classroom: Professional Responsibility or Constitutional Right? A Conversation with Teachers," *Education Law Reporter* 227 (2008): 505–524.

48. Fries, Connelly, and DeMitchell, "Academic Freedom in the Public K-12 Classroom," 518.

49. DeMitchell and Cobb, "Teachers: Their Union and Their Profession," 19.

50. The five point scale directed the respondents to select one of the following responses to the statement: 1 = strongly disagree, 2 = disagree, 3 = neutral, 4 = agree, and 5 = strongly agree. The higher the mean the higher the agreement with the statement.

51. Todd A. DeMitchell and Casey D. Cobb, "Teacher as Union Member and Teacher as Professional: The Voice of the Teacher," *Education Law Reporter* 220 (2007): 25–38.

52. DeMitchell and Cobb, "Teacher as Union Member and Teacher as Professional," 28.

53. DeMitchell and Cobb, "Teachers: Their Union and Their Profession," 13. It is interesting to note that the National Education Association has been classified as a union since 1976 by the Bureau of Labor Statistics and the Internal Revenue Service, yet one would be hard pressed to find an NEA affiliate that used the term union in its title.

54. Ibid., 12–13. Union leaders differed from non-union leaders in which the former tended to find little conflict between hardball tactics and professionalism while the latter found hardball tactics troubling.

55. Ibid., 13.

56. Ibid., 18. Union leaders (M = 3.34) responses are significantly different (p = 0.002) from non-leaders (M = 2.40). There is a real disconnect between the two groups of teachers on the influence of the contract on quality teaching—the heart of the professional activity of teachers.

57. Ibid.

58. Ibid., 17.

59. Ibid., 20.

60. DeMitchell and Cobb, "Teacher as Union Member and Teacher as Professional," the total of 77 responses included 33 elementary school, 26 middle school, and 18 high school teachers, 31.

61. Ibid.

62. Ibid.

63. DeMitchell and Cobb, "Teachers: Their Union and Their Profession," 18. The mean for this statement is 2.08, the lowest mean in the study.

64. DeMitchell and Cobb, "Teacher as Union Member and Teacher as Professional," 32.

65. DeMitchell and Cobb, "Teachers: Their Union and Their Profession," 11.

66. DeMitchell and Cobb, "Teacher as Union Member and Teacher as Professional," 33.

67. Ibid., 32.

68. Ibid.

69. DeMitchell and Cobb, "Teachers: Their Union and Their Profession," 18.

70. Ibid., 18, $M = 2.54$. Further confounding the issue, as stated earlier, on the statement the teacher looks first to the union rather than the school district to meet their inservice needs, 83.5 percent disagreed or strongly disagreed. Just over one-quarter (26%) of the respondents held the position that they would first turn to the union for assistance.

71. DeMitchell and Cobb, "Teacher as Union Member and Teacher as Professional," 33.

72. "Unions protect, advocate for, and support professionalism according to these 71 respondents. The themes developed from the support professionalism prompt mirror the mean ($M = 3.63$) for "The union supports my ability to provide a professional service to my students." Ibid., 34.

73. Ibid.

74. Ibid.

75. The concern about protection has been echoed by several commentators. For example, Terry Moe writes, "most people would be shocked" at collective bargaining agreements that "make it virtually impossible to dismiss teachers for poor performance." Terry M. Moe, "Union Power and the Education of Children," in *Collective Bargaining in Education: Negotiating Change in Today's Schools*, ed. Jane Hannaway and Andrew J. Rotherham (Cambridge, MA: Harvard Education Press, 2006): 229–255, 237. And, "The burden of removing weak teachers has meant that principals often find it easier to shuffle poor teachers around the district than to remove them." Frederick M. Hess and Martin R. West, *A Better Bargain: Overhauling Teacher Collective Bargaining for the 21st Century* (Cambridge, MA: Program on Education Policy and Governance, Harvard University, n.d.), 29.

76. Todd A. DeMitchell, "A Reinvented Union: A Concern for Teaching, Not Just Teachers," *Journal of Personnel Evaluation in Education* 11 (1998): 255–268, 263.

77. DeMitchell and Cobb, "Teacher as Union Member and Teacher as Professional," 34–35.

78. Ibid. 35, comment from an elementary school teacher.

79. Ibid., 36, comment from a middle school teacher.

80. Ibid., 35, emphasis in original.

81. Ibid., 36.

82. Julia E. Koppich, "The As-Yet-Unfilled Promise of Reform Bargaining: Forging a Better Match between the Labor Relations System We have and the Education System We Want," in *Collective Bargaining in Education: Negotiating Change in Today's Schools*, ed. Jane Hanaway and Andrew J. Rotherham (Cambridge, MA: Harvard Education Press, 2006), 203–227, 208.

83. DeMitchell and Cobb, "Teachers: Their Union and Their Profession," 15. There is no significant difference between union leaders and non-union leaders on these statements.

84. Ibid.

85. DeMitchell and Cobb, "Teacher as Union Member and Teacher as Professional," 36.

86. DeMitchell and Cobb, "Teachers: Their Union and Their Profession," 13. "A Bonferroni correction was made to the alpha level resulting in an adjusted significance level of .002." 10.

87. Ibid., 12.

88. DeMitchell and Cobb, "Teacher as Union Member and Teacher as Professional," 38.

89. Terry M. Moe, "Union Power and the Education of Children," in *Collective Bargaining in Education: Negotiating Change in Today's Schools*, ed. Jane Hannaway and Andrew Rotherham (Cambridge, MA: Harvard Education Press, 2006), 229–255, 255.

90. Bess Keller, "Seattle Teachers Approve Tentative Contract With Broad New Evaluation, Hiring Policies," *Education Week* (September 17, 1997). Site visited April 10, 2015, at https://www.edweek.org/ew/articles/1997/09/17/03seattl.h17.html.

91. Ronald D. Henderson, "Teacher Unions: Continuity and Change," in *Teacher Unions and Education Policy: Retrenchment or Reform?* ed. Ronald D. Henderson, Wayne J. Urban, and Paul Wolman (Boston: Elsevier), 1–32, 12–13.

Section 3

LAW AND POLITICS IN UNCERTAIN TIMES

RETRENCHMENT AND ASSAULT

Chapter 7

Power, Money, and Politics

Responses to Teacher Unions

In January 2019, following a charter school teacher strike, the Chicago Teachers Union president Jesse Sharkey said the message to charter school teachers was to "give the union a call."[1]

Teacher unions have been around for over a century. The two major unions followed two divergent paths to the present. The National Education Association (NEA) grew from more of a top-top down orientation dominated by college professors and school administrators. The American Federation of Teachers (AFT) has clearly traceable roots to labor. Professionalism and issues of social justice arose with varying degrees of emphasis in both organizations. Whatever the differences in the beginning they are overshadowed by their commonalities today. The institution of state employee collective bargaining rights, some two and one-half decades after Congress passed the National Labor Relations Board Act in 1935, moved the two organizations toward each other, at least in focus—representing teachers at the bargaining table.

As discussed in chapter 2, the nascent public education system of the colonial period took on a dynamic transformation after the War of 1812. The rise of the Common School movement sought to professionalize and centralize education. As public education grew through compulsory education and child labor laws, it became more standardized, thus sowing the seeds for standardizing, centralizing, and formalizing effects of collective bargaining.[2]

In the late 1950s, starting in Wisconsin, various states granted public sector employees, including teachers the right to bargain collectively with their employer. The AFT Local No. 2, in 1962, won the right to represent the New York City Schools and Albert Shanker ascended the national stage. The NEA responded at the Denver Convention in the same year marked the entry of the NEA into collective bargaining. And the race was on between the NEA and the AFT to organize and represent public school teachers. As bargaining expanded sweeping in more school districts so did the scope of issues that could be brought to the bargaining table. Class size limits, mandated evaluation procedures, and a guaranteed voice for teachers in school-wide curriculum decisions became common provisions.[3]

A LEGAL RETRENCHMENT UP TO 2010

The roots of public sector collective bargaining are planted deeply in the soil of legal mechanisms. While legislatures and governors through the latter decades of the second half of the twentieth century were passing laws to create and define public sector collective bargaining, there may well be a retrenchment, a pulling back of the reach of those laws. As of 2014, five states prohibited public sector collective bargaining (Georgia, North Carolina, South Carolina, Texas, and Virginia) while Arizona had no law allowing or prohibiting public sector bargaining.[4]

"Overall, the 1990s redefined collective bargaining for education employees in the public sector as a fragile right that can be threatened by an unfriendly state legislature and/or governor."[5] The scrutiny of the unions has also occurred at the federal level.

For example, the U.S. Labor Department in 2003 considered rule changes, which would allow for greater detailed reporting about a union's finances. The federal rule change would only apply to the largest of teacher unions. The move was prompted by embezzlement within the Washington Teachers Union and the United Teachers of Dade (Florida).[6]

Several states in the 1990s, in many ways, reversed or stemmed the tide of legislation that strengthened public sector bargaining. Michigan has historically been a strong labor state given the dominance of the auto industry. Yet, in 1994, Governor Engler signed legislation (PA 112) that targeted teachers by changing the collective bargaining statute. The argument for the limits was to avoid work stoppages and teacher strikes. The legislation increased the number of prohibited subjects of bargaining thus preserving those topics to the sole authority of the school district. It also allowed school districts to unilaterally impose their "last best offer." One union leader called it a "stake through the heart."[7]

Oregon in 1995, made similar major revisions to its collective bargaining laws. Among the changes were a reduction in the number of mandatory subjects of bargaining and the definitions of managerial and supervisory employees were altered. The latter resulted in the exclusion of employees who were previously covered under the law. In the same year Illinois amended the collective bargaining law limiting the scope of bargaining for K–12 and community college employees in Chicago. These changes to state law limited the scope of bargaining by declaring certain topics to be prohibited. This short-ened the reach of collective bargaining.

Another example of retrenchment in which the rights of labor were rolled back is found in New Hampshire. Prior to August 29, 2003, a union and a school board could negotiate into the grievance clause due process rights for a probationary teacher who was nonrenewed for the following year. State law does not grant the right to a hearing for a probationary teacher whose contract is not renewed for the following year. However, the state public labor board had previously upheld contract provisions negotiated into a CBA that resulted in advisory or binding arbitration for grievances filed regarding a nonrenewal. The legislature with the support of the governor eliminated the ability to bargain such a right. The legislation also provided for a sunset for any contracts that had such a provision declaring them null and void at the expiration of the contract.[8]

Another statutory change occurred in New Mexico. In 1992, the governor signed a public sector collective bargaining law. The bill had a sunset provi-sion for July 1, 1999, thus forcing the legislation to be renewed. The legislature passed a successor bill but failed to muster enough votes to override the veto of the governor—different governor from the one who signed the original legisla-tion. Public sector bargaining in New Mexico had a seven-year tenure before it was retired. However, in 2003 it was resurrected, but the reauthorization allowed school districts to refuse to bargain with teachers' unions.[9]

The genesis of public sector collective bargaining is state law. The changes in the 1990s, underscore the reality of a law-based right created within the crucible of the give and take of politics: times change and new values and interests force their way onto the public agenda. The strength of issue partisans in one decade may not be as robust in a later decade. The argument is never won forever. Critics of unions and public sector collective bargaining hail these changes with the refrain, "it is about time." Proponents of unions worry over what they perceive is an erosion of their important and hard-won rights.

For example, there were several ballot measures placed before the public in the general election of 2008. Colorado residents failed to pass Amend-ment 49, which would have prohibited public employee payroll deductions for union dues as well as fees for other organizations. Payroll deductions is a negotiable item, one that unions seek because it ensures a steady stream of dues without having to spend money on billing their membership and dun-ning delinquents. Collecting union dues is done for them by the school dis-trict and not by the union. This amendment would likely have had a negative financial impact on unions. What was protected by the ballot box was lost in the Courts a decade later (see the discussion on the *Janus* decision).

Voters in Oregon also rejected a measure that would have impacted the unions and its members. Measure 60 was written to prohibit school districts from giving raises based on seniority and would have instituted raises based on classroom performance.[10]

BEYOND 2010: THE STRUGGLE OVER
UNIONS, POWER, AND INFLUENCE

Wisconsin, in 1959, captured the attention of workers throughout America passing the first public sector collective bargaining law allowing public employees, including teachers, to bargain collectively with their public employer. This began the heyday of public sector collective bargaining in which all states except for five (Georgia, North Carolina, South Carolina, Texas, and Virginia) either required school boards to bargain with the teachers exclusive representative or permitted local districts to do so.

Wisconsin's Budget Repair Act: It's About Money and Unions

However, the nation once again focused on Wisconsin in February and March of 2011, when thousands of workers descended on the state capitol for a different purpose just over half a century earlier. This time they came not celebrate their victory but, in their minds, to save that victory. Workers, including teachers, arrived, some with children in tow, carrying signs, and loudly proclaiming their opposition to the pending legislation.

It is possible to see the drama of thousands of workers, many with their children in tow beating drums and carrying signs, with legislators walking through the gauntlet with counterdemonstrators chastising the demonstrating teachers, as a struggle over money, power, and the relevance of the public sector union. While Wisconsin governor Scott Walker cast the argument as repairing the budget and addressing the deficit, for many the subtext is the need to loosen what they characterized as the stranglehold of unions and their self-entitled and privileged workers. They argued that the taxpayers' pocketbooks must be protected from the avarice and voracious union bosses who want to protect their privilege. However, union leaders and their rank and file members, such as classroom teachers, and other supporters believed the governor and the state's Republican Party real goal was to bust their union and that the worker would be left without protection from the will and whim of the employer and that they will be turned out of the middle class. They believed that they were being unfairly targeted as the reason for the economic recession and asserted that their contracts are bilaterally negotiated and not unilaterally forced on the public. The irony that this is happening in the first state to allow for public sector collective bargaining is not lost on either side: "how can this happen here" and "it is about time" bookend the controversy.

Both sides are right. The controversy was about money. The governor's policy would address the budget shortfall by compelling targeted public employees with paying a greater share of their benefits and their retirement contribution. The unions agreed to the changes. Collective bargaining is always about money. Management tries to balance how little it can pay and still attract and retain the right workforce. Unions represent the self-interests of employees who want to maximize the pay they receive for their labor. Both sides pursue legitimate ends. This is the essence of private or public sector collective bargaining, an employee asking for a raise, or a corporate executive seeking a pay raise, enhanced benefits, and perks such as expanded business expenses to cover the use of their car with their board of directors. There is a conflict of interest between management and labor and there is a community of interest between the parties. Conflict drives bargaining and the community allows for resolution.

However, the Wisconsin governor went further than just money while trying to repair the budget. The governor wanted to limit public sector bargaining to just wages with a requirement that any raise over the consumer price index must be referred to the voters on a referendum. In addition, the governor wanted to force the union to have a certification election every year, allow employees who benefit from the collectively bargained contract to not pay a fee for the work performed on their behalf, ban the public employer from collecting the dues of the union members, and the legislation would eliminate all collective bargaining for employees in the University of Wisconsin System.

The question is how do these acts repair the budget. Since the police and fire unions are exempt from many of these restrictions is the argument that public sector unions undermine the economic viability of Wisconsin, or does it mean that only specific unions undermine the long-term economic health of the state? The answer lies with power.

If the governor breaks the power of the union by severely limiting bargaining to only wages the union will have no ability to influence the working conditions, a staple of union successes, and benefits would entirely be the province of the school district. The relationship between wages and benefits would be severed even though unions are often forced into tradeoffs of pursuing wages or benefits. The legislation also tries to negate the relationship between wages and benefits in that the increase of salary automatically translates into increased benefits. If a union must hold an election each year, the apparent hope is that it will be too much of a hassle for the union members and it will die a death that would be laid at the hands of the workers—they don't want a union.

While appealing to the American sense of freedom, the argument that teachers and other public employees are compelled to join a union is false. Closed union shops are illegal. Where unions have gained the right through bargaining with the public managers of assessing agency fees in which members of the bargaining unit must pay the cost of bargaining through a fee or join the union, the budget repair essentially outlaws the practice.

Unions are required to provide fair representation to the members it represents without regard for whether the employee is a union member or not.

Employees who do not support the political agenda of the union may opt for the agency fee, which does not include that portion of dues used for political activity. The relationship between the individual paying for a benefit provided by another and the cost to the public seems so slight as to be inconsequential. If it does not repair the budget, what does it do except for eliminating the concept of fairness providing for free riders who gain benefits on the work of others and paid for by others?

Reducing the power of unions appears to be the underlying rationale for Governor Walker's Budget Repair Act. While Governor Walker stated, "We must take immediate action to ensure fiscal stability in our state."[11] Does the elimination of all bargaining rights of the employees of the University of Wisconsin, family child-care workers, and home health care workers balance the budget now and into the foreseeable future? Since these workers have been able to bargain in the past is the budget crisis laid at the feet of these workers because their managers caved into their unreasonable demands? Legislating away the traditional bargaining subjects of benefits and working conditions may implicitly assume the position that public managers at the bargaining table are unable to say no to the union proposals, even when no should be the answer to the proposals of the union.

The relevance of public sector unions is called into question in the second decade of the twenty-first century. Republican governors and legislatures rallied the public against the public employee and its union. Can a public sector union, the largest unionized workforce in America, remain relevant? Two questions arise from the retrenchment in Wisconsin and potentially other states such as Ohio in which the Senate passed (March 2, 2011) Senate Bill 5 to curtail the bargaining rights of public employees.

First, can public sector unions maintain their ability to provide a voice and a buffer for public employees or will public employees return to the conditions of employment that existed prior to collective bargaining in which they worked at the pleasure of the employer? Second, will the voice of the union which speaks for the workers be reduced or eliminated so that the only the voice of the employer remains in the public sphere?

Some are concerned that an workforce represented by an irrelevant union will be weakened as a counterbalance to business interests who lobby government for their political purposes. Governor Walker's legislation appears to take the position that public sector unions must be rendered irrelevant.

Wisconsin is part of a pattern of states pushing back the power of unions and the voice of the employees. Public sector collective bargaining laws were typically passed to foster harmonious relations between the public employer and its public employees who provide a governmental service. Will the reduction of union power, and its elimination in some instances, foster harmonious relations? Or is harmony in the workplace no longer the goal?

The public employer will face the real challenge of retrenchment. In the new power relationship will the employer seize the moment to keep or improve the relationship with its employees or will it grab the opportunity to impose its will on those employees?

RIGHT TO WORK: STARVE THE BEAST
OR PROTECT WORKERS' RIGHTS?

While making a number of changes to the Wagner Act in 1947 to place restraints on labor unions, three changes in the Taft-Hartley Act declared that closed shops in which employees are required to join a union were prohibited. The second major change allowed the practice of nonunion employees being required to pay a fee (agency fee) to the union for the bargaining and enforcement of the collective bargaining agreement, too which those employees enjoyed full access and representation. The third point is that it allowed states to pass legislation in which states can prohibit the implementation of agency fees.

Right to Work (RtW) laws were adopted in the 1940s following the adoption of the Taft-Hartley Law (1947), which revised the 1935 Wagner Act, which established the right of unions to bargain with private employers under specified conditions. "One of the most pervasive purposes of the [Taft-Hartley] Act was to protect the rights of the individual against his[/her] union."[12] The National Right to Work Committee states, "A Right To Work law guarantees that no person can be compelled, as a condition of employment, to join or not to join, nor to pay dues to a labor union."[13]

In the 1940s, twelve states passed RtW laws, and in the 1950s, six states passed the legislation; however, the rate slowed from 1958 to 2001 (one new state in 1963, one in 1976, one in 1985, and one in 2001). However, since 2012, six states, Indiana, Michigan, Wisconsin, West Virginia, Kentucky, and Missouri, on February 6, 2017, have passed RtW laws. The total number of RtW states as of February 6, 2017, is twenty-eight.[14] However, by a 2-1 margin, voters in August of 2018 rejected the Missouri RtW legislation intended to "curb union power."[15]

New Hampshire may join in the future, but if a Republican governor who campaigned on implementing RtW with a Republican Legislature did not pass the legislation, is the prospect for the near future more rosy? Just four and one-half score years ago, the individual states were given the right to adopt RtW legislation, yet just over half have taken advantage of this opportunity.

The New Hampshire State Legislature, in 2017, held a floor vote on SB 11. This is approximately the thirty-fifth time, since the late 1970s, that New

Hampshire considered passing legislation called Right to Work[16]—antiunion legislation. The legislation failed once again.

The core of New Hampshire's SB 11, the Right To Work Act is found in the requirement to furnish and post a copy of "Employees Freedom of Choice." This notice states:

> Under the law of the state of New Hampshire, employees are protected in the exercise of their free choice to join or refrain from joining labor unions, and it is unlawful for an employer and a labor union to enter into a contract or agreement requiring them to pay dues, fees, or charges of any kind to a labor union as a condition of obtaining or keeping a job. Under this law, an employer may not discharge or otherwise discriminate against an employee because of joining or refusing to join a labor union, or to pay dues, or other charges to a labor union.[17]

One of the arguments used by opponents is that right-to-work is really a right-to-work-for-less;[18] proponents push back.[19] In other words, states that have a RtW law have lower wages than states they do not have such a law. Using the Bureau of Labor Statistics, GoBankingRates calculated the mean salaries of elementary, middle and high school students to arrive at the mean salary for each state. Brenda Lasevoli, in an *Education Week* blog, Teacher Beat, listed the salaries of the top ten states and the salaries of the bottom ten states.[20] The following chart tends to support opponents' contention that RtW is a right to work for less. All ten of the lowest paid states are right-to-work states, whereas nine of the ten highest paying states are not right-to-work states.(table 7.1).

In two of the lowest paying states, lawmakers have recognized the problem of low salaries and its impact on recruitment and retention of teachers. Both Oklahoma and Arizona are pushing to increase teacher salaries.[21]

It is worthwhile asking whether states that have adopted right-to-work has positively impacted student outcomes because of the protections afforded to its teachers. A review of the Nation's Report Card, the National Assessment of Educational Progress comparing the 2015 scores for fourth grade mathematics showed that of the top ten places three were RtW states (Wyoming, Virginia, and North Dakota) and seven of the bottom ten spots were filled by RtW states (Michigan, Arkansas, West Virginia,[22] Louisiana, Mississippi, Nevada, and Alabama). The highest performing state was Massachusetts (251) and the lowest was Alabama (231), a RtW state.[23] It appears that right-to-work may not be a magic bullet for improved student outcomes by freeing teachers from being forced to join a union; a right they already possess. This diminishes the argument that union membership restrains educators from either entering the public schools (Have "excellent" teachers who have waited on the sidelines until the role of unions has been diminished through RtW legislation now flooded to RtW states to improve student outcomes?)

Table 7.1   Teacher Mean Salaries by States: Right-to-Work and Not Right-to-Work

State	Salary	Right-to-Work	Not Right-to-Work
Top Ten States with the **Highest** Average Teacher Salaries			
1. Alaska	$77,853		YES
2. New York	$76,593		YES
3. Connecticut	$75,867		YES
4. California	$72,050		YES
5. Massachusetts	$71,857		YES
6. New Jersey	$70,700		YES
7. Rhode Island	$67,533		YES
8. Maryland	$65,257		YES
9. Illinois	$65,153		YES
10. Virginia	$63,493	YES	
Top Ten States with the **Lowest** Average Teacher Salaries			
1. Louisiana	$48,587	YES	
2. Kansas	$47, 127	YES	
3. Idaho	$47,063	YES	
4. Arkansas	$47,053	YES	
5. West Virginia	$45,477	YES	
6. Arizona	$43,800	YES	
7. North Carolina	$43,587	YES	
8. South Dakota	$43,200	YES	
9. Oklahoma	$42,647	YES	
10. Mississippi	$42,043	YES	

or keeping those who are in the public schools from significantly raising the outcomes of their students?

It can reasonably be asserted that RtW legislation seeks to "starve the beast," unions, of their stream of revenue, so that they wither and die with a shrug of shoulders and not my fault attitude. If the real purpose is to weaken and destroy unions, this debate must be held on grounds that all understand and not on grounds shrouded in fog and misdirection. If proponents of RtW want to destroy the influence of unions and leave employees with just the power of employers, this policy debate should be held in the light of day. Will silenced teachers better serve the needs of children and the community? No!

THE *JANUS* DECISION:
FREE SPEECH AND FREE RIDERS

For almost fifty years the prevailing constitutional position held that an employee's constitutional right to free speech was not abridged by a requirement that she/he pay a fee to the union that bargained the wages, benefits, and conditions of employment in lieu of joining the union. The fee was confined to the costs of bargaining and management of the contract and could not be used to support the political positions and activities of the union. The concepts of *Abood v. Detroit Board of Education*[24] were that these arrangements support labor peace and prevent free ridership by which employees could benefit from the services of the union but not pay for it.

The Supreme Court in 2018 decided *Janus v. American Federation of State, County, and Municipal Employees Council, 31*[25] which upended precedence of the 1971 *Abood* case. In this case, plaintiff Mark Janus, a public employee in the Illinois Department of Healthcare and Family Services as a child support specialist, stated that he did not support many of the positions of the union including its positions in bargaining. The union's "behavior" in bargaining, in his estimation did not appreciate the current fiscal crisis. He stated that "if he had a choice, he would not pay any fees or otherwise subsidize [the Union]."[26]

Justice Alito wrote the decision of the court for *Janus*. The primary question was whether an agency fee was subsidized compelled speech. Employees who are represented by a union that was elected by their colleagues do not have to join the union but assert that the requirement to pay their share of the service that the union provides in way of bargaining for wages, benefits, terms and conditions of employment. The argument is that paying a fee to the union is a tacit if not implicit statement of support for the political positions that the union holds and pursues, as is their right of speech but is not held by an employee.

The court overruled *Abood* stating that it was wrongly decided finding that "States and public-sector unions may no longer extract agency fees from nonconsenting employees."[27] However, agency fees can be collected only if the employee "affirmatively" consents to pay the fee.

Questions Raised[28]

> It is also not disputed that the State may require that a union serve as exclusive bargaining agent for its employees—itself a significant impingement on associational freedoms that would not be tolerated in other contexts. We simply draw the line at allowing the government to go further still and require all employees to support the union irrespective of whether they share their values.
>
> Justice Alito, *Janus* v. *American Federation of State, County, and Municipal Employees Council, 31*, 138 S.Ct. 2448, 2478 (2018).

Justice Alito opines that government establishing a process for employees to select an exclusive representative for a recognized unit of employees (e.g., teachers) "substantially restricts the rights of individual employees."[29] Thus, the union is required to fairly represent all members of the bargaining unit, members and nonmembers alike. One issue the majority pointed to is processing grievances. The court recognizes that processing a grievance (and its potential arbitration) is a burden. Rather than address the burden by implementing an agency fee, Justice Alito suggests that the nonmember could be required to pay for the service or could be denied representation altogether.

While this approach is appealing—no fee for the service, no service—it is problematic. The CBA covers all employees, thus the resolution cannot abridge the rights of all of the members of the unit. In other words, management cannot accept a resolution of the grievance that runs counter to the CBA; the CBA is standardized for all employees. While the union may not be "paid" to represent the employee, their presence will be felt. If management resolves the grievance in a way that the union believes is inimical to the contractual rights of the members of the unit, it can file a grievance, and the procedure starts all over again.

The majority also found that even though an exclusive representative violates the free association rights of employees, that such a "significant" violation was allowed to stand. However, the requirement to pay a fair share of the labor that the exclusive representative bargained for the interest of the employees it represents is unconstitutional. It is subsidizing the speech of the employee who may not agree with the various stances/values/positions that the union holds and pursues. This decision may become noted as a watershed in educational labor relations. However, here are a few questions that are raised by this decision:

1. If the Right of Association significantly impinged on a First Amendment Right of Association, why would the majority not strike it down as unconstitutional? Instead it elevated the right to free speech of the employee and ignored the right to association. Focusing on the right of association would also eliminate the issue of subsidized compelled speech, because the employee would not be required to be part of any one organization, or individuals, who seeks to bargain collectively or individually with the school board. The employee would pursue his or her interests in a marketplace of options.

The court asserted the benefit of requiring a duty to represent, considering it as concomitant to its authority to be an exclusive representative. It only quoted *Abood* for its reasons why exclusive representation is important. It offered no rationale of its own other than a rationale for why the nonmember's right to be fairly represented would be treated unfairly.[30]

2. The union is not overburdened and may benefit from its status as the exclusive representative thus negating the concept of the free rider, Justice Alito argues. Two arguments are advanced for this assertion. First, the

exclusive representative does not have to pursue the designation. Thus it is voluntary. Second, the union gets benefits that "greatly outweigh any extra burden imposed by the duty of providing fair representation for nonmembers."[31]

The first reason essentially says, if you don't like what the conditions are, don't seek to be a representative, there are plenty of others who will do it. For the second reason the majority offers as benefits that outweigh resources expended to support bargaining; the exclusive representative has a favored place in negotiations (there are only two places at the bargaining table, the union and management and there is no extra money for this privileged position to cover the costs of bargaining, it is what the union must do), obtaining information about the members they are representing (this is no offset of expenses for free riders, this is the information that the union needs and is entitled to under good faith bargaining, these data are not sold to make money for the union), and finally dues and fees are deducted from wage by the school district.

This last one is a benefit, but it is also one that state legislatures are taking away. Is there no public interest served by having an exclusive representative, these seem weak and unconvincing compared to the extent of the responsibility?

3. The compelled speech argument asserts that employees who do not support the union cannot be compelled to pay a fee to the union but can be compelled to accept the fruits of the labor of the negotiated contract by adhering to the sections of the contract. The plaintiff stated that he did not support the bargaining position of the union.

If the employee does not support the speech of the union and has the constitutional right not to support that speech through not paying a fee for a service rendered; what about the tangible outcome of the speech of the union—the collectively bargained contract? Did the majority carve out an exception for noncompliance with the contract because an employee may take issue with the union's position on sections of the contract that the union pursued and was accepted by the school district?

The question becomes, if the contract is speech, whose speech is it? If both sides bilaterally agree to the speech through enforcement of the contract, are both the speakers? The speech of the contract compels action—expressive conduct? Have both the union and the school district compelled speech as well as conduct? Consequently, has the school district violated their employee's free speech rights? If yes, this flies in the face of the concept that teachers are hired to further the speech (curriculum) of the school district.

Justice Alito states that unions speak out as part of collective bargaining on "sensitive political topics" that are "matters of profound value and concern to the public."[32] An Ohio court wrote, "An employee has no more right to ignore a collective bargaining agreement than does an employer."[33] However, according to the free speech rights of the teacher to not "mouth" the position of the union can the teacher be compelled to follow the contract even if the teacher disagrees with sections of the contract? How can the nonunion employee be held harmless and not pay an agency fee so as to not support the principles and positions of the union and yet, as stated by the majority collective bargaining, involves union positions that the employee has to adhere to even though it may embody those very principles he/she eschews? If speech is not compelled by an agency, conduct resulting from the speech is compelled as a condition of employment.

If the contract through collective bargaining includes sensitive political topics that the teacher disagrees with, is the teacher compelled to follow the dictates of the union position? Nonunion employees receive protection from concepts/ideas/positions by not paying an agency fee for what was bargained, but there is no relief from having their conduct structured by those very concepts.

Teachers who do not support positions of the union are free to speak out against those positions. Union members or nonunion teachers have the same right of free speech to denounce union stances in the crucible of the marketplace of ideas. In addition, they have the right to seek to decertify the exclusive representative and either find one more in tune with their positions or have no union representing them. They have the right to form advocacy groups against union positions just as they have the right to associate with the union. These options are consistent with free speech and the right of association. Is an agency fee compelled speech or is it the price for a service rendered by and accepted, and enforced by a third party? While the argument of the majority is that the nonunion members were not free riders in a ride to a place they did not want to go, did they eschew and refuse to accept the benefits of the destination of the trip?

VAMMING TEACHERS: "RANK AND YANK"[34]

This chapter has explored several legislative and judicial responses to teachers and their unions. One such legislative agenda aimed at teachers is the process by which they are evaluated. The following chapter reviews a legal challenge to teachers' security seeking to make it easier to fire teachers and thus improve student outcomes. The highly touted new evaluation system, value-added modeling (VAM) is central to the California court case on tenure (*Vergara v. State of California*) discussed in the next chapter. However, caution flags have been raised from educators, scholars, and policy makers regarding the efficacy and wisdom of using evaluation of teachers through VAM type systems as a policy approach to improving schools. One such policy maker, U.S. Secretary of Education Arne Duncan, commented, "This country is going to need a million new teachers. You can't fire your way to the top."[35]

The constant in schools from Plato through the American Common School movement to current system of education is the role and the importance of the teacher. "A mountain of empirical evidence shows that teacher quality is the *schooling* factor that most influences student test achievement."[36]

State policy makers, largely in response to the *Race to the Top* competition for federal funds, increasingly sought to hold teachers individually accountable in very public ways for the academic achievement of their students.[37] Based on the premise that teachers have the single-largest impact on student achievement of all the factors that schools can control the evaluation of teacher quality has shifted to focus on outcomes through the use of student test scores.

The method of their evaluation for high stakes employment decisions seeks to hold teachers accountable for student learning. "Efforts to revamp public education are increasingly focused on evaluating teachers using student test scores, but school districts nationwide are only beginning to deal with the practical challenges of implementing those changes."[38]

The lodestone of this culture of accountability is teachers make a difference. Consequently, teacher effects on student learning have taken on a central role in determining effectiveness leading to high stakes personnel decisions about merit and retention. How to improve student achievement and how to hold schools and teachers accountable for that achievement is a hotly discussed topic in education policy deliberations from coast to coast.[39] Stephen Sawchuk in *Education Week*, commented: "It has generated sharp-tongued exchanges in public forums, in news stories, and on editorial pages. And it has produced enough policy briefs to fell whole forests."[40]

The process of using student test scores to measure and evaluate teachers is commonly called VAM. While questioning their utility, Professor Mark Paige acknowledges that value-added models are irresistible but a mistake.[41] "Value-added measurement changed pretty much everything in our national conversation about student achievement"[42]—the chief work of teachers and their schools.

VAM is offered up as a "rational" basis for deciding whether a teacher is incompetent and can/should be fired. First they are "ranked" using VAM and then they are "yanked" from their employment. "In the simplest of terms, VAMs (e.g., Tennessee's TVAAS) are statistical models used to measure the predicted and the actual "value" a teacher "adds" to (or detracts from) student achievement from the point at which students enter a teacher's classroom to the point students leave."[43] This form of statistical modeling uses past student test scores to predict future student's score, and, ultimately, whether or not individual teachers "add value" to children's learning in language arts and math. Thus advocates seek to "fire" their way to establishing a successful system of public education.

While it is intuitive and rationale that the work of effective teachers should lead to positive student outcomes, the reality of using assessments designed to measure student knowledge and skills as valid and reliable for the assessment of teacher effectiveness may be counterintuitive and unreasonable. However, researchers and much of the educational research community have raised red flags about the use of VAM for high stakes employment decisions.

For example the American Educational Research Association issued a statement on the use of VAMS in evaluation systems cautioning "against VAM being used to have a high-stakes, dispositive weight in evaluations."[44] Similarly, the American Statistical Association position on the use of VAM in teacher high-stakes decisions concludes, "VAMs typically measure correlations and not causation,"[45] thus, to what degree can teachers be held accountable for the scores of students, or are there other variables that also effect student learning beyond a teacher's control?

VAM places teachers at the core of student outcomes. Teachers in Florida reacted by bringing suit against this new evaluation system. A federal district court[46] and the Eleventh Circuit of Appeals[47] ruled VAM to be rational but questioned whether it was fair. Federal district court Judge Mark E. Walker, in the Florida case, *Cook v. Stewart* (2014), upheld a state law that used VAM as part of the evaluation system holding teachers accountable for student scores in math and language arts, teachers who did not teach those subjects. Judge Walker wrote:

> Needless to say, this Court would be hard-pressed to find anyone who would find this evaluation system fair to [teachers who did not teach math or language arts], let alone be willing to submit to a similar evaluation system.[48]

Assessment of students is designed to improve student learning by guiding curricular decisions of flow and sequencing. Dana Goldstein accurately posits, "When testing practices are set up to select teachers to fire, educators are incented to raise test scores at any cost, not use tests to help children learn."[49] Consequently, will the educational process be distorted by unconscious and/or conscious decisions that distort the educational process—lobbying for selected students who score well in specific subject areas, focusing on students who are "on the bubble" and can "raise my VAM score," and will VAM harm morale and hinder collaboration among teachers – ranking teachers tends to pit teachers against each other to get the higher score and not be targeted for dismissal for incomptence?

Another potential unintended consequence asks whether VAM can be used as a lever to overcome the defects that have characterized educational malpractice.[50] Researchers Carla Evans, Jade Caines (Lee), and Winston Thompson offer a caution regarding VAM. They write, "Making decisions about the design and/or implementation of teacher evaluation systems without considering the intended and unintended consequences, especially ethical ones, is ill-advised."[51]

RATIONAL, BUT IS IT REASONABLE?

The Florida Northern Federal District Court denied relief to plaintiff teachers who argued that the VAM type model of evaluation was unconstitutional violating their substantive due process and equal protection by holding teachers responsible for student scores when they did not teach subject tested (math or language arts). The court held that the evaluation policy was legally rational. However it noted in its conclusion, "The unfairness of the evaluation system as implemented is not lost on the Court."

Cook v. Stewart, 28 F. Supp. 3d 1207, 1215 (N.D. Fla. 2014)

VAM is a simple solution for measuring a complex activity: how to direct, organize, teach, and inspire someone else to learn. Is it the right solution or just the easy solution? Given the limitations of VAMs, caution is not just prudent it is necessary. While legislation that requires the use of student performance data, such as VAM, remains on the books, there seems to be a diminished policy discussion in the literature about its role. Has prudence surfaced in the discussion?

CHARTER SCHOOLS AND TEACHER UNIONS: A NEW HORIZON FOR UNIONS

Not all changes have been negative for unions. Charter schools have been touted as reform lighthouses for public education because they are unburdened from many regulations loosening the web of rules that ensnares other public schools. This release from "unnecessary" rules frees charter schools for innovation, as proponents assert. A charter school appears to have questioned the argument as applied to a collectively bargained contract. Teachers at the Conservatory Lab Charter School in Brighton, Massachusetts in

November of 2008 broke ranks with all charter schools in the state when they organized into a union (American Federation of Teachers Massachusetts).

The twenty charter school teachers stated that they wanted a more persuasive voice in educational decisions. But the Chairwomen of the trustees noted that there had been friction around pay and health insurance (bread and butter issues). Similarly, teachers in the Pennsylvania Online Regional Cyber Charter School voted to unionize.[52]

The AFT continued its recruitment efforts within charter schools and ramped up their efforts.[53] From 2012 to 2017 charter school unionization grew from seven percent to ten percent.[54] The move toward unionization of charter schoolteachers took a step forward when unionized Chicago charter schoolteachers in June of 2017 were set to vote on whether they would join the Chicago Teachers Union.[55] Boston, Chicago, New Orleans, and Washington, DC: charter schools all faced a move toward unionization. All of these examples are from large urban centers, but what about suburban charter schools, do they appear to also be potential targets for unionization?

ONCE UNIONIZATION OCCURS, IT IS VERY DIFFICULT TO REMOVE THE UNION

Response from the Alliance College-Ready Public Schools charter school network to a unionization movement.
Mel Lenor. (February 13, 2017). "Teacher Unions Ramp Up Recruitment Efforts at Charter Schools." *Politico*. Site visited July 3, 2017, available at http://www.politico.com/story/2017/02/teachers-unions-ramp-up-recruitment-efforts-at-charter-schools-234958. (emphasis in original)

Do teachers who sought to work in charter schools, possibly for their distance from unionization, find that the protection of the union is desired over the conceptual argument of reform through loosening the burden of unnecessary rules? "Interest in forming teachers' unions is bubbling up at charter schools in big cities, and the national unions are pitching in to help–but that doesn't mean they've shed their wariness about the charter movement as a whole."[56] This bears watching and studying, why the change, what does unionization bring to the work of these teachers in their schools?

One clear indication that unionization is taking hold in charter schools is the selection of the union as the exclusive representative (approximately 11% of charter schools). The other indicator is whether charter school teachers adopt the tactics of a union, for example strikes. In February of 2019, teachers at four Chicago charter schools operated by the Civitas Education Partners went on strike for increased pay, more counselors and social workers, smaller class sizes, and better benefits including paid parental leave.[57] This was the third strike in the first two months of 2019 by teachers at charter schools.

The legitimate needs of employees for security, reasonable wages and benefits, and working conditions that support the important work of the teacher often competes with the equally legitimate need for the efficient delivery of important public services. Unions, like most organizations which operate in the public sphere, find themselves beset from many sides, must find ways to adapt the external environment while maintaining and appropriately adjusting its internal integration to maintain its essential core function. Unions exist within a political environment developing enforceable policies through collective bargaining.

#REDFORED:
TEACHER PROTESTS/STRIKES/WALKOUTS

The decade has witnessed protests, strikes, and walkouts. For example, Five thousand Seattle teachers went on strike on what would have been the first day of school in September of 2015. A spokesperson for the school district stated, "Our goal is a contract that puts students first, honors, but is also fiscally sound. It is our duty to protect the district financially as we support teachers."[58] One year later the Chicago Teachers Union, on April 1st, called a one-day walkout forcing the cancellation of classes for 330,000 students. This followed their strike four years earlier in 2012.[59] And Chicago teachers once again walked the picket line in the fall of 2019.

The Keystone Oaks Education Association (Pittsburg, PA) gave the required forty-eight-hour strike notice to the school district on Monday, March 27, 2017. The teachers had taught without a contract since June 30, 2016. Their news release stated:

> Negotiations will resume at 7 pm Wednesday evening and continue until the midnight deadline so that a strike can be avoided," [union president] Gallagher added. "We are committed to the students of this community and education is out top priority. We stand in solidarity as a membership to call for a strike unless we are presented a district proposal that recognizes our worth to the students and the community.[60]

The strike was averted when a tentative agreement was reached that extended the existing contract until June 30, 2017.

#RedforEd is a grassroots movement that started on Facebook. It has a following of teachers, parents, and community members. While it focuses on supporting public education, it has "made itself a force in the push to win pay increases for tens of thousands of teachers across the nation."[61] Carrying signs and attired in red teachers swept into state capitals in states not known for a close relationship with the union movement. As of the late spring of 2019, RedforEd wave rolled into North and South Carolina. This was North Carolina's second protest, 2018 & 2019. The 2018 labor action was billed as "March for Students and Rally for Respect."[62]

> This was the second year (2018) teachers reached their breaking point. From West Virginia to Arizona, they walked out en masse to protest at their state capitols. Many were tired of working multiple jobs and wanted higher salaries. Even more demanded better school funding for their students to replace crumbling textbooks and archaic supplies. Sometimes they got what they wanted. Other times, they didn't.
> Holly Yan, "Here's what teachers accomplished with their protest this year," *CNN* (May 29, 2018). Site visited August 20, 2019, at https://www.cnn.com/2018/05/29/us/what-teachers-won-and-lost/index.html.

In 2018, statewide walkouts, with almost 400,000 teachers striking, occurred in primarily Republican-leaning states starting in West Virginia, where the #RedforEd movement began and spread to Oklahoma, Kentucky, Colorado, Arizona, and North Carolina. While strikes like the 2012 Chicago strike, the 2019 strikes in Los Angeles teachers, Oakland, Sacramento, and were reflective of district-level relationships and local contexts, while the statewide strikes were less about the contract and more about the level of support for schools and teachers identifying legislatures as failing to provide the necessary support for students' education. For example, researchers at the Center on Budget and Policy Priorities in a November 2017 report wrote:

> Most states cut school funding after the recession hit, and it took years for states to restore their funding to pre-recession levels. In 2015, the latest year for which comprehensive spending data are available from the U.S. Census Bureau, 29 states were still providing less total school funding per student than they were in 2008.[63]

Striking teachers, parents, and even some students advocated for the funding necessary to attract and retain effective teachers, support instructional programs, reduce class sizes, and provide for capital improvements to old and inadequate school buildings and classrooms. These are not just bread-and-butter issues, they are educational issues. Education is a federal interest, a state responsibility, and a local function. The teachers and their allies targeted the responsibility of their state to provide an adequate education.

The strikes of 2018 yielded some results. A March 6, 2019, report on the teacher strikes of 2018 found that four states, Arizona, North Carolina, Oklahoma, and West Virginia, substantially increased their funding for schools. These states made deep cuts to their funding formula over the prior decade. Unfortunately, even with these increases, the funding level "remains well below 2008 levels for these states." And there is a concern that three of these four states increases will be short lived "unless they raise revenue in more sustainable ways."[64]

Hardball union tactics resulted in some wins financially, raised the profile of the importance of low teacher salaries and support for public education generally. It is worthwhile to contrast the district and state level strikes at the end of the second decade with the public response to the teacher protests in Wisconsin at the turn of the decade. Public sentiment appears to have shifted. At the beginning of the decade there was great angst about the economic condition of the nation and now with a much stronger economy, teachers feel that they are still being left behind. They believe that they sacrificed when needed and expected that they would be rewarded when things turned around. They weren't.

CONCLUDING COMMENTS

The decade since 2010 has been a time of change, and uncertainty. It started with the pitched battle in Wisconsin between the Republican governor and legislature as it basically dismantled much of the public sector collective bargaining that started there in 1959. Teachers were scorned and vilified and unions were blamed for bad, budget-busting contracts that were ratified by elected and appointed officials as well as the union. There was a strong sense that teachers and unions in particular were under siege.

As 2019 closes, teachers are being supported in states that are not normally considered strong union states as they walked out and protested. The move to statewide protests, not so much to gain something in a specific contract but to seek a hearing to redress their concerns for not only better pay but better conditions for their students is a major change in tactics. Pay for teachers has continued to stall, even in economic conditions that are considered strong. An Economic Policy Institute study concludes, "The opportunity cost of becoming a teacher and remaining in the profession becomes more and more important as relative teacher pay falls further behind that of other professions."[65] Teacher compensation has become part of the public agenda through state actions and is part of the Democratic policy positions of a number of the presidential candidates in 2019."[66]

Unions registered few gains on the legislative and judicial fronts. Right-to-work legislation passed in a number of states but was rejected in Missouri and New Hampshire. Probably the biggest loss for unions and the biggest gain for opponents of public sector bargaining was the *Janus* decision which overturned *Abood* and held that agency fees are a constitutional violation of nonunion members' free speech rights.

The next chapter will focus on tenure and the California case *Vergara* and legislative responses.

NOTES

1. Madeline Will, "Los Angeles Charter School Teachers Are Back In School After Eight-Day Strike," *Education Week* (January 28, 2019). Site visited August 22, 2019, at http://blogs.edweek.org/edweek/teacherbeat/2019/01/los_angeles_charter _school_teacher_strike.html.

2. Nina Bascia and Pamela Osmond, *Teacher Unions and Educational Reform: A Research Review* (Washington, DC: National Education Association, 2012), 1.

3. Bascia and Osmond, *Teacher Unions and Educational Reform.*

4. Milla Sanes and John Schmidt, *Regulation of Public Sector Collective Bargaining in the States* (Washington, DC: Center for Economic and Policy Research, March 2014), 5.

5. David J. Strom and Stephanie S. Baxter, "From the Statehouse to the Schoolhouse: How Legislatures and Courts Shaped Labor Relations for Public Education Employees During the Last Decade," *Journal of Law & Education* 30 (2001): 296.

6. Julie Blair, "Labor Dept. Proposes to Heighten Scrutiny of Teachers' Unions," *Education Week* (July 9, 2003): 26.

7. William Lowe Boyd, David N. Plank, and Gary Sykes, "Teacher Unions in Hard Times," in *Conflicting Missions? Teacher Unions and Educational Reform*, ed. Tom Loveless (Washington, DC: Brookings Institution Press, 2000), 174–210, 180.

8. New Hampshire RSA 273-A:4.

9. Benjamin A. Lindy, "The Impact of Teacher Collective Bargaining Laws on Student Achievement: Evidence from a New Mexico Natural Experiment," *The Yale Law Journal* 120 (2011): 1130–1191, 1135. Site visited August 25, 2017, at https ://law.yale.edu/system/files/documents/pdf/Student_Organizations/Benjamin_Lindy. _The_Impact_of_Collective_Bargaining_Laws.pdf.

10. Author, "State Ballot Measures," *Education Week* (November 12, 2008): 18–19.

11. Office of the Governor, Scott Walker, *Governor Walker Introduces Budget Repair* (February 11, 2011). Site visited March 4, 2011, at http://www.wisgov.state. wi.us/journal_media_detail.asp?locid=177&prid=5622.

12. Clyde W. Summers, "A Summary of the Taft-Hartley Act," *Faculty Scholarship Series*. Paper 3900. *Yale Law School Legal Scholarship Repository* (1958): 407–408. Site visited February 1, 2017, at http://digitalcommons.law.yale.edu/cgi/v iewcontent.cgi?article=4895&context=fss_papers.

13. Author, "Right to Work is ..." *Right to Work Committee* (n.d.). Site visited June 30, 2019, at https://nrtwc.org/facts/right-work-mean/.

14. National Right to Work Legal Defense Fund, "Right to Work States." Site visited July 15, 2017, at http://www.nrtw.org/right-to-work-states. The site provides a map of right to work states and "forced unionism states."

15. Noam Scheiber, "Missouri Voters Reject Anti-Union Labor Law in a Victory for Labor," *New York Times* (August 7, 2018). Site visited July 2, 2019, at https://www.nyt imes.com/2018/08/07/business/economy/missouri-labor-right-to-work.html?action=cl ick&module=inline&pgtype=Homepage. A *New York Times* editorial the following day regarding the ballot proposal rejection of RtW concluded, "That is welcome news for long-suffering American workers." Editorial Board, "The Wind at Labor's Back," *New York Times* (August 8, 2018). Site visited July 2, 2018, available at https://www.nyt imes.com/2018/08/08/opinion/missouri-labor-unions-vote.html?action=click&pgtype= Homepage&clickSource=story-heading&module=opinion-c-col-left-region&region= opinion-c-col-left-region&WT.nav=opinion-c-col-left-region.

16. Jacob Bennett, "What's Wrong with 'Right-to-Work' in New Hampshire," an unpublished paper, University of New Hampshire, Education Department (May 23, 2017) located in the files of Todd A. DeMitchell.

17. Site visited January 16, 2017, at https://legiscan.com/NH/text/SB11/2017.

18. See Elise Gould and Will Kimball, "'Right-to-Work' States Still Have Lower Wages," *Economic Policy Institute* (April 22, 2015). Site visited September 16, 2017, at http://www.epi.org/publication/right-to-work-states-have-lower-wages/.

19. See Erin Shannon, "Frequently Asked Questions About Work-to-Right Laws," *Washington Policy Center: Improving Lives Through Market Solutions* (December 2014). Site visited September 16, 2017, at https://www.washingtonpolicy.org/library /docLib/FAQ_RTW.pdf.

20. Brenda Lasevoli, "Which States Pay Teachers the Most (and Least)," *Education Week* (February 10), 2017. Site visited September 14, 2017, at http://blogs.ed week.org/edweek/teacherbeat/2017/02/which_states_pay_teachers_the_.html?int c=highsearch.

21. Lasevoli, "Which States Pay Teachers the Most (and Least)."

22. West Virginia was included in the list of RtW states because the State's Supreme Court overturned a preliminary injunction that stayed the implementation of a 2016 law that made West Virginia a RtW state. Associated Press, "West Virginia's Top Court Clears 'Right-to Work' Law," *U.S. News & World Report* (September 15, 2017). Site visited January 14, 2018, at https://www.usnews.com/news/best-states/ west-virginia/articles/2017-09-15/west-virginia-top-court-clears-right-to-work-law.

23. Author, "State Performance Compared to the Nation," *The Nation's Report Card* (N.D.). Site visited January 14, 2018, at https://www.nationsreportcard.gov/p rofiles/stateprofile?chort=1&sub=RED&sj=&sfj=NP&st=MN&year=2015R3.

24. *Abood v. Detroit Board of Education*, 431 U.S. 209 (1971). "Congress determined that it would promote peaceful labor relations to permit a union and an employer to include an agreement requiring employees who obtain the benefit of union representation to share its cost, and that legislative judgment was surely an allowable one." Ibid., 219.

25. *Janus v. American Federation of State, County, and Municipal Employees Council, 31*, 138 S.Ct. 2448 (2018).

26. Ibid., 2461.

27. Ibid., 2486.

28. Justice Kagan speaking for the dissent (Justices Ginsburg, Breyer, and Sotomayor) wrote, "Across the country, the relationships of public employees and employers will alter in both predictable and wholly unexpected ways." Ibid., 2487 (Kagan, J, dissenting).

29. Ibid., 2460.

30. Ibid., 2469. "That is why we said many years ago that serious 'constitutional questions [would] arise' if the union were not subject to the duty to represent all employees fairly" Ibid. Does the Court define fairness if the union does not provide a service for grievances and arbitration for nonmembers?

31. Ibid., 2467.

32. Ibid., 2476. Justice Alito listed such fundamental questions of the subsidized union speech as teacher pay based on seniority, merit-pay, transfer, and procedures for discipline or dismissal. These are typical subjects of bargaining. Ibid.

33. *Provens v. Stark City Board of Mental Retardation & Developmental Disabilities* (1992), 64 Ohio St.3d 252, 262, 594 N.E.2d 959, 966 (Douglas, J., concurring).

34. I acknowledge and gratefully thank Carla M. Evans, Associate, Center for Assessment, Dover, NH, for her insightful comments and helpful suggestions about the role of VAM.

35. Deborah Solomon, "The School of Hard Drives," *The New York Magazine* (September 16, 2010). Site visited August 12, 2017, at http://www.nytimes.com/20 10/09/19/magazine/19fob-q4-t.html.

36. Dan Goldhaber, "Evidence-Based Teacher Preparation: Policy Context and What We Know," *Journal of Teacher Education* 70 (2019): 90–101, 90 (emphasis in original). Professor Goldhaber finishes the sentence writing, ". . . and newer evidence shows a relationship between teacher quality and outcomes such as high school graduation, college-going, and labor market earnings.") Ibid.

37. Clarin Collins and Audrey Amrein-Beardsley, "Putting Growth and Value-Added Models on the Map: A National Overview," *Teachers College Record* 116 (2014): 1–34.

38. Stephanie Banchero, "Teacher Evaluations Pose Test for States," *Wall Street Journal* (March 8, 2012): 1. Site visited February 26, 2016, at http://online.wsj.com/articles/SB10001424052970203961204577267562780533458.html?mod=djemPJ_t.

39. *See* Jason Song and Jason Felch, "L.A. Unified Releases 'Value-Added' Method," *Los Angeles Times* (April 12, 2011). Site visited February 26, 2016, at http://www.latimes.com/news/local/la-me-0413-value-add-20110414,0,1675000.s tory; Michael Winerip, "Evaluating New York Teachers, Perhaps the Numbers Do Lie," *The New York Times* (March 6, 2011). Site visited February 26, 2016, at http://www.nytimes.com/2011/03/07/education/07winerip.html?emc=eta1. See page 1 for a VAM model formula.

40. Stephen Sawchuk, "Wanted: Ways to Measure Most Teachers," *Education Week* (February 2, 2011): 1.

41. Mark A. Paige, "A Legal Argument Against the Use of VAMS in Teacher Evaluation," *Teachers College Record* (December 21, 2014) ID Number 17796.

42. Dana Goldstein, *Teacher Wars: A History of America's Embattled Profession* (New York: Doubleday, 2014), 205.

43. Mark A. Paige, Audrey Amrein-Beardsley, and Kevin Close, "Tennessee's National Impact on Teacher Evaluation Law & Policy," *Tennessee Journal of Law & Policy* 13 (2019): 523–574, 530.

44. AERA Council, "AERA Statement on Use of Value-Added Models (VAM) for the Evaluation of Educators and Educator Preparation Programs Educational Researcher," *American Education Research Association* 44 (November 1, 2015): 448.

45. Author, ASA "Statement on Using Value-Added Models for Educational Assessment," *American Association of Statistics* (April 8, 2014). Site visited August 8, 2017, at https://www.scribd.com/document/217916454/ASA-VAM-Statement-1. The ASA offers several key questions that should be address regarding the use of VAMs.

46. *Cook v. Stewart*, 28 F. Supp. 3d 1207 (N.D. Fla. 2014).

47. *Cook v. Bennett*, 792 F.3d 1294 (11th Cir. 2015).

48. *Cook v. Stewart*, 28 F. Supp. 3d at 1216.

49. Goldstein, *supra* 39, 269.

50. Todd A. DeMitchell, Terri A. DeMitchell, and Douglas Gagnon, "Teacher Effectiveness and Value-Added Modeling: Building a Pathway to Educational Malpractice?" *Brigham Young University Education and Law Journal* (2012): 257–301.

51. Carla M. Evans, Jade Caines, and Winston C. Thompson, "First, Do No Harm?: A Framework for Ethical Decision-Making in Teacher Evaluation," in *Student Growth Measures in Policy and Practice: Intended and Unintended Consequences of High-Stakes Teacher Evaluations*, ed. K. K. Hewitt and Audrey Amrein-Beardsley (New York: Palgrave Macmillan 2016), 169–188, 170.

52. James Vaznis, "Teachers Unionize at Charter School, a First for Mass," *The Boston Globe* (November 26, 2008): 1, 10.

53. Mel Lenor, "Teacher Unions Ramp Up Recruitment Efforts at Charter Schools," *Politico* (February 13, 2017). Site visited July 3, 2017, at http://www.poli tico.com/story/2017/02/teachers-unions-ramp-up-recruitment-efforts-at-charter-sc hools-234958.

54. Lenor, "Teacher Unions Ramp Up Recruitment Efforts at Charter Schools."

55. Juan Perez Jr., "Charter School Teachers to Vote on Joining CTU," *Chicago Tribune* (June 5, 2017). Site visited August 8, 2017, at http://www.chicagotribune .com/news/local/breaking/ct-charter-school-unions-vote-met-20170604-story.html.

56. Liana Loewus, "More Charter School Teachers See Unions as an Option," *Education Week* (June 30, 2017). Site visited July 5, 2017, at http://www.edweek.or g/ew/articles/2017/06/30/at-big-city-charter-schools-more-teachers-see.html.

57. Yana Kunichoff, "Why Chicago's Second Charter School Strike Is the One to Watch," *Chalkbeat* (February 11, 2019). Site visited August 22, 2019, at https:// chalkbeat.org/posts/chicago/2019/02/11/why-chicagos-second-charter-strike-is-one-t o-watch/.

58. Ahiza Garcia, "Teacher Strike Closes Seattle Schools," *CNN Money* (September 10, 2015). Site visited July 15, 2017, at http://money.cnn.com/2015/09/10/new s/seattle-teachers-union-strike/index.html. A picture in the article underscores the

conundrum of being a professional being a member of the union involved in a labor dispute. The picture showed teachers walking a picket line with signs wearing what appears to be a red Seattle Teachers Education Association T-shirts. The sign that the teacher is carrying says "ON STRIKE! SEA/WEA/NEA. Attached to the union sign is a hand written sign that says I My KIDS." Ibid.

59. Author, "5 Things to Know About the Chicago Teachers Strike," *Chicago Tribune* (March 31, 2016). Site visited July 15, 2017, at http://www.chicagotr ibune.com/news/local/breaking/ct-chicago-teachers-walkout-5-things-to-know-met-0 401-20160331-story.html.

60. Keystone Oaks Education Association, "Keystone Oaks Education Association Gives 48-hour Strike Notice to School District," *Keystone Oaks Education Association* (facebook) (n.d.). Site visited July 15, 2017, at https://www.facebook.com/ koeacares/.

61. Daarel Burnette III, "#Redfor ED? Behind the Hashtag That's All the Rage in Teacher Strikes," *Education Week* (Blog) (May 3, 2018). Site visited April 22, 2019, at http://blogs.edweek.org/edweek/teacherbeat/2018/05/what_exactly_is_red fored.html.

62. Liana Heitin Loewus, "North Carolina Teachers Turn Out in Droves for Day-long Protest," *Education Week* (May 16, 2018). Site visited May 17, 2018, at http:// blogs.edweek.org/edweek/teacherbeat/2018/05/scenes_from_the_north_carolina_tea cher_protest.html.

63. Michael Leachman, Kathleen Masterson, and Eric Figueroa, "A Punishing Decade for School Funding" (Washington, DC: Center on Budget and Policy Priorities, November 29, 2017), 1. Site visited on April 29, 2019, at https://www.cbpp.org /sites/default/files/atoms/files/11-29-17sfp.pdf.

64. Michael Leachman and Eric Figueroa, "K-12 School Funding Up in Most 2018 Teacher-Protest States, But Still Well Below Decade Ago," (Washington, DC: Center on Budget and Policy Priorities, March 6, 2019), 1. Site visited May 28, 2019, at https ://www.cbpp.org/research/state-budget-and-tax/k-12-school-funding-up-in-most-201 8-teacher-protest-states-but-still.

65. Sylvia Allegretto and Lawrence Mischel, "The Teacher Pay Penalty Has Hit a New High," *Economic Policy Institute* (September 5, 2018). Site visited August 20, 2019, at https://www.epi.org/publication/teacher-pay-gap-2018/.

66. See, for example, Author, "Teacher Pay," *Politico* (July 24, 2019). Site visited August 30, 2019, at https://www.politico.com/2020-election/candidates-views-on-t he-issues/education-reform/teacher-pay/.

Chapter 8

Teacher Tenure

Necessary Protection or Boondoggle for the Incompetent? The Courts and State Legislatures Respond

By Todd A. DeMitchell and Joseph J. Onosko

Evidence has been elicited in the trial of the specific effect of grossly ineffective teachers on students. The evidence is compelling. Indeed, it shocks the conscience.[1]

Today the ineffective tenured teacher has emerged as a feared character, a vampiric type who sucks tax dollars into her bloated pension and health care plans, without much regard for the children under her care.[2]

HEREIN LIES TENURE: RIP. MAYBE?

Prior to 2009, all states provided some form of tenure for public school teachers. As Professor Elizabeth Blankenship pointed out, "Since January 2009, teacher tenure legislation has come under particular scrutiny."[3] Historically, the policy argument justifying tenure laws states that they are a valuable employment benefit.[4] However, teachers and their tenure have become a hot button item in the last several years.[5] By 2011, eighteen state legislatures— more than a third of the nation—had modified their tenure laws,[6] with seven states by 2014 passing legislation that returned tenured teachers to probationary status if they are rated "ineffective."[7]

Several states passed laws that essentially eliminated teacher tenure, including Florida, South Dakota, Idaho, Louisiana, Kansas, and North Carolina. Idaho and South Dakota replaced tenure with one- and two-year contracts; however, both plans were rejected by statewide referendums.[8] The Louisiana, Florida, and Kansas tenure-repeal statutes were upheld by their respective courts, while the North Carolina Supreme Court ruled that the legislature's tenure-repeal law[9] violated the Contract Clause of the U.S. Constitution "without adequate justification."[10]

Professor Blankenship's review of state legislative initiatives between January 2009 and July 2013 identified five types of change to tenure laws: (1) increased length of the probationary period, (2) teacher performance/evaluations added to the tenure granting process, (3) poor performance added to "just cause" dismissal criteria, (4) "reduction in force" decisions not based entirely on seniority, and (5) tenure protections removed after receiving a poor performance evaluation.[11]

The controversy over teacher tenure divides sharply and is of central importance to public education. One side views tenure as a safe harbor for the ineffective, with teacher unions harming public education by protecting teachers rather than serving the interests of students.[12] Nearly 71 percent of just over 7,000 responding principals in the National Center for Education Statistics' study, *Principal Questionnaire: 2007–2008*, identified tenure as the major barrier for dismissal of poor performing and incompetent teachers.[13]

Chester E. Finn, Jr., president emeritus of the Thomas B. Fordham Institute, asserted that human resource practices in nontenure granting private and charter schools are better than their public school counterparts because school leaders are more "nimble in regrouping, restaffing, and redirecting their schools" by hiring and firing employees according to "shifting pupil needs and organizational priorities."[14]

However, the other side argues that tenure is beneficial to public education, as teachers are insulated from the political vagaries of shifting ideologies and overzealous or vindictive administrators, including protections to speak candidly about school policies and practices with the community.[15] Furthermore, supporters assert that tenure is not a guarantee of employment; it is nothing more than a requirement that government act fairly when dismissing its employees.

The debate over tenure has shifted from policy considerations to the courts, a move that education historian Diana D'Amico asserts is a thinly veiled strategy to achieve a broader objective; "Thwarting tenure laws is a first step in the larger, well-publicized project of dismantling teacher unions."[16] In 2014, the most notable case to challenge the constitutionality of tenure and other teacher protections, *Vergara v. State of California*, played out in Judge Treu's California Superior Court chamber.

On August 27th of that year, just as California teachers and students were returning to school, Judge Treu rocked the nation's education community by rendering a scathing rebuke of California's tenure statutes. He ruled that both students and teachers are unfairly, unnecessarily, and for no legally cognizable reason (let alone a compelling one), disadvantaged by the current Permanent Employment Statute.[17] Judge Treu struck down four California *Education*

Codes on tenure and one code on teacher layoff procedures (that implicates tenure), ruling the codes violate students' fundamental rights, specifically their constitutional right to receive an equal and "quality" education.[18]

In response to the ruling, there was a genuine concern on one side that teachers were being scapegoated, and on the other side there was a resonate refrain, "finally!" *Vergara* was immediately heralded as "A New Battle for Equal Education" by the editorial board of the *New York Times*.[19] An opinion piece in the *Washington Post* carried this headline: "'*Vergara*' decision signals the start of a third wave of education reform,"[20] with the author asserting this new third wave would prioritize "student outcomes over adult interests."[21]

Terry Moe, Stanford University professor and critic of teacher unions, wrote, "[T]enure is also enormously beneficial for teachers, essentially guaranteeing them a job for life. Who wouldn't want that, if they were only thinking of themselves?"[22] President Obama's education secretary, Arne Duncan, also weighed in on *Vergara*, praising the decision as "a mandate to fix educational inequities" and an opportunity to "build a new framework for the teaching profession."[23] In short, supporters of Judge Treu's decision see tenure as a fortress for the ineffective, with teacher unions manning the ramparts to protect the incompetent rather than serving the needs and interests of children and the broader public.

> The court's historic decision in *Vergara v. California* reaffirmed the fundamental, Constitutional right of every student to learn from effective teachers and have an equal opportunity to succeed in school.
>   Students Matter, *Vergara v. California SudentsMatter* (n.d.). Site visited August 6, 2017, available at http://studentsmatter.org/case/vergara/

Defenders of tenure were also quick to respond to the *Vergara* decision. Erwin Cherminsky, dean of the School of Law at the University of California at Irvine, noted the persistent challenges of teacher retention and predicted that "Getting rid of tenure and due process will not encourage more teachers to stay in the profession. It will drive out and discourage other qualified people from entering the profession in the first place."[24]

This diminished sense of job security will negatively impact the difficult and important professional work of preparing students to participate as public citizens in our democratic forms of self-governance and to become economically self-sufficient private individuals enjoying and abiding by their natural rights, the argument asserts. Finally, a *Slate* magazine headline wrote "Tenure is Not the Problem," further explaining, "Racial segregation continues to bedevil American society and . . . Concentrations of poverty have much more to do with why poor and minority students often end up with the worst teachers than do tenure laws."[25]

Though *Vergara* did not directly challenge teacher unions, they were clearly the unspoken "guests" at court. Harvard Kennedy School professor Paul E. Peterson hoped that the legal reach of *Vergara* would include breaking "the union stranglehold over teacher-tenure policy."[26] Teacher unions respond to attacks like Peterson's by arguing that tenure protects teachers and communities from questionable employment decisions by management and allows teachers to speak freely to the community about school practices that are of questionable educational value or even detrimental to students.

The legal shockwave of *Vergara* was short-lived, as Judge Treu's decision was stayed due to an immediate appeal by the California Teachers Association. Nearly two years later, a three-judge panel of the Second District Court of Appeals overturned Treu's ruling in a 3-0 vote, thus restoring tenure to California public school teachers.[27]

Four months later the California Supreme Court refused to review the Court of Appeals decision but on a very divided 4 to 3 vote.[28] One dissenter, Justice Cuellar, asserted that a review was needed due to the "staggering failures that threaten to turn the right to education for California schoolchildren into an empty promise."[29] The judicial death notice of teacher tenure was premature but across the nation it was still a target.

In the next section, we will clarify the meaning of "tenure," a protection accorded public schoolteachers through procedural and substantive due process.

> The need for change is now. We cannot waste another day, cannot waste another child.
>
> John Fensterwald, "Judge Strikes Down All 5 Teacher Protection Laws in *Vergara* Lawsuit" *EDSOURCE* (June 10, 2014). Site visited January 29, 2015, available at http://edsource.org/2014/judge-strikes-down-all-5-teach er-protection-laws-in-vergara-lawsuit/63023

WHAT IS TENURE?

The Fourteenth Amendment states that before government can take away a person's life, liberty, or property, it must only do so with the due process of law.[30] At its core, due process means fundamental fairness. Boiled down, due process requires government to implement fair laws in a fair manner, specifically if government action infringes upon a person's life, liberty, or property.

The history of teacher tenure in the United States stretches back about eleven decades, when New Jersey passed the first tenure law in 1909.

Progressive era "good-government" reformers in Chicago lobbied for tenure in Illinois in response to the attack on the Chicago Teachers Federation and teacher's rights. Good government reform also took place in New York, as chronicled by the Official Journal of the National Civil Service Reform League, *Good Government*.[31] Dana Goldstein points out that "the new three-year probationary period followed by tenure was seen as a clean government reform after decades of politically influenced teacher appointments, in which schools were part of the patronage machine."[32]

In 1921, California passed the Teachers' Tenure Act, establishing probationary and permanent classes of teachers.[33] Historian Diana D'Amico identified several reasons for the development of tenure laws in the early twentieth century: (a) paperwork associated with rehiring a growing teaching force each year was time-consuming and inefficient, and (b) a desire to entice the "right" teachers to stay in the system, as too often teachers were hired and fired "based on personal connections, whims, and politics."[34]

In a 1939 California Court of Appeals case involving the dismissal of a teacher, defenders of the state's tenure law argued that it ensures "an efficient permanent staff of teachers for our school whose members are not dependent upon caprice for their positions as long as they conduct themselves properly and perform their duties efficiently and well."[35] D'Amico commented, "The California ruling further legitimized the historic finger wagging at teachers. Not only is this unfair to teachers, it is detrimental to the nation's children."[36]

Forty years later, the New York Court of Appeals (the state's highest court) noted that tenure is a public good, writing, "the interests of the public in the education of our youth can best be served by a system designed to foster academic freedom in our schools and to protect competent teachers from the abuses they might be subjected to if they could be dismissed at the whim of supervisors."[37] Another New York Court of Appeals decision at this time underscored the importance of tenure in protecting teachers from "arbitrary suspension and removal."[38] The court noted that the state's tenure law safeguards "tenured teachers from official or bureaucratic caprice."[39]

But what is teacher tenure? First, it is not a job guarantee; it is, however, protection "against termination of employment in cases where there are no grounds for termination or where a teacher has no fair opportunity to present a defense."[40] Tenure is due process applied to educators in public school contexts "against arbitrary action of government."[41] The idea of due process is rooted in common law dating back to that nascent, revolutionary document of 1215, *Magna Carta Libertatum* (or "The Magna Carta," or the "Great Charter for Liberties") that served to check monarchic power by inscribing protections for members of the aristocracy in written rules of law. Over the centuries, protections against unilateral government authority have expanded to include many other citizen classifications, including public school teachers.

Today, teacher tenure is guaranteed by the U.S. Constitution via the Fifth and Fourteenth Amendments, once it has been identified as a property right through state legislative action. When teachers receive tenure under the applicable state law, they gain "a legitimate claim" of property[42] and thus are entitled to due process protection when their property (employment) is threatened.[43] In short, tenure becomes property, as there is a continuing expectation of employment.[44]

Due Process: Procedural and Substantive Rights

Due process is a protection against government taking away a person's life, liberty or property without the "due process of law," as stated in both the Fifth and the Fourteenth Amendment. Tenure, as due process, guarantees teachers fundamental fairness when the government acts against them, individually or collectively. Due process requires that government implement laws, codes and regulations that are fair whenever a person's life, liberty or property may be affected; that is, it "protects against policies and practices which violate precepts of fundamental fairness."[45] There are two elements that comprise due process; procedural due process and substantive due process.

Procedural due process guarantees that a person is entitled to a fair process, including fair notice and a fair hearing, prior to the deprivation of a person's life, liberty, or property. The notice must contain specific information about the day, time and place of the hearing. It must also include, with sufficient specificity, notice of the charges against the person so that she/he can prepare an adequate defense. The hearing must be held before a neutral tribunal that has authority in the matter. There must be an orderly proceeding and the "accused" must have the opportunity to cross-examine witnesses. The hearing, except in the matter of exigency of immediate harm, must be held prior to the desired government action. As a Texas federal district court ruled in 2017, "In short, due process is designed to foster government decision-making that is both fair and accurate."[46]

These protections are modified or limited by the special characteristics of the public school and the state's compelling interest to provide an efficient service to the public. The U.S. Supreme Court in *Morrissey v. Brewer* opined, "Once it is determined that due process applies, the question remains what process is due."[47] The extent of procedural due process is "tailored" according to the extent of the deprivation a person may suffer at the hands of government. For example, a first-grade student facing a suspension of one day is entitled to due process prior to the suspension;[48] however, the extent of the due process is greater for a teacher facing dismissal.

Substantive due process is concerned with the substance of the law, rule or regulation; that is, any deprivation to an individual's life, liberty, or property must be reasonable and consistent with the American sense of fairness, and must be clearly and rationally related to a lawful state function or responsibility. The reasonable person test is used in substantive due process cases. The test asks: "Could a reasonable person understand what to do or not do after reading the law, rule, or regulation?" Substantive due process challenges involve questions of vagueness or overbreadth of the law, rule, or regulation, as well as questions about fundamental fairness of the decision made by government (e.g., is the behavior of government to take away a person's life, liberty, or property conscious-shocking).

Understanding conscious-shocking behavior, while rarely found by the courts in education cases, is an important consideration when we examine the *Vergara* decision and its view of tenure. In *Rochin v. California* (1972), the Supreme Court held that substantive due process is violated when government conduct "offend[s] those canons of decency and fairness."[49] In other words, a "sense of justice" must not "shock the conscience." Similarly, substantive due process is violated when government conduct reaches "a demonstrable level of outrageousness."[50]

Our legal system has viewed teacher tenure as a property right that is granted by the state when certain conditions have been met, such as completing a specific number of years of service. The U.S. Supreme Court in *Cleveland Board of Education v. Loudermill* (1985) asserted that property interests "are created and their dimensions defined by existing rules or understandings that stem from an independent course such as state law."[51] When a teacher has been granted tenure, his/her job becomes "property" in that there is a continuing expectation of employment and, therefore, government can take away that property right only after due process has been satisfied.

Tenure is not a guarantee of lifetime employment despite the assertions of opponents. School boards have discretion in deciding whether a teacher will be granted tenure. Education law professor, Perry Zirkel, writes, "It is a myth that teacher tenure provides a guarantee of lifetime employment."[52] Instead, tenure assures that school leaders must demonstrate just cause for termination. As the U.S. Supreme Court asserted in *Loudermill*, "Tenure, as originally designed, only protects teachers from frivolous dismissals, not for legitimate reasons such as incompetence, inadequate performance, immoral conduct, insubordination, willful neglect of duties, or any other sufficient cause."[53]

Just cause terminations must (a) explain the basis for the decision, as well as (b) provide a hearing in which the school employer must (c) produce a preponderance of evidence (a legal standard) to support the denial of the teacher's property.[54] In addition, (d) the burden is on the government to prove the case for dismissal rather than on the employee to prove his or her competence.

Public school teachers who have not been granted tenure have not attained a "property" right and, therefore, are not entitled to due process if their contracts are not renewed. They are typically granted due process rights if the school district seeks to dismiss the teacher during the yearlong contract period (typically August to June). Teachers have an expectation of employment during the contract period but not beyond the contract period.

Private sector employees—including teachers in religious and secular private schools—cannot claim a property right, as the U.S. Constitution only protects citizens of their "life, liberty and property" from government action, not the actions of privately owned organizations. Consequently, private sector workers, including private school teachers, are referred to as "at-will" employees, except in the state of Montana.[55] At-will employment means that an employer can terminate a worker at any time and for any reason, or for no reason at all, without incurring legal liability.[56]

Therefore, without tenure statutes public school teachers would likely have at-will employment status; they could be dismissed for any or no reason if the administration does not violate state or federal anti-discrimination laws (which, by the way, are much narrower in scope than due process rights).

Having laid the groundwork for what constitutes tenure (i.e., a constitutional right of due process requiring that government treat its employees fairly), the next section will examine how this due process right was challenged in the courts using the high profile case, *Vergara v. State of California*. Following the *Vergara* analysis, we will then explore legislative attacks on tenure.

Attacking Tenure through the Courts: Vergara v. State of California

As mentioned earlier, Judge Treu's Superior Court decision was overturned by the Court of Appeals and affirmed by the California Supreme Court, preserving the due process protections of California teachers. Nonetheless, it is important to explore Treu's legal reasoning in *Vergara*, especially given the California Supreme Court's narrow 4-3 decision not to review the two lower court decisions. The *Vergara* complaint and holding will be explored in some detail because it is the likely "playbook" for future plaintiffs, such as New York's, *Davids v. State*.[57]

The Complaint

Attacks against public education—and teachers specifically—may have reached a watershed around 2010, with the rollback of collective bargaining rights in Wisconsin (see chapter 7). Tenure became a target for those seeking to remake education. In 2012, California became a lightning rod for the movement to rid the public schools of tenure. In a widely publicized case, *Vergara v. State of California*, nine student plaintiffs, ages seven to fifteen years,[58] sought declaratory and injunctive relief, as well as continuing jurisdiction over the matter and an award for costs and attorneys' fees.

First, the complaint asserts, using *Serrano v. Priest* and other school finance cases,[59] that students have a fundamental interest in a publically supported education. Consequently, where substantial disparities exist in the "quality and extent of educational opportunities . . . the State has a duty to intervene and ensure equality of treatment to all pupils of the state."[60] Essentially, *Vergara* was cast as a civil rights case regarding the equal protection of students in schools that serve a large population of minority and economically disadvantaged students. These students, it was argued, received an education of lesser quality than their nonminority and economically advantaged peers due to the targeted tenure statutes.

The complaint focused on five California statutes that "prevent school administrators from prioritizing—or even meaningfully—considering the interests of their students in having effective teachers when making employment and dismissal decisions."[61] Consequently, by "perpetuating" the employment of "grossly ineffective teachers" the identified students are being denied equal access to quality teaching. The complaint cited research on the central role of teachers in the education of students, reflecting Harvard education professor, Susan Moore Johnson's admonishment, "Who teaches matter."[62]

The plaintiffs asserted that California schools hire and retain grossly ineffective teachers at alarming rates, and that the five targeted statutes "make it virtually impossible" for school administrators to dismiss them. The five contested statutes pertain to (i) the attainment of tenure after approximately eighteen months of service,[63] the dismissal statute that includes (ii) written charges,[64] (iii) correct and cure,[65] (iv) dismissal procedures,[66] and, finally, (v) the layoff statute mandating the use of seniority.[67]

While the plaintiffs asserted that "recent research studies" have found that the dismissal statutes "effectively" prevent California school administrators from dismissing teachers for poor performance, the only data cited by the plaintiffs is the cost and time associated with the dismissal process. Evidence was not presented that established any type of causal relationship between the dismissal statutes and administrator inability to dismiss or force the resignation of teachers.

These statutes, the plaintiffs asserted, denied students equal access to California's "fundamental right" to receive an education, because they led to the retention of grossly ineffective teachers. Furthermore, these grossly ineffective teachers "are disproportionately assigned to schools serving predominantly minority and economically disadvantaged students."[68] In the absence of these statutes, the complaint asserted, school administrators could make employment (layoff) and dismissal decisions based on the best interests of students.

The Tenure Analysis: "Uber Due Process"[69]

Former Texas governor, Rick Perry, told the Greater Miami Chamber of Commerce, "Good teachers know they don't need tenure. There is no reason to have it except to protect those that don't perform as they should"
Trip Gabriel & Sam Dillon, "G.O.P. Governors Take Aim at Teacher Tenure." *The New York Times* (January 31, 2011). Site visited September 7, 2015, available at http://www.nytimes.com/2011/02/01/us/01tenure .html?_r=1.

First, there is wide agreement that an incompetent teacher does great harm to the education of his/her students and to the overall performance and reputation of the school. Among the many school-related variables, teacher effectiveness is usually, if not always, considered to be the most important in shaping students' academic performance. In short, teachers are the school variable that matters most and, therefore, incompetent teachers must be weeded out through a fair and transparent process. In fact, the U.S. Supreme Court in 1952 declared "that school authorities have the right and the duty to screen the officials, teachers, and employees as to their fitness to maintain the integrity of schools as a part of ordered society cannot be doubted."[70]

Consequently, issues about the validity and reliability of teacher evaluation data are critically important when making decisions about who to place in front of students in a classroom, how to help teachers reach higher levels of performance, when and how to identify deficiencies, and when dismissal is justified. In *Vergara,* Judge Treu accepted, without comment, the teacher effectiveness research findings of economics professors Raj Chetty, John N. Friedman, and Jonah Rockoff[71] that were based on "value-added modeling" (VAM) of student standardized test scores.[72] Chetty et al. asserted:

Replacing a teacher whose [VAM Assessment] is in the bottom 5% with an average teacher would increase the present value of students' lifetime income by more than $250,000 for the average classroom in our sample. We conclude that good teachers create substantial economic value and that test score impacts are helpful in identifying such teachers.[73]

However, the Chetty et al. findings have been disputed, calling into question the causal connection the court made between tenure and ineffective teachers.[74]

Judge True cast *Vergara* as essentially a civil rights case; that is, do the California statutes on teacher tenure, dismissal, and seniority layoff negatively affect the education of students generally, and minority and low-income students specifically? And, relatedly, do these statues violate students' constitutional right to receive an equal and "quality" education?

The factual issue for Treu was to determine if the five Challenged Statutes "cause the potential and/or unreasonable exposure of grossly ineffective teachers to all California students in general and to minority and/or low income students in particular, in violation of the equal protection clause of the California Constitution."[75] Given the VAM research of Chetty and the testimony of others, the judge found that "the Challenged Statutes impose a real and appreciable impact on students' fundamental right."[76]

In addition, by determining that California students possess a "fundamental" constitutional right to a quality education, "strict scrutiny analysis" is triggered, the most rigorous standard or test that government entities must satisfy. ("Heightened scrutiny" and "rational basis" _ the easiest standard for government to meet – are two other legal standards used by the courts.) Strict scrutiny analysis presumes that the disputed state action is unconstitutional and will only survive if the government articulates a "compelling state interest" that justifies the challenged law, and that the law uses "necessary means" to achieve that interest. In short, there is no higher legal test for schools to meet.[77]

1. The Tenure Statute

The court analyzed first the critically important Permanent Employee statute, as it grants permanent status and, therefore, triggdue process tenure rights after two years of service. (In practice, tenure in California is granted after eighteen months of service because of the required March 15th notice of nonrenewal of the contract.) Judge Treu argued, along with several expert witnesses, that this statutory two-year period does not provide administrators with enough time to make an informed tenure decision.

He found that this short time frame denies teachers an adequate opportunity to establish their competence and deprives "students of potentially competent teachers."[78] Consequently, he concluded, "that both students and teachers are unfairly, unnecessarily, and for no legally cognizable reason (let alone a compelling one), disadvantaged by the current Permanent Employment Statute."[79] (It should be noted that Judge Treu never provided a definition of a "potentially competent" and, equally important, that he questionably used value-added modeling to identify "grossly ineffective teachers," not "potentially competent" teachers.)

2. Dismissal Statutes

Judge Treu then moved to the remaining three tenure statutes that defined dismissal. He found that the time demands and cost restraints of firing a tenured teacher may cause school districts to be reluctant to commence dismissal proceedings, adding that the competing parties would instead begin the "Dance of the Lemons" and the "Turkey Trot." According to the court, substantial evidence was presented that dismissals could take anywhere from two to almost ten years and could cost \$50,000 to \$450,000.[80] All the while, these grossly ineffective teachers were left in the classroom.

Judge Treu moved from discussing the dearth of teacher dismissals to an examination of the "uber due process" rights of teachers. While asserting that due process protections are cumbersome in terms of time and money, he conceded that affording teachers due process is a "legitimate issue."[81] In his summary judgment of the dismissal statutes, Treu found that "[t]here is no question that teachers should be afforded reasonable due process when their dismissals are sought."[82] However, because the process is time consuming and expensive, it makes the process for a "fair dismissal of a grossly ineffective teacher illusory."[83] Treu, therefore, ruled that the defendant (i.e., teachers and their unions) did not carry the burden of demonstrating a compelling state interest.

As already indicated, both the judge and the plaintiffs sought to maintain some due process rights for teachers facing dismissal. In his decision, Treu tried to do this by linking these rights to those of nonteaching personnel under *Skelly v. State Personnel Board*.[84] In short, the judge believed that *Skelly* could ensure the retention of due process protections for teachers (after the contested statutes were struck down as unconstitutional), and that *Skelly* rights would involve much less time and community expense in cases involving teacher dismissal.

However, *Skelly* pertains to California "classified personnel" (i.e., government employees who do not possess a teaching or administration credential to hold their position, such as school secretaries, bus drivers, and custodians), as well as "certificated employees" who already have a property right (e.g., tenured teachers). Neither the court nor the plaintiff seeking to graft *Skelly* to teachers demonstrated that *Skelly* was applicable. As discussed earlier, due process rights associated with tenure are predicated upon a recognized property right. It is the attainment of "permanent status" that triggers a public employee's property right and tenure. But *Skelly* rights are only available when there is a separate, existing and legally enforceable employee property right granted by civil service laws. In other words, *Skelly* does not create a property right, it only ensures due process after a property right has been established.

Judge Treu writes, "There is no question that teachers should be afforded reasonable due process when their dismissal is sought."
    Vergara v. State of California, No. BC484642, 2014 WL 6478415 at *13 (Sup. Crt. Cnty. Los Angeles Aug. 27, 2014)

The problem here is that teachers are granted permanent status (i.e., property) and due process rights (i.e., tenure) by the very statute (§44929.21) that Judge Treu declared null and void. Stated another way, *Skelly* rights cannot be stretched to include public school teachers because teachers are not covered under California civil service laws. As the *Skelly* court asserted (by citing to *Board of Regents v. Roth*), "To have a property interest in a benefit, a person clearly must have more than an abstract need or desire for it. He must have more than a unilateral expectation of it. He must, instead, have a legitimate claim of entitlement to it."[85] Judge Treu tried to preserve due process protections for teachers but unwittingly removed the statutory basis for an enforceable property right. Thus, Judge Treu unwittingly removed the trigger for due process protections for teachers.

3. Last In, First Out (LIFO)

The strict scrutiny analysis of the LIFO statute was cursory and simplistic; that is, it framed LIFO as a choice between retaining a "gifted junior teacher" or a "grossly ineffective senior teacher." This Hobson's choice led to two conclusions: keep the gifted teacher and get rid of the grossly incompetent one. In this flawed construction, there are only two types of California teachers; gifted new teachers and grossly incompetent veterans. However, retention decisions in public schools involve a rather long continuum of teachers, from first-year novice teachers to veterans who've plied their craft for decades. In Treu's analysis, teaching experience seems to count for nothing.

In summary, the *Vergara* decision reconfirmed that California public school students have a fundamental constitutional right to equitable educational opportunity and Judge Treu created a new fundamental student right to a "quality education." All five Challenged Statutes failed strict scrutiny analysis and, therefore, all were found unconstitutional.

The Appeal

The decision in *Vergara* was stayed pending the appeal. Twenty months after Judge Treu's decision, the California Court of Appeals in April of 2016 reversed and remanded the matter to the Superior Court, directing it to enter a judgment in favor of the defendants on all causes of action.[86] For its analysis, the Court of Appeals defined two distinct classes of students; Group 1 was the "unlucky subset" of students who were taught by grossly ineffective teachers and Group 2 were poor and minority students.[87]

The Appellate Court held that the plaintiffs failed to establish an equal protection claim; that is, "they did not show that the statutes inevitably cause a certain group of students to receive an education inferior to the education received by other students."[88] In fact, the court held that there was no "identifiable class sufficient to maintain an equal protection claim."[89] Critically, the plaintiffs were not able to demonstrate how the statutes themselves make any specific group of students more likely than any other group of students to be assigned incompetent teachers.

Central to the analysis is the degree of cause that can be attributed to the statutes themselves for the concentration of incompetent teachers in certain schools. The salient point made by the court is that the law does not dictate where teachers—competent or incompetent—are assigned. The court did note drawbacks to the current tenure, dismissal, and layoff laws; however, it did not find that the statutes created a facial constitutional violation. The court wrote:

> The evidence also revealed deplorable staffing decisions being made by some local administrators that have a deleterious impact on poor and minority students in California's public schools. The evidence did not show that the challenged statutes inevitably caused this impact.[90]

The plaintiffs lost on appeal. Essentially, the California Court of Appeals found that if poor and minority students' constitutional rights to "basic educational equality" are infringed because of more frequent encounters with grossly ineffective teachers, it "is the product of staffing decisions, not the challenged statutes."[91] Importantly, the court questioned whether there would have been a different outcome in this case had the plaintiffs targeted local administrative decision-making rather than the laws themselves.

The plaintiffs appealed to the California Supreme Court. The appeal was denied on a 4-3 vote in May of 2016 without a written opinion, though statements from three dissenting judges were filed. Justice Liu argued that the issue of incompetent teachers is of statewide importance and that the serious harm to students requires further review to determine if the challenged statutes are to blame.[92] Justice Cuellar noted the need to achieve a balance between honoring students' fundamental right to an education and "retaining protections for public employees from arbitrary dismissal."[93] He asserted that the Supreme Court should have heard the case to differentiate between the usual "blemishes" of governance and "those staggering failures that threaten to turn the right to an education for California schoolchildren into an empty promise."[94]

LEGISLATIVE ATTACKS ON TEACHER TENURE

Both sides of the tenure controversy are correct; all students deserve to be taught by competent teachers and all teachers deserve to be protected from arbitrary and capricious actions by school administrators and school boards. But how can the nation thread this needle? Judge Treu tried in *Vergara* but his legal remedy failed. Let us now turn to legislative attempts to address the controversy.

North Carolina's Legislation Is Declared Unconstitutional

In 2013, the Republican-run North Carolina General Assembly, similar to the move by Wisconsin, repealed the state's 1971 teacher tenure law[95] starting five years into the future (i.e., July of 2018). The law allowed North Carolina teachers to retain their due process rights if acquired by the end of the 2013–2014 academic year.[96] Tenure would be replaced by one-, two-, or four-year contracts. Nonrenewal of a contract would be based on any reason not "arbitrary, capricious, discriminatory, for personal or political reasons, or on any basis prohibited by State or federal law."[97] Local school boards would decide whether to hear an appeal from a nonrenewed teacher.[98] In effect, the due process rights of North Carolina teachers were now exclusively in the hands of local school boards.

Not all North Carolina school districts welcomed the diminishment of the due process rights of their teachers. In 2015, the Wake County School Board, drafted a policy that restored the due process rights of teachers eliminated by the new state law. Specifically, teachers were to be given notice of the reason(s) for their dismissal and, upon request, would be given a hearing before the school board. The policy applied to teachers with at least five years of experience who had received good evaluations the prior three years.[99] The school board also acknowledged the importance of employment security for teachers. Wake County's assistant superintendent for human resources stated, "Our goal is to make sure our teachers felt they had protection and support. With the elimination of career status, our policy was written to provide as much support as we could."[100]

In April of 2016, two years before the tenure-removal legislation would take effect, the North Carolina Supreme Court in a unanimous decision, *North Carolina Association of Educators v. State of North Carolina*,[101] struck down the 2013 law as unconstitutional. The court conducted a contract analysis of the 1971 Career Status law that had established teacher tenure and found an implied contract. The court also highlighted the importance of employee due process rights when hiring teachers, that tenure had "value to prospective teachers which 'makes up for not having better monetary compensation.'"[102]

The court's contract analysis also examined if there was a legitimate public purpose for eliminating the contract and whether the method adopted was necessary and reasonable. While the North Carolina Supreme Court recognized the legislature's valid concern for flexibility when dismissing low-performing teachers, the justices unanimously found the action not to be necessary and reasonable.[103] Instead of instituting a "drastic impairment" of the contract, the court asserted there were more moderate alternatives, such as identifying additional grounds for dismissal and refining the definition of inadequate performance.

Successful Legislative Attacks on Tenure: Louisiana and Kansas

While North Carolina's legislative attempt to abolish its tenure laws failed, other states were successful. For example, the Louisiana legislature in 2012 passed Act 1, a sweeping repeal of multiple tenure-related statutes and the enactment of new teacher performance and retention requirements. The pertinent changes for this discussion include: (a) requiring superintendents and principals to make employment-related decisions based on "performance and effectiveness"; (b) prohibiting seniority from being used as the "primary criterion" for personnel decisions, including reduction in force; (c) tenure acquired by September 1, 2012, is retained but only if the teacher received a rating of "highly effective" in five of the six preceding years; (d) teachers without tenure as of September 1st will forever remain at-will employees; and, (e) teachers paid with support from federal funds are not eligible for tenure.[104]

A suit for declaratory judgment was brought by the Louisiana Federation of Teachers (LFT) and other plaintiffs. Among the many complaints, the plaintiffs argued that Act 1 violated due process protections because it allowed superintendents to dismiss tenured teachers without a hearing or the opportunity for judicial review. The Superior Court, in its second ruling, agreed with the plaintiffs and held that Act 1 was unconstitutional.

The legislature responded in June 2014 by passing Act 570 which amended sections of Act 1. The amended sections now required a hearing and judicial review for dismissed or disciplined tenured teachers. (When the Louisiana Supreme Court finally heard the case, Act 570 made this portion of the LFT's appeal moot.) However, significant sections of Act 1 remained under scrutiny, including requirements for gaining tenure and the transfer of employment decision-making from the school board to the superintendent. The plaintiffs also argued that legislation must focus on a single subject to increase public transparency and reduce the possibility of "logrolling" (i.e., combining unrelated subjects into a single bill in an effort to get legislators to vote for one portion of a bill in exchange for a vote on another section). However, Louisiana's highest court held that the Act 1 statutes addressed only one subject; that is, "improving elementary and secondary education through tenure reform and performance standards based on effectiveness."[105] Louisiana had successfully eliminated due process rights for all current public school teachers not granted tenure status by September 1, 2012, as well as all future teachers.

Kansas educators faced legislation similar to their colleagues in Louisiana, and in a state that also restricted legislative initiatives to a single subject. In 2014, the Kansas legislature was forced to respond to the state Supreme Court's order to pump more money into the state's public school system due to inequitable funding. At the last minute, a provision was added to the bill that stripped teachers of their sixty-year-old right to due process before being fired.[106] The Kansas National Education Association brought suit alleging that the process evaded proper legislative review and violated the single subject rule. The Supreme Court heard the case and voted unanimously in January of 2017 that the budget and the elimination of tenure were a single subject and, therefore, the legislation was constitutional.

This did not end the issue; the Kansas National Education Association filed suit challenging the application of the tenure repeal on behalf of several teachers in February of 2017.[107] The Plaintiffs were tenured teachers before tenure was eliminated by the 2014 legislation. Their contracts were not renewed at the end of the 2014–2015 academic year and without the benefit of a hearing or a statement of reasons for the nonrenewal. The suit asserts that the school board's application 2014 amendments to the Teacher Due Process Act are an unconstitutional violation of due process rights.[108] This case is pending and will be watched closely.

ATTACKING TENURE: CONTEXT AND IMPACT

It has often been said that organizational leaders cannot fire their way to success and excellence. Does an educational reform strategy that is grounded in quick and easy firing practices with little to no concern for building the capacity of its teachers, drive educators from the profession and dissuade others from considering teaching as a career? Does a focus on the percentile ranking of teachers according to student test scores (using VAM) and reducing or eliminating any sense of job security for teachers working in high-stress environments help or harm efforts to attract and retain our nation's best and brightest? More specifically, did Louisiana and North Carolina's indiscriminant; slash-and-burn approaches to removing incompetent teachers improve the overall quality of their state's corps of public school teachers? Were student educational outcomes positively affected by these legislative actions?

The backdrop or context to reduce or remove tenure is occurring at a time of teacher shortages. Valerie Strauss describes the current crisis facing our nation's public schools:

Teacher shortages are nothing new—most states have reported some since data started being kept more than 25 years ago—but the problem has grown more acute in recent years as the profession has been hit with low morale over low pay, unfair evaluation methods, assaults on due-process rights, high-stakes testing requirements, insufficient resources and other issues.[109]

Compounding the teacher shortage is the shrinking pipeline from teacher preparation programs to employment as first-year teachers. The Learning Policy Institute (2016) estimates a demographic increase of roughly 3 million K to 12 students over the upcoming decade and the need to hire approximately 300,000 teachers a year (after factoring in retirements and the profession's already high annual attrition rate). The Economic Policy Institute's 2019 report, "The Perfect Storm in the Teacher Labor Market," states that the teacher shortage is real and has significant consequences, especially for high poverty schools.[110] Unfortunately, this teacher shortage is occurring at a time when enrollments in teacher education programs have dropped 35 percent.[111]

California illustrates the challenges of teacher shortages when teacher tenure, a valued condition of employment, is under serious attack. During the recession period and before the *Vergara* case, 2008–2012, California lost 82,000 teaching positions; however, in 2015 alone the state had to fill 21,500 teaching slots.[112] This yo-yo effect of cutting teaching positions followed by a period of high teacher demand but low supply is detrimental to stability in educational programming and attracting teachers to the profession. Derek Black makes this point in his law review of tenure, "Some have already suggested that new teacher evaluation systems and attacks on teacher tenure are playing a role in the teacher shortage that developed in California in 2015."[113] And, as mentioned earlier, compounding this teacher shortage is a precipitous drop in candidates entering teacher preparation programs, the primary pipeline for our next generation of educators.

It should be of no surprise that many teachers responded to the legislative changes in North Carolina and Louisiana by leaving the state or the profession. The North Carolina Department of Public Instruction reported that 1,082 North Carolina teachers took jobs in other states in 2015, roughly triple the number who moved away in 2010.[114] Compounding the mounting staffing pressures was the fact that enrollments in the state's fifteen schools of education had dropped by 30 percent since 2010.[115] (This precipitous drop is surprising given the devastating economic recession of 2008 and the usual effect of increased interest in government employment due to greater job security. We speculate that the removal of due process protections contributed to this decline.)

While the significant rise in teacher attrition and reduced enrollment in teacher preparation programs following North Carolina's elimination of tenure seems more than coincidental, researchers Strunk, Barrett and Lincove directly examined the impact of Louisiana's tenure removal law on teacher turnover. They found that after the law's passage there was a significant increase in the number teachers exiting the profession:

> Our estimates suggest that the tenure reform is responsible for the exit of 1,500 to 1,700 teachers in the first two years after the removal of tenure protections, a loss of 3.0 to 3.5% of Louisiana's teacher workforce.[116]

Third-year teachers, who under the old law were very close to the prospect of tenure, showed a significant increase in departures; however, the largest percentage of teacher exits occurred among fourth-year teachers—the ones who formerly had received tenure. There was also a large jump in exits among teachers who were retirement eligible. Finally, the lowest-performing schools (i.e., those with an "F" rating),[117] saw teachers exiting these typically high poverty schools beyond their already staggeringly high annual attrition rates.

The tenure reform created substantial churn in the Louisiana teacher workforce.

Katharine O. Strunk, Nathan Barrett, & Jane Arnold Lincove, *When Tenure Ends: Teacher Turnover in Response to Policy Changes in Louisiana*, Policy Brief Education (New Orleans, LA: Research Alliance for New Orleans, February 22, 2017): 5.

In short, while the intent of the Louisiana law was to make removal of incompetent teachers easier, it also led to competent teachers leaving the profession. The exodus of competent teachers, smarting from the loss of due process protections against arbitrary administrative action, does not serve the educational needs of schoolchildren. Worse, the greater "churn" of teachers in low-performing schools moves us further away from equality of educational opportunity, a cornerstone principle and justification for any truly meritocratic society. Finally, the additional cost of recruitment, hiring, and preparation needed to replace these departing Louisiana teachers was estimated at $4,000 to $18,000 per position.[118]

At a time when the nation desperately needs to attract talented young people to public service through teaching, the prevailing school reform stance is to reduce due process protections for teachers and somehow fire our way to educational excellence. And, inexplicably, this reform strategy is to be carried out in an environment of increased teacher attrition, a shrinking pool of new teacher candidates, and reduced pay relative to other professions. (In a new international study, the Organization for Economic Development and Cooperation found that "U.S. teachers make less than 60 cents on every dollar made by others with their education level, the biggest gap of any OECD country.")[119] Bottom line, public school reformers cannot narrowly focus on just one part of a complex multidimensional problem.

SHOULD TENURE PRACTICES BE MODIFIED? YES!

Protection of teachers from arbitrary and capricious dismissals serves the public good. Even Judge Treu and the plaintiffs in *Vergara* did not want to cast teachers adrift without protection from the vagaries of shifting political winds and questionable motives of administrators. Will easy dismissal of teachers result in significant student gains as envisioned by opponents of tenure? M. J. Stephey offers a counterpoint:

> Abolishing tenure doesn't address problems of underfunding, overcrowding or improving students' home environments. And despite more than a century of social progress, the need to protect teachers from the whims (or the tyranny) of the community remains as important as ever—especially in science classrooms where the battle over evolutionary biology and creationism rages on.[120]

For example, in *Stachura v. Truzkowski* (1985), a life science teacher was accused of improper teaching when using a school board-approved textbook and set of films.[121] The unfounded complaints nonetheless sparked vehement protests, including calls to tar and feather Stachura. In the ensuing court case brought by Stachura for being disciplined by the administration, the court noted, "when public protest arose neither the administrative officials of the school board nor the School Board itself saw fit to defend this embattled teacher, or publicly to assume responsibility for their own decisions."[122]

The court concluded that Stachura was never given a fair opportunity to present his defense and that the Board failed to act in good faith. He won compensatory and punitive damages against the school board for $321,000. Tenure provided protection against this travesty; however, it could not shield a teacher's reputation from being damaged or prevent the loss of taxpayer monies and school personnel time and energy on a needless lawsuit. Cases like this make clear that due process protections are necessary but not sufficient when administrators shirk their leadership responsibilities.

The court in *Donahoo v. Board of Education* two-thirds of a century ago asserted that tenure improves the school system "by assuring teachers of experience and ability continuous service" by providing protection from "political, partisan, or capricious" reasons for dismissal.[123] Decades later, we support this Illinois court—the court got it right.

Beyond protections from arbitrary and capricious dismissals, tenure serves the public good by attracting a larger talent pool and by providing greater stability in the workforce. Judge Hopgood, in the Superior Court case *North Carolina Association of Educators, Inc. v. State of North Carolina* discussed earlier, wrote that eliminating tenure would make it "harder for school districts to attract and retain quality teachers."[124] In addition, due process rights for tenured teachers (a) eliminates the constant distraction and fear of termination, (b) contributes to greater teacher experimentation and creativity, (c) promotes richer and more authentic relationships with students, and (d) increases teacher willingness to inform the community about questionable reform strategies and practices advocated by school leaders. In short, government acting fairly toward its schoolteachers benefits the community in a variety of important ways.

Modifying but not eliminating due process protections for teachers is a reasonable and necessary reform to maximize the public good. As former U.S. Secretary of Education Arnie Duncan stated in defense of unions and teacher tenure, "You can't fire your way to the top."[125] However, we also know that the status quo regarding tenure practices is not in the public interest.

Beyond the obvious need to extend the pre-tenure review period to at least three years or more, we offer five modifications: (1) only effective teachers are granted tenure; (2) ensure that teacher evaluations are much more than ceremonial congratulations that result in the automatic protection of incompetence; (3) enhance clarity about what constitutes incompetence and "just cause" for dismissal; (4) keep seniority as a factor in layoffs but not the only factor; and (5) hold administrators and school boards accountable.

(1) Only Effective Teachers Are Granted Tenure: Tenure is a property right that should be earned. In higher education, the process is difficult and involves a longer time period, with high standards required in the areas of teaching, scholarship, and service. The community of scholars takes responsibility for upholding its standards of effectiveness; tenure is not gained through the passage of time. Tenure must be earned through a demonstration of competence as a professional educator who serves the best interests of their students. Given that the vast majority of teachers continue to develop their competence and professionalism over many years, K to 12 tenure decisions should not be made prior to the conclusion of the third year of service.

Further, tenure is a statement of competence that must be continually earned in order to protect and serve the public good. When a tenured teacher's competence is questioned (a) using a thorough, transparent, and fair documentation system and (b) attempts at remediation have failed, it is in the public interest to terminate employment. The issue of nontenured teachers who are coming up for a tenure decision, but who are on improvement plans or under investigation for unprofessional behavior must receive additional scrutiny in the tenure approval process. The default position in these situations when there is doubt should be what is in the best interests of students. Students must not languish in classrooms that lack a competent educator, and the public should not foot the bill for salaries and benefits when a public employee provides incompetent service.

(2) Improve Teacher Evaluations: Evaluation systems should be designed to reveal weaknesses, identify strengths, and assist in improving teacher performance. The Supreme Court of South Dakota wrote, "The purpose of any evaluation is to monitor changes in performance and make improvements where necessary."[126] Evaluations cannot focus on a narrow range of learning outcomes (as was the case under NCLB and RTTT), nor can evaluations be too broad and vague. Too many evaluation systems either resort to the checklist of traits and actions or have such detailed standards and substandards that the system becomes byzantine and overly burdensome.[127] Teachers and administrators want to use evaluation systems that are holistic, fair, transparent, and efficient.

To preserve due process protections for teachers going forward, unions need to abandon their all-too-often automatic legalistic posture and combative stance and, instead, work with community and/or state representatives to construct and confirm the legitimacy of evaluation systems that provide reliable and valid measures of teacher effectiveness. Teachers want to work with respected, effective colleagues and, therefore, in addition to unions speaking for the profession, teachers must advocate for higher and clearer performance standards.

(3) Clarify Grounds for Dismissal: DeMitchell and Fossey have observed that teachers and their unions, to their own peril, have not identified commonly shared beliefs and values about what constitutes proper grounds for teacher dismissal.[128] Stated another way, persistent union defense of questionable teacher behaviors throughout the country and over many years has contributed to today's polarizing crisis regarding tenure. While the extremes of behavior are generally easy to identify and prosecute, the "grey area" between competence and incompetence is where the needle has yet to be threaded. For example, in a Wyoming study of principal and superintendent perceptions of teacher incompetence, researchers found the school leaders' descriptions to be vague.[129]

Union and community representatives must engage in the candid and difficult dialogue to better define professional expectations and responsibilities, including what actions will not be condoned by either side. These expectations and responsibilities must be incorporated into the evaluation system.

Fair protection of teachers is necessary; however, blind protection ill-serves the profession by elevating the needs of the employee over the needs of students and the community. The NEA and AFT consider their organizations to be comprised of professionals; incompetent teachers harm students and harm the profession.

(4) Temper Seniority Practices: The role of seniority, a staple of collective bargaining agreements, in layoffs needs to be reconsidered. We reject the assertion by opponents of tenure that it is axiomatic that newer teachers are better than veterans, and we reject the standard union argument that seniority is the only objective, transparent way to address layoff decisions. The curricular, instructional, and other programmatic and financial needs of the community should receive first consideration, and these needs must be clearly and transparently articulated. In situations requiring layoffs, these needs must then be applied fairly using recent teacher evaluations, with comparable evaluations resolved in favor of the more senior teachers.

A teacher who has received a series of unsatisfactory evaluations (that include remediation attempts) must not be retained over a teacher with satisfactory to excellent reviews, regardless of seniority. This applies to retaining a nontenured competent teacher over a tenured "unsatisfactory" teacher. Also, layoffs must not be used as a strategy to remove teachers who administrators are unwilling to terminate using established due process procedures or for personal, vindictive reasons. In short, layoffs must be motivated by the legitimate programmatic and financial needs of the community in order to maintain any semblance of fairness with public employees.

(5) Administrators and School Boards Must Meet Their Professional Responsibilities for Evaluation: With the support and backing of local school boards, school administrators are central to the effective implementation of performance evaluation systems, including the identification and removal of incompetent teachers. School leaders must possess the intestinal fortitude, assessment skills, and energy necessary to make informed, reasoned, fair, and, at times, difficult employment decisions.[130] Their responsibilities involve the sometime conflicting roles of supporting and evaluating teachers. As one former teacher expressed in the "reader comment" section of a recent *Washington Times* article regarding tenure:

> I've been a union "building rep" and have sat with sub-par teachers in meeting with the principal. In most cases they corrected their poor behavior, in some cases they disappeared. The unions simply fulfill their contractual

> obligation to their members. The problem is gut-less administrators who won't sit across from a sub-par employee and demand improvement and do it properly within the contract and within civil service laws. Telling an incompetent employee the ugly facts is not pleasant...We need more principals and superintendents with backbone.[131]

The public must be served through its public schools and, therefore, the citizenry must stay informed and demand "transparent, rigorous, and fair systems"[132] of teacher evaluation. Attracting and retaining effective teachers is critical to the public good. It is up to school administrators and school boards, informed by teacher and union input, to institute evaluation systems that are fair and effective at identifying performance deficiencies and removing teachers if remediation measures fail.[133]

If principals, superintendents, and school boards are unwilling to accept the difficult responsibility of serving as gatekeepers of educational excellence, who will? Tenure as a property right can no longer remain a watered-downed interest of teachers irrespective of the public good. Tenure must be a status of continued effectiveness.

Note that our recommendations do not reduce or remove the history and spirit of tenure protections; they serve to identify and retain competent teachers in support of the public good. Developing more robust teacher evaluation systems, clarifying professional expectations and grounds for dismissal, delimiting the status of seniority, and requiring that administrators and school boards to uphold high standards of instruction do not erode teachers' due process protections. Teachers can and should expect a fair notice of deficiencies in their performance using sound, transparent evaluation systems, along with fair hearings and reasonable but time-sensitive opportunities for remediation.

As asserted throughout this chapter, due process for teachers serves the public interest in a variety of ways, including the assurance of a stable workforce of teachers. Teachers are the core, indispensable part of the educational system; in fact, they are the most important educational resource provided by the state for students' academic, intellectual, civic, and social development. Maximizing the capacity of this vital community resource is better social policy and more effectively serves the interests of the community than reducing teachers to at-will employees without recourse when terminated. Tenure is an essential public good.

NOTES

1. *Vergara v. State of California*, No. BC484642, 2014 WL 6478415 at *7 (Sup. Crt Cnty Los Angeles Aug. 27, 2014). See discussion on Due Process: Procedural and Substantive Rights, note 45.

NOTE: A tentative decision was rendered by Judge Treu on June 10, 2014 (2014 WL 2598719), which was followed by the judgment on August 27, 2014. The two decisions are virtually the same with some slight modifications if organization. The holding and reasoning of the court remains unchanged from the tentative decision to the judgment.

2. Dana Goldstein, *The Teacher Wars: A History of America's Most Embattled Profession* (New York: Doubleday, 2014), 5.

3. Ann Elizabeth Blankenship, "Teacher Tenure: The Times, They Are a Changin'," *Education Law & Policy Review* 1 (2014): 193.

4. Katharine O. Strunk, Nathan Barrett, and Jane Arnold Lincove, *When Tenure Ends: Teacher Turnover in Response to Policy Changes in Louisiana*, Policy Brief Education (New Orleans, LA: Research Alliance for New Orleans, February 22, 2017), 2. Site visited August 11, 2017, at https://deutsch29.files.wordpress.com/20 17/02/022217-strunk-barrett-arnold-lincove-when-tenure-ends-teacher-turnover-in-response-to-policy-changes-in-louisiana.pdf.

5. *See* Christine Emmons, "No Teacher Is an Island," *Education Week* 44 (April 6, 2011): 44, writing, "The current educational climate seems riddled with blame, especially blame of teachers. Teacher-bashing is very much in favor."

6. Kathy Christie and Jennifer Dounay Zinth, "Teacher Tenure or Continuing Contract Laws," *Education of the States* (August 2011). Site visited September 11, 2015, at http://www.ecs.org/clearinghouse/94/93/9493.pdf.

7. Jennifer Thomsen, "A Closer Look: Teacher Evaluations and Tenure Decisions," Education Commission of the States (May 2014). Site visited December 29, 2017, at https://files.eric.ed.gov/fulltext/ED561923.pdf.

8. Blankenship, "Teacher Tenure," 210. The vote in Idaho (2011) was 58% to 42% to reinstate tenure, while South Dakota voters rejected the change in tenure by a vote of 114,590 for the change and 235, 064 against the change.

9. *North Carolina Educators Association, Inc. v. State*, 786 S.E.2d 255 (2016).

10. Ibid., 266. The court held that there was no demonstrated problem with dismissing ineffective teachers. The Supreme Court mirrors the Court of Appeals decision writing, the affidavits from the State asserting that tenure "creates insurmountable obstacles to dismissing ineffective teachers" as vague and conclusory. North Carolina Association of Educators, Inc. v. State, 776 S.E.2d 1, 15 (N.C. Ct. App. 2015).

11. Blankenship, "Teacher Tenure," 200.

12. Author, "Protecting Bad Teachers," *Teachers Union Exposed* (n.d.). Site visited April 26, 2015, at http://teachersunionexposed.com/protecting.php (writing, "As long union leaders possess the legal ability to drag our termination proceedings for months or even years—during which time districts must continue paying teachers and substitute teachers to replace then, and lawyers to arbitrate the proceedings—the situation for students will not improve.").

13. Vincent J. Connelly, Todd A. DeMitchell, and Douglas Gagnon, "Teacher Evaluation: Principal Perceptions of the Barriers to Dismissal. Research, Policy, and Practice," *Education Law & Policy Review* 1 (2014): 183 (noting the next highest barrier was the effort required for the documentation for dismissal [67% responding yes]).

14. Chester E. Finn, Jr., "Will Teacher Tenure Die?" *Thomas B. Fordham Institute* (April 19, 2017). Site visited January 1, 2018, at https://edexcellence.net/articles/will-teacher-tenure-die.

15. See Michael Hiltzik, "Why That Ruling Against Teacher Tenure Won't Help Your School Children," *Los Angeles Times* (June 11, 2014). Site visited June 12, 2014, at http://touch.latimes.com/#section/-1/article/p2p-80476702/ (writing, "Eviscerating the due process protection of teachers on the job won't guarantee quality; it will only give administrators more leeway to harass or promote teachers for any reasons they choose.").

16. Diana D'Amico, "The Myth of Teacher Tenure," *Teachers College Record,* ID Number 17620 (July 23, 2014).

17. *Vergara v. State of California*, No. BC484642, at *10.

18. For a critique of Judge Treu's finding that California students have a constitutional right of equal and quality education, *see* Note: "Minimally Adequate Education," *Harvard Law Review* 130 (March 10, 2017): 1458. Site visited January 1, 2018, at https://harvardlawreview.org/2017/03/the-misguided-appeal-of-a-minimally-adequate-education/. The Note, asserts "there is the potential that excessive and more expansive constitutional litigation may actually make things *worse*." Ibid. 1478. See also, Todd A. DeMitchell and Joseph J. Onosko, "*Vergara v, State of California*: The End of Teacher Tenure or a Flawed Ruling?" *Southern California Interdisciplinary Law Journal* 25 (2016). They argue that making an equal and quality education requires the use of strict scrutiny analysis (serving a compelling state interest using the necessary means to achieve that interest) "is a high hurdle for schools to meet." Ibid., 619.

19. Editorial Board, "A New Battle for Equal Education," *New York Times* (June 11, 2014). Site visited June 12, 2014, at http://www.nytimes.com/2014/06/12/opinion/in-california-a-judge-takes-on-teacher-tenure.html?_r=0 (concluding, "Teachers deserve reasonable due process rights and job protections. But the unions can either work to change the anachronistic policies cited by the court or they will have change thrust upon them."). What is interesting about this quote, is the case does not directly deal with any collective bargaining agreement that the teacher unions would have control over. Unions, like school districts, will adapt to any legislative changes, but unions cannot change the laws associated with tenure, dismissal, or layoffs.

20. Joshua Lewis, "'*Vergara*' Decision Signals the Start of a Third Wave of Educational Reform," *Washington Post* (August 14, 2014). Site visited August 15, 2014, at http://www.washingtonpost.com/opinions/vergara-decision-signals-the-start-of-a-third-wave-of-education-reform/2014/08/14/4abe128a-1f28-11e4-ae54-0cfe1f974f8a_story.html.

21. Lewis, "'*Vergara*' Decision Signals the Start of a Third Wave of Educational Reform."

22. Terry M. Moe, *Teachers Unions and America's Public Schools* (Washington, DC: Brookings Institution Press, 2011), 102.

23. Editorial Board, "A School Reform Landmark," *The Wall Street Journal* (June 20, 2014). Site visited June 22, 2014, at http://www.wsj.com/articles/a-school-reform-landmark-1402442804.

24. Erwin Cherminski, "Teacher Tenure: Wrong Target," *New York Daily News* (October 23, 2014). Site visited October 25, 2014, at http://www.nydailynews.com/opinion/teacher-tenure-wrong-target-article-1.1983826.

25. Richard D. Kahlenberg, "Tenure Is Not the Problem," *Slate* (June 13, 2014). Site visited August 5, 2017, at http://www.slate.com/articles/life/education/2014/06/vergara_v_california_the_court_s_decision_to_gut_teacher_tenure_will_not.html.

26. Paul E. Peterson, "Teacher-Tenure Decision Is NOT an Abuse of Judicial Power," *EducationNext* (July 31, 2014). Site visited August 5, 2017, at http://educationnext.org/teacher-tenure-decision-abuse-judicial-power/.

27. *Vergara v. State of California*, 246 Cal.App.4th 619 (2016). The court held, "In sum, the evidence presented at trial highlighted likely drawbacks to the current tenure, dismissal, and layoff statutes, but did not demonstrate a facial constitutional violation. The evidence also revealed deplorable staffing decisions made by some local administrators that have a deleterious impact on poor and minority students in California public schools." 651.

28. *Vergara v. State of California (California Teachers Association)*, Case Number S234741. Appellate Courts Case Information. Petition for review denied (August 22, 2016). Site visited August 6, 2017, at http://appellatecases.courtinfo.ca.gov/search/case/dockets.cfm?dist=0&doc_id=2142232&doc_no=S234741.

The California Supreme Court's decision is appended to the Court of Appeals decision; see above.

29. Ibid., 652n.

30. In public education, claims for a property right in employment thus triggering due process are supported by *Board of Regents v. Roth*, 408 U.S. 564 (1972) and *Perry v. Sinderman*, 408 U.S. 593 (1972).

31. See *Good Government*. (1909). Volumes 26-27 site visited January 9, 2018, at https://books.google.com/books?id=HzI2AQAAMAAJ&pg=PA80&lpg=PA80&dq=Tenure+in+New+York+during+clean+government+period&source=bl&ots=wZ2AuzTsPp&sig=qA_EKBgcovW4vmw_vPOS4_hvo3w&hl=en&sa=X&ved=0ahUKEwj98ryth8zYAhWh1IMKHXVODU4Q6AEIVjAI#v=onepage&q=Tenure%20in%20New%20York%20during%20clean%20government%20period&f=false.

32. Goldstein, *The Teacher Wars*, 85.

33. Stats. 1921, ch.878.

34. Diana D'Amico, *The Myth of Teacher Tenure*, Commentary Teachers College Record 1 (July 23, 2014): 2.

35. *Fresno City High School District v. Caristo*, 33 Cal. App.2d 666, 673 (1939).

36. D'Amico, *The Myth of Teacher Tenure*, 3.

37. *Ricca v. Board of Education, City School District of City of New York*, 47 N.Y.2d 385, 391 (1979).

38. *Holt v. Board of Education, Webutuck Central School District*, 52 N.Y.2d 625, 632 (1981).

39. Ibid.

40. Jennifer Thomsen, "Teacher Performance Plays Growing Role in Employment Decisions," *Education Commission of the States* (May 2014): 4. Site visited June 23, 2015, at http://www.nnstoy.org/download/Various/11242.pdf.

41. *County of Sacramento v. Lewis*, 523 U.S. 833, 845 (1998).

42. *Board of Regents v. Roth*, 408, U.S. 564, 576 (1972). (further writing, as opposed to an "abstract need or desire for it . . . [or] a unilateral expectation of it."). Ibid.

43. *Cleveland Board. of Education. v. Loudermill*, 470 U.S. 532, 546–48 (1985).

44. For a discussion of due process and critiques of tenure, Todd A. DeMitchell and Joseph J. Onosko, "*Vergara v. State of California:* The End of Tenure or a Flawed Ruling," *Southern California Interdisciplinary Law Journal* 25 (2016): 589–624, 593–602.

45. Author, "Generally: The Principle of Fundamental Fairness," *Justia US Law* (n.d.). Site visited April 12, 2016, at http://law.justia.com/constitution/us/amendment-14/52-procedural-due-process-criminal.html.

46. *Houston Federation of Teachers, Local 2415 v. Houston Independent. School District*, 251 F. Supp. 3d 1168, 1176 (S.D. Tex. 2017) (quoting *Carey v. Piphus*, 435 U.S. 247, 262 (1978).

47. *Morrissey v. Brewer*, 408 U.S. 471, 481 (1972).

48. *See Goss v, Lopez*, 419 U.S. 565, 584 (1975) (discussing the flexibility needed for the suspension of public school students.).

49. *Rochin v. California*, 342 U.S. 165, 169 (1972).

50. *Hampton v. United States*, 425 U.S. 484, 495n.7 (1976).

51. *Cleveland Board. of Education v. Loudermill*, 470 U.S. 532, 539 (1985).

52. Perry Zirkel (Guest for Valerie Strauss), "The Myth of Teacher Tenure," The Answer Sheet (Blog), *Washington Post* (July 13, 2010). Site visited May 2015, 2017, at http://voices.washingtonpost.com/answer-sheet/teachers/the-myth-of-teacher-tenure.html.

53. Laura McNeal, "Total Recall: The Rise and Fall of Teacher Tenure," *Hofstra Labor & Employment Law Journal* 30 (2013): 509.

54. *Cleveland Board. of Education v. Loudermill*, 470 U.S. at 544.

55. National Conference of State Legislatures, "The At-Will Presumption and Exceptions to the Rule" *National Conference of State Legislatures* (n.d.). Site visited June 2, 2016, at http://www.ncsl.org/research/labor-and-employment/at-will-employment-overview.aspx.

56. See, e.g., *Collins v. KCEOC Community Action*, 455 S.W.3d 421, 423 (K. App. 2015) (stating, "it has long been the law in Kentucky that an at-will employee may be discharged for good cause, for no cause, or for a cause that some might view as morally indefensible.").

57. *Davids v. State*, No. 101105/14 (N.Y. Sup. Ct. June 30, 2014). Having two motions to dismiss, the case is proceeding to trial. See *Notice of Appeal, Davids*, No.101105/14 (N.Y. Sup. Ct. December 7, 2015).

58. First Amended Complaint for Declaratory and Injunctive Relief, *Vergara v. State* No. BC484642 (Cal. Super. Ct. L.A. Cty. May 14, 2012).

59. *Serrano v. Priest* (1971) 5 Cal.3d 584; *Serrano v. Priest* (1976) 18 Cal.3d 728.

60. *Vergara v. State of California, supra* note 1 at *2.

61. First Amended Complaint for Declaratory and Injunctive Relief, *Vergara v. State* No.BC484642 (Cal. Super. Ct. L.A Cty. May 14, 2012), 3.

62. Susan Moore Johnson, *Teachers at Work: Achieving Success in our Schools* (New York: Basic Books, 1990), xii. See also, Eric Hanushek, *The Economic Value of Higher Teacher Quality* (Washington, DC: National Center for Analysis of Longitudinal Data in Education Research, 2010), 257. Writing, "First, teachers are very important; no other measured aspect of schools is nearly as important in determining student achievement."

63. First Amended Complaint, *supra* note 30 at *12, citing California Education Code § 44929.21.

64. Ibid., *13, citing California Education Code § 44934.

65. Ibid,. citing California Education Code § 44938(b)(1)(2).

66. Ibid., *13–14.

67. Ibid., *13 citing California Education Code § 44944.

68. Ibid., *5.

69. *Vergara v. State of California*, Case No. BC484642 at *11 (writing, State/Defendants/Intervenors raise the entirely legitimate issue of due process. However, given the evidence above stated, the Dismissal Statutes present the issue of *uber* due process."). Ibid.

70. *Adler v. Board. of Education*, 342 U.S. 485, 493 (1952).

71. *Vergara*, No. BC484642 at *7–8. Judge Treu cites, Raj Chetty, John N. Friedman, and Jonah E. Rockoff, *The Long-term Impacts of Teachers: Teacher Value-Added and Student Outcomes in Adulthood* (Working Paper 17699) (National Bureau of Economic Research, December 2011). Site visited February 6, 2015, at http://www.nber.org/papers/w17699.pdf. For a critique of this research relied upon by Judge Treu, see Moshe Adler, "Findings vs. Interpretation in 'The Long Term Impacts of Teachers' by Chetty et al," *Education Policy Analysis Archives* 21 (February 1, 2013). Site visited February 7, 2015, at http://epaa.asu.edu/ojs/article/view/1264 (writing, "There is just one problem: as we explain below, the study does not show what the authors claim it shows") 2; Bruce D. Baker, "Revisiting the Chetty, Rockoff and Friedman Molehill," *National Education Policy Center* (June 10, 2013). Site visited February 7, 2015, at http://nepc.colorado.edu/blog/revisiting-chetty-rockoff-friedman-molehill (concluding, "Indeed it's an interesting study, but to suggest that this study has important immediate implications for school and district level human resource management is not only naive, but reckless and irresponsible and must stop.").

72. Chetty et al., *The Long-term Impacts of Teachers*.

73. Ibid., Abstract. For a discussion of VAM see Chapter 7.

74. Derek W. Black, "The Constitutional Challenge to Teacher Tenure," *California Law Review* 75 (2016): 104, 130.

75. Ibid., *3.

76. *Vergara* No. BC48642 at *8. See also *Butt v. State of California,* (1992) 4 Cal. 4th, 668, 683. (writing, "the unique importance of public education in California's constitutional scheme requires careful scrutiny of state interference with basic educational rights").

77. For a critique of *Vergara's* strict scrutiny analysis as applied to the five disputed statutes, see Todd A. DeMitchell and Joseph J. Onosko, "*Vergara v. State of California*: The End of Teacher Tenure or a Flawed Ruling?" *Southern California Interdisciplinary Law Journal* 25 (2016): 612–615.

78. *Vergara* No. BC48642 *10.

79. Ibid.

80. Ibid., *11.

81. Ibid.

82. *Vergara* No. BC48642 *13.

83. Ibid.

84. *Skelly v. State Personnel Board*, 15 Cal.3d 194 (1975).

85. *Skelly v. State Personnel Board*, 15 Cal.3d at 206–07, citing to *Board. of Regents v. Roth*, 408 U.S. 564, 577 (1972).

86. *Vergara v. State of California*, 246 Cal. App. 4th 619, 652 (2016).

87. Ibid., 645.

88. Ibid., 627.

89. Ibid., 648.

90. Ibid., 651.

91. Ibid.

92. Ibid., 652b.

93. Ibid., 652l.

94. Ibid., 652n.

95. See https://canons.sog.unc.edu/north-carolina-public-school-teachers-and-t he-status-of-tenure/. Site visited December 28, 2017.

96. Craig Jarvis, "NC Supreme Court Rejects State's Repeal of Teacher Tenure," *The News Observer* (Raleigh, NC) (April 15, 2016). Site visited August 10, 2017, at http://www.newsobserver.com/news/politics-government/state-politics/article72033 607.html.

97. N.C.G.S. § 115C–325.3(e) (2015).

98. Ibid.

99. T. Keung Hui, "Wake County School Board Looking to Restore Tenure Rights for Teachers," *The News Observer* (Raleigh, NC) (February 2, 2015). Site visited December 31, 2017, at http://www.newsobserver.com/news/local/education/a rticle10246418.html.

100. Ibid.

101. *North Carolina Educators Association v. State*, 786 S.E.2d 255 (2016).

102. Ibid., *20.

103. Ibid., *25.

104. *Louisiana Federation of Teachers v. State of Louisiana*, No. 14-CA-0691 (Supr. Crt. Louisiana, October 15, 2014) *2-6. Site visited January 1, 2018, at http: //media.nola.com/education_impact/other/Act%201%20Supreme%20Court%20ru ling.pdf.

105. Ibid., *22.

106. Sam Zeff, "Kansas Supreme Court Upholds Law Ending Teacher Tenure," *KCUR* (January 20, 2017). Site visited January 1, 2018, at http://kcur.org/post/kans as-supreme-court-upholds-law-ending-teacher-tenure#stream/0.

107. *Scribner and McNeme v. Board of Education of U.S.D. No. 492*, No. 16-116818-A Appellants Brief Kansas Supreme Court, February 28, 2017). Site visited January 1, 2017, at http://mediad.publicbroadcasting.net/p/kcur/files/201707/knea_app eal_brief.pdf?_ga=2.121729422.427783846.1514840873-1537509985.1514840873.

108. Ibid., 2.

109. Valerie Strauss, "Teacher Shortages Affecting Every State as 2017-2018 School Year Begins," *The Washington Post, Answer Sheet* (August 28, 2017). Site Visited January 2, 2018, at https://www.washingtonpost.com/news/answer-sheet/wp/2017/08/28/teacher-shortages-affecting-every-state-as-2017-18-school-year-begins/?utm_term=.f1d6139814f8.

110. Emma Garcia and Elaine Weiss, "The teacher shortage is real, large and growing and worse than we thought," *Economic Policy Institute* (March 26, 2019). Site visited August 17, 2019, at https://www.epi.org/files/pdf/163651.pdf.

111. Leib Sutcher, Linda Darling-Hammond, and Desiree Carver-Thomas, "A Coming Crisis in Teaching? Teacher Supply, Demand, and Shortages in the U.S.," *Learning Policy Institute* (September 15, 2016). Site visited December 31, 2017, at https://learningpolicyinstitute.org/product/coming-crisis-teaching.

112. Motoko Rich, "Teacher Shortages Spur a Nationwide Hiring Scramble (Credentials Optional)," *New York Times* (August 9, 2015). Site visited August 11, 2017, at https://www.nytimes.com/2015/08/10/us/teacher-shortages-spur-a-nationwide-hiring-scramble-credentials-optional.html.

113. Black, "The Constitutional Challenge to Teacher Tenure," 146.

114. Editorial Board, "Battling the Teacher Shortage," *The Times News* (Burlington, NC) (February 14, 2016). Site visited May 5, 2017, at http://www.thetimesnews.com/article/20160213/OPINION/160219608.

115. Editorial Board, "In NC, a Teacher Shortage Developed by Design," *The News & Observer* (Raleigh, NC) (February 4, 2016). Site visited May 5, 2017, at http://www.newsobserver.com/opinion/editorials/article58519968.html#storylink=cpy.

116. Strunk, et al., *When Tenure Ends*, 5.

117. Ibid., 3–4.

118. Ibid., 5.

119. Sarah D. Sparks, "Teachers' Pay Lags Furthest Behind Other Professionals in U.S., Study Finds," *Education Week* (September 12, 2017). Site visited September 15, 2017, at http://blogs.edweek.org/edweek/inside-school-research/2017/09/us_ranks_last_in_relative_teacher_pay.html?cmp=eml-enl-eu-news2&M=58189858&U=1171185.

120. M.J. Stephey, "Tenure," *Time* (November 17, 2008). Site visited December 29, 2017, at http://content.time.com/time/nation/article/0,8599,1859505,00.html.

121. *Stachura v. Truszkowski*, 763 F.2d 211, 213-14 (6th Cir. 1985).

122. Ibid., 213–214.

123. *Donahoo v. Board of Education*, 109 N.E.2d 787, 789 (Ill. 1952).

124. *North Carolina Association of Educators, Inc. v. State of North Carolina*, No. 13 CVS 16240, 2014 WL 495210 (N.C. Super. Ct. June 5, 2014) at *4.

125. Deborah Solomon, "The School of Hard Drives," *The New York Magazine* (September 16, 2010). Site visited August 12, 2017, at http://www.nytimes.com/2010/09/19/magazine/19fob-q4-t.html.

126. *Iverson v. Wall Board of Education*, 522 N.W.2d 188, 193 (S.D. 1994).

127. See Connelly et al., "Teacher Evaluation," for a discussion of the challenges that principals perceive hinder their ability to work with ineffective teachers.

128. Todd A. DeMitchell and Richard Fossey, *The Limits of Law-Based School Reform: Vain Hopes and False Promises* (Lancaster, PA: Technomic Publishing Co. Inc., 1997), 88.

129. Bret G. Range, Heather E. Duncan, Susan Day Scherz, and Courtney A. Haines, "School Leaders' Perceptions About Incompetent Teachers: Implications for Supervision and Evaluation," *NASSP Bulletin* 96(4) (2012): 302,322,311.

130. For a discussion of the importance of principal's gaining and utilizing the knowledge and skills of documenting ineffective and incompetent teacher conduct, see Todd A. DeMitchell and Mark A. Paige, *Threading the Evaluation Needle: The Documentation of Teacher Unprofessional Conduct* (Lanham, MD: Rowman & Littlefield, 2019).

131. Farmboy-ed comment, Richard Berman, "Teachers Who Can't Teach," *The Washington Times* (February 8, 2016). Site visited January 10, 2018, at https://www.washingtontimes.com/news/2016/feb/8/richard-berman-ending-teacher-tenure-would-get-rid/.

132. Connelly et al., "Teacher Evaluation," 175.

133. Richard F. Elmore, *Bridging the Gap Between Standards and Achievement: The Imperative for Professional Development in Education* (New York: Albert Shanker Institute, 2002), 5. Writing, "For every increment of performance I demand from you, I have an equal responsibility to provide you with the capacity to meet that expectation."

Section 4

THOUGHTS ON AN
UNCERTAIN FUTURE

Chapter 9

Labor Relations in an Uncertain Time

We can't hope to build a more equitable economy unless working people have strong organizations of their own.[1]

[T]he history of American public education shows that teachers are uniquely vulnerable to political pressures and moral panics that have nothing to do with the quality of their work.[2]

AN UNCERTAIN TIME FOR TEACHERS

It has been a turbulent time, an uncertain time, in public education this past decade; teachers, tenure, and unions have been the subjects of intense scrutiny. Teachers have fought back in the courts, at the ballot box, and through traditional labor tactics such as strikes, protests, and walkouts but in unlikely places with evolving union demands beyond just bread and butter. The education labor terrain appears to be altering as its tectonic plates are shifting. The new landscape is still unsettled with its new features still not clearly in view as the dust of change settles.

The right of a union to bargain for the wages, benefits, and terms and conditions of employment has been under concerted pressure if not attacked from primarily Republican governors, legislatures, and well-heeled issue partisans. Since 2010, it has been a particularly pointed, and in many ways a successful, assault. The pressure has resulted in the diminishment of security, the addition of right-to-work states with its antiunion bias, the increase of prohibited subjects of bargaining, and the loss of agency fees as a tactic to starve the two-headed beast of unions and collective bargaining.

179

Is American society ready to write the epitaph of teacher unions? Sixty years after public collective bargaining began in Wisconsin is public sector collective bargaining and teacher unions still pertinent? The answer is yes.

An August 2018 Gallup poll found that support for unions has remained steady at just a tick above 60 percent.[3] The last time since the polling started in 1936 that it dipped below 50 percent was in August of 2009 during the Great Recession when it hit 48 percent. The surveys show that higher unemployment corresponds with less support for unions. Support for unions is not consistent between political affiliations. Forty-five percent of Republicans supported unions whereas 62 percent of independents indicated support, while 80 percent of Democrats approve of unions. Legislative enactments designed to diminish the influence of public sector unions clearly center in the red states.

However, a takeaway is that the majority of the citizenry supports having unions as part of the nation's labor relations providing a voice for employees. The 2018 referendum in red state Missouri in which right-to-work legislative was overturned may be a runway light that leads to a safe but bumpy landing for unions. It could be that the union provides a voice in an environment tilted toward management; one that the public does not want silenced.

However, just because there is support for unions, that support must not be taken for granted as a given for the future. As long as unions and collective bargaining are perceived by a majority of Americans as worthy, support will follow. The challenge is how to find the path forward in which unions meet their legal requirement to pursue the legitimate interests of its members and those it represents without being perceived as a force that is insulated from and in opposition to the public's interests.

The work environment for teachers is unlike most other professions. "They work in a fishbowl environment, with parents and community members having access throughout the year to many aspects of their daily work with children."[4] Consequently, their actions are scrutinized to a much higher degree than most employees, and, in part, because parents view the work of teachers as having enormous short and long-term consequences for their children. Consequently, recommendations for improving the labor relations in education must be tailored to its unique environment.

This book explored the roots of educational labor and focused on the last decade of uncertainty and change. Will and should teacher unions survive appears to be a question that was asked in several ways in several venues. A statement by law professor Ronald C. Brown in 1973, during the rise of public sector bargaining, still resonates today. He wrote, "Public sector collective bargaining has proven itself to be a fact of life rather than a passing phenomenon."[5] However, like all facts of life, life changes to meet the challenges of the present and the promise of tomorrow.

> Although K–12 education historically has not been a driving force in national elections, the nation is in a unique moment in time. Teacher protests and strikes over the past year have catalyzed increased public support for both teachers and for funding public education more broadly. Across the country, people are recognizing that after a decade of disinvestment following the Great Recession, the support that students, teachers, and schools need is simply not being provided—and the consequences are evident.
>
> Scott Sargrad, Khalilah Harris, Lisette Partelow, Neil Campbell & Laura Jiminez. *A Quality Education for Every Child: A New Agenda for Education Policy* (Washington, DC: Center for American Progress, July 2, 2019). Site visited July 2, 2019, available at https://www.americanprogress.org/issues/education-k-12/reports/2019/07/02/471511/quality-education-every-child/.

The book concludes with two foci for change: loosening the constraining straps of the industrial union model and balancing the legitimate interest of only placing and retaining effective teachers in classrooms with the necessary protections that teachers need in order to meet the high demands of their responsibilities.

A necessary beginning point for moving forward is to leave behind the denigration of teachers as individuals and the discounting of their important contributions as a group. For example, former Maine governor LePage of Maine at the unveiling of a new vocational school described teachers as "a dime a dozen."[6] Does the governor mean that teachers are of so little value that they can be found everywhere and can be replaced easily? Words matter and these words of a leader do little to recruit and retain teachers, the core of the educational system. It is not a good practice or policy to demean the very people who provide a necessary service, most often under stressful conditions.

LOOSENING THE GRIP OF THE INDUSTRIAL LABOR MODEL

As stated previously, teachers labor but they are not laborers. The concept of the regulated workplace that can be captured in a standard form through a negotiated contract is inadequate for our classrooms and schools. We must reduce or break the hold of an ill-fitting model and replace it with a more flexible one.

Specifically, the following are good beginning points for reducing the industrial labor hold on education.

Us-and-Them

The us-and-them established by a decade-old model of labor relations no longer works in business and has never worked in education. The rhetoric that sustains the distinction between educators must be reduced. The us-and-them dichotomy must make room for "we/educators." This involves both teachers and administrators reconceptualizing the relationship and acting on that new view. This, however, does not mean that there will no longer be a conflict of interests. There will always be some conflict. It does mean that educators allow for the "we" of a community of interest to be just as visible and just as influential as the us-and-them, the conflict of interests of collective bargaining.[7]

The us-and-them model tends to exaggerate differences which supports and needs conflict. Too often cooperation becomes a lull in the permanence of conflict. It has been well established that cooperation among teachers and between teachers and school administrators is an important factor in creating a successful school.

Standardization versus Flexibility

Julie Koppich's caution, just over a quarter of a century ago, is still salient today. The noted commentator on teacher unions wrote, "The union as an organization must be prepared to 'let go' of standardized and centralized work rules."[8] The standard union work rules found in contracts contribute to an inflexible environment.

The standardizing effect of collective bargaining must be rethought. What aspects of a negotiated contract should include standardization and how do we support flexibility when it is needed to further professional practice? Standardizing work behavior may have the unintended consequence of calling for "managing" teachers through the policing and enforcement of a contract while inhibiting the empowerment of them. Shedd and Bacharach write, "Rather than negotiating rules that restrict flexibility, [the union] will look for ways to relax restrictions on both teachers and administrators."[9]

A spider web of rules that standardizes and scripts practice rather than empowering teachers' professional practice ill-serves teaching. Professional practice demands flexibility and differential action based on the context of the learning situation. Teacher professionalism is highly subject to contextual factors. Too many of the standard union work rules found in contracts contribute to an inflexible environment. The old union adage "if it is not in the contract, it does not exist" does not work in a professional environment. Professional practice is not easily shoehorned into the prescriptive language of a contract.

A community of professionals cannot easily thrive within the confines of standardized, centralized work rules rigidly enforced, like those found in industrial union labor contracts.

The Role of Seniority

Management decisions based on seniority is a staple in industrial union contracts and workplace decision-making. But like shoes that are a size too small they soon become uncomfortable, pinched and work against their purpose. In education, shoe size matters.

Teachers, in a study by DeMitchell and Barton, rated transfer as the most negative contract section affecting reform. One teacher in the study wrote: "Use of seniority to assign teachers to grade, track, etc.; experience, education, training, etc. for a special grade, etc. just doesn't count! The senior teachers can just grab anything they want."[10]

Interestingly, in the same study, principals along with teachers rated this section of the contract as one of the most negative affecting school reform efforts. In contrast, building union representatives rated it as the second most positive section after the evaluation section. The difference in the view of teachers and principals with union representatives is stark and significant. Rigid seniority may be a union goal but not necessarily a goal of teachers and administrators.

However, school administrators who make decisions such as transfer in support of favored faculty members is a legitimate concern. A seventeen-year veteran teacher who sat on the Board of the United Teachers of Los Angeles summed the issue in the following way: "Workers fought for seniority rights because there was a problem with managers trying to curry favor with certain folks. And that certainly has not gone away."[11]

In an interesting twist to the debate over seniority and favoritism, a teacher of the year nominee was laid off based on seniority just prior to the final decision of who will be the New Hampshire teacher of the year.[12] In this case seniority trumped a finding of excellence.

This concern places the onus on administrators to use any relaxation in the use of seniority to show that the decision was unbiased, neutral, and based on defensible criteria. However, the union should not wave the flag of an ancient history of past wrongs by administrators who may no longer work in the school district, and that bears no relation to the current administrators or current history. A past wrong may no longer be a current problem. Caution should be exercised so that contracts not become an archive of previous concerns that no longer exist.

The call is not to abandon all use of seniority. The question how does seniority impact this decision should be asked. Is the decision to use seniority in the best interest of the senior employee and the easiest for the administrator, or is seniority the factor that should determine what best serves the interests of students and the school? Seniority should not be the first and only factor for decision-making.

RETAINING EFFECTIVE TEACHERS:
SERVING THE COMMON GOOD

Both administrators and the union have an interest in attracting, retaining, and supporting effective teachers. While they have conflicts of interest at the bargaining table, this is a community of interest that both can pursue.[13]

The Union

Unions are too often associated with the defense of its least competent members to the detriment of the competent and the profession as a whole. Teachers take pride in their work. Most are troubled by the presence of incompetent teachers in their school building. One union building representative commented, "We have, on our staff, a few people who should leave teaching, perhaps 2 or 3 out of 70. It has been difficult to remove them due to contract language."[14]

Teacher unions are caught in a dilemma; they must provide representation for teachers, even the incompetent ones, yet their members want to only work with competent colleagues. The union must be seen by its membership as protecting their own from unfair accusations and unfair processes, yet they are aware of the public perception that they protect incompetent teachers which harms students and the community. Compounding this challenge, Harvard professor Johnson notes, "For most teachers, being part of a good school took precedence over union membership."[15] Similarly, DeMitchell and Cobb identified the concern of teachers that the union provides "blind protection" for teachers.[16]

Placing the protection of union members without regard for competence in the classroom is to elevate the interests of the employee over the needs of the recipient of the professional service. A union that seeks a place at the policy table too easily becomes perceived as an issue partisan, like other issue partisans, pursuing a narrow agenda within the policy discussion of the public good of education if it pursues blind protection. The focus should be the entitlement of an education and not a job.

Unions must protect the due process rights of teachers. They do not have to, nor should they protect incompetence. Unions protect the process by which incompetence is addressed so that the problem can be identified and addressed fairly. Blind protection ill-serves the profession, fair protection does. The due process of tenure calls for a fair process using fair rules to arrive at a fair decision.

The need for fairness in employee discipline is self-evident. Al Shanker, the driving force for the AFT, stated, "We fought to have due process, to give to teachers a fair trial. We did not fight to protect incompetence."[17] Can unions move from the industrial labor model, which calls for the defense of its least competent members to a professional model, which seeks to protect the public from incompetence in its ranks? They must.

Unions can meet their responsibilities to their teachers they represent. They can and must pursue the best wages, benefits, and terms and conditions that they can achieve given the realities of their school district. Unions do not seek to bankrupt the employer nor do they seek to replace the school administrators. They seek to work under positive conditions that allow teachers to act as professional educators serving the best interests of their students and their community. Unions pursue these subjects of bargaining in good faith with a pragmatic eye. They must also balance whether to and how far to support and represent teachers being disciplined.[18]

Similarly, the union and its members should seek contract sections that also are pragmatic and create a professional working environment. Reflexive responses to employee discipline of all-out and unconditional support without concern for the requirements of the ethics of the profession do not serve the students, the school, the community, or the profession. Unions that are only public adversaries regarding employee discipline and do not stand for teaching do not serve a public good which is the basis for the profession of education.

As stated at the beginning of this section, administrators are the other major player. Attracting, supporting, and retaining effective teachers is a core responsibility of administrators. Administrators must earn the respect of teachers through the demonstration of their commitment to effective teaching and their skills in implementing that commitment.[19]

Ethical teacher evaluation policies coupled with the ethical application of the policy through the use of these principles should be an important part of the evaluation system and its documentation component. Placing and retaining effective teachers in classrooms and removing ineffective teachers must be grounded in an ethical approach. Providing proper supervision that assists with strengthening the instructional skills of the teacher and maintaining a professional classroom is an important responsibility of the principal. Knowledge of how to fairly and properly document performance is important, if not a critical skill for school leaders.

Consistently using a fair process in evaluations and observations assists in supporting the perception by the school faculty that pettiness, vindictiveness, and the vagaries of decision-making are not the modus operandi of the principal. Consequently, the decisions of whom to place and to keep in front of students, how to assist that teacher to reach higher levels of excellence, when to identify deficiencies, and when to dismiss are critical.

The evaluation process cannot just be a ceremonial congratulation; the awarding of a certificate of participation in the school's activities. Who we place and retain in our classrooms is a challenge demanding an imperative of transparent, fair, and ethical action for school leaders. It must be undertaken with the application of skills and knowledge, and pursued with a high-level of professional responsibility. Fair procedures reduce the recurring fear of an unwarranted termination. "In short, government acting fairly towards its schoolteachers serves the public good."[20]

It takes careful and dedicated hard work and documentation to remove a teacher who is detrimental to the well-being of the school.
Steve Permuth & Robert Egley, "Letting Teachers Go—Legally," *Principal Leadership*, 3 (September 2002): 22–26, 26.

MOVING FORWARD

The future of labor relations in education involves choices of policies, politics, and practices. Two basic truths are a foundation for these choices of what policies to pursue, what is traded off, and who gains and who shares power through politics, and what practices will be implemented as a result of the politics in pursuit of what policies. First, providing for an educated citizenry is one of the most important functions of government. Second, elementary and secondary education is delivered through the work of people; it is people intensive.

Students stand at the center of education but teachers stand at the crossroads that lead toward or away from educational achievement; toward or away from economic success; and toward or away from meaningful citizen participation.

A consequence of these two truths is that in order to provide an effective educational system, government requires qualified professionals working in the best interests of students. Because the majority of public schools deliver education in a unionized environment, the work of unions and the effects of collective bargaining influence public education; labor relations are structured around the relationship between unions and management.

For too long this relationship has been grounded in the industrial labor model. The consequences of this model have not been good for education.

Unions provide a legitimate service, one that teachers clearly value and want and which society largely supports. While they may not identify with unions as part of their daily work, teachers want the protection that they believe unions provide. There will always be a conflict of interest but there is also a community of interest that needs to be vigorously pursued.

Education is an essential public good. Teachers are instrumental in providing the educational experiences needed by both students and the community: thus, they are necessary to the public good. Quality labor relations must support teachers in their educational efforts. Unions support teachers as part of their responsibility, but their support should also be part of the public good formula. Remaining a narrow special interest group that only supports their critical needs and interests without a grounding in the important role played in serving the public good is a challenge for educators, elected officials, the union, and the community.

Becky Malone, a parent of two students in the Chicago Public Schools and a member of the 19th Ward Parents organization stated in response to the Chicago teachers strike of 2012, stated, "As parents we support our teachers, because . . . our teachers' working conditions are our children's learning conditions."

Adam Mertz, "A Century of Teacher Organizing: What Can We Learn?" The Labor and Working Class History Association (LAWCHA) (n.d.). Site visited August 18, 2019, at https://www.lawcha.org/century-teaching-organizing/.

The book concludes with the following observations:

- The success of bargaining is not defined by signing a contract. The success of bargaining is measured by the quality of the relationship between the parties.
- Labor relations must emphasize the relations part of the term. Once the grievance is settled, the contract signed, the conflict resolved we have the educators in the school who need to work together, and in most instances want to work together. The relationship between people who must work together must not get lost in the labor relations built on an industrial model that separates more than it brings together.
- Labor and management must work to ameliorate the negative impact of the industrial labor model. The challenge for teachers and their unions is to reconcile professionalism and unionism, service to other and self-interest. Administrators face a similar challenge in that if they treat teachers as

"employees" during bargaining and contract administration, but as valued professionals on curricular and instructional matters they also support the wrong model.

- The union must be able to move beyond the self-interest of its membership but still meet that self-interest. It must be able to stand tall for what is right for the profession and the community and set aside the expedient of just being a reflexive advocate for its membership. It is a fine line that unions walk to transform themselves into a union of professionals. Management must assist in this effort. This is not a solo journey but rather a shared expedition of educators. The need for a new model is clear; the old one does not work. That does not mean that it will be easy to fashion a new model from which to transform labor relations to conform to professional relations.
- The bargaining table is a legitimate place for both labor and management to pursue their interests. Because there is a community of interests and not just a conflict of interests, the table must not be viewed as disconnected from the rest of the places in which educators interact. Both parties, labor and management, may come to the table separately, but they are joined in many ways after leaving the table.
- We must find ways to replicate the concept of good faith required in bargaining and make it part of the regular relationships between educators. Good faith should not only occur at the bargaining table; it must be a staple in the ebb and flow of a school. It must characterize the relations between educators.
- Neither side should be involved in practices at the bargaining table that attack and demean people and then expect that the behavior which targeted individuals can be forgotten with an understanding that the table is somehow a special place devoid of consequences for personal attacks. The table should not be a place for demonizing. The public sport of union bashing and administrator trashing will no longer work in a new age of professionalism. Confidence in public education is destroyed both inside and outside the schoolhouse gate when the public is left with the impression that the inept are leading the callous and the indifferent.
- We must find ways through working with teachers and the union to consistently strive to change community perceptions to coincide with the reality that educators are members of a learned profession. Once again pursuing the tenets of a union of professionals is more than worthwhile; it is necessary. The tension between teacher as professional and teacher as member of an industrial style union must be reduced.

As stated throughout this book, teachers are central to education. We must attract, support, and retain the best and brightest to the profession. They deserve and must have wages and benefits commensurate with the high duty that is expected of them. They need working conditions that support student learning and professional practice. They need the ongoing and high-level professional development to hone skills and to learn new ones. They need to work in an environment that provides security from the political forces that always lurk at the schoolhouse gate and access the autonomy necessary to meet their responsibilities.

Unions can and must play an important role in securing the structures that support teachers in these endeavors. They provide a voice for teachers. However, unions must also rethink the contract sections that trade off what is best for students for what is easiest for educators. Inflexible rules that reinforce standardization and centralization must be replaced. Professional practice demands flexibility and differential action based on the context of the learning situation. Reflexive approaches to these challenges of unions and administration result in the continued tangled fit of being a union member within the broader work context of being a professional. Recognition by all parties that reconciliation of union member and professional can be untangled, or at least be made less tangled.

Administrators and school boards must speak and act for the students and the community. They must also speak and act for teachers and teaching, and that includes working effectively and in good faith with the teachers' elected representative. They must be good stewards of the community's purse. They must provide the resources and support necessary to meet the goals and serve the vision of an educated populace.

The CBA is one of the means in which effective educators can be attracted, supported, and retained. It must be more than a constraining document, an instrument of compliance. More interests are shared than are in conflict. There are no silver bullets, no magic incantations—there is only hard work in building and maintaining relationships, including labor relationships. Changing the model for collective bargaining and focusing on attracting, supporting, and retaining effective educators is critical. The bilateral decision-making of a bargained contract is a bilateral responsibility ensuring that the public good of education is provided by effective professional educators in an environment that reflects the high values the community holds for its children.

NOTES

1. William E. Forbath and Brishen Rogers, "A New Type of Labor Law for a New Type of Worker," *New York Times* (September 4, 2017). Site visited September 4, 2017, at https://www.nytimes.com/2017/09/04/opinion/labor-laws-workers.html?action=click&pgtype=Homepage&clickSource=story-heading&module=opinion-c-col-left-region&region=opinion-c-col-left-region&WT.nav=opinion-c-col-left-region&_r=0.

2. Dana Goldstein, *The Teacher Wars: A History of America's Most Embattled Profession* (New York: Doubleday, 2014), 230.

3. Lydia Saad, "Labor Union Approval Steady at 15-Year High," Gallup (August 30, 2018). Site visited July 6, 2019, at https://news.gallup.com/poll/241679/labor-uni on-approval-steady-year-high.aspx.

4. Todd A. DeMitchell and Joseph J. Onosko, *"Vergara v. State of California*: The End of Teacher Tenure or a Flawed Ruling," *Southern California Interdisciplinary Law Review* 25 (2016): 589–624, 620.

5. Ronald C. Brown, "Public Sector Collective Bargaining: Perspective and Legislative Opportunities," *William and Mary Law Review* 15 (1973): 57–92, 58.

6. Associated Press, "LePage: Teachers 'a dime a dozen'," *Portsmouth Herald* (Portsmouth, NH, August 19, 2017): A4.

7. See Todd A. DeMitchell, *Educators at the Bargaining Table: Successfully Negotiating a Contract That Works for All* (Lanham, MD: Rowman & Littlefield, 2018), 10–11 for a discussion of the Conflict of Interest and the Community of Interests that structures collective bargaining: "Collective bargaining embraces both conflict and community," (10).

8. Julia E. Koppich, "Getting Started: A Primer on Professional Unionism," in *A Union of Professionals: Labor Relations and Educational Reform*, ed. Charles Taylor Kerchner and Julia E. Koppich (New York: Teachers College Press, 1993), 194–204, 202.

9. Joseph B. Shedd and Samuel B. Bacharach, *Tangled Hierarchies: Teachers as Professionals and the Management of Schools* (San Francisco: Jossey-Bass Publishers, 1991), 168.

10. Todd A. DeMitchell and Richard M. Barton, "Collective Bargaining and Its Impact on Local Educational Reform Efforts," *Educational Policy* 10 (1996): 366–378, 375.

11. Jeff Archer, "Districts Targeting Seniority in Union Contracts," *Education Week* (April 12, 2000): 5.

12. Patrick Cronin, "Teacher of Year Nominee Laid Off: Union: Seniority Rule Enacted as School Cuts Jobs," *Portsmouth Herald* (Portsmouth, New Hampshire) (April 27, 2009): A1, A2.

13. For a discussion of "Conflict and Cooperation: The Tension in Bargaining" see Todd A. DeMitchell, *Educators at the Bargaining Table: Successfully Negotiating a Contract that Works for All* (Lanham, MD: Rowman & Littlefield, 2018), 9–11.

14. DeMitchell and Barton, "Collective Bargaining and Its Impact on Local Educational Reform Efforts," 375.

15. Susan Moore Johnson, *Teacher Unions in Schools* (Philadelphia; Temple University Press, 1984), 163.

16. Todd A. DeMitchell and Casey D. Cobb, "Teacher as Union Member and Teacher as Professional: The Voice of the Teacher," *Education Law Reporter* (2007): 220, 25–38.

17. Kathy Checkley, "The New Union: Helping Teachers Take a Lead in Educational Reform," *Education Update* (Association for Supervision and Curriculum Development August 1996): 1, 3–5, 7–8, 3.

18. While the United States Supreme Court in *Humphrey v. Moore*, 375 U.S. 335 (1967) stated that unions have a duty to represent employees in an honest manner, without fraud or deceit, that duty has limits. Unions are given considerable discretion regarding what claims to press to grievance and arbitration. They do not have to take every employee grievance through all of the grievance steps and on to arbitration.

19. For a discussion of effective documentation, see Todd A. DeMitchell and Mark A. Paige, *Threading the Evaluation Needle: The Documentation of Teacher Unprofessional Conduct* (Lanham, MD: Rowman & Littlefield, in press).

20. DeMitchell and Onosko, "*Vergara v. State of California*," 621.

Index

Also by Todd A. DeMitchell

ALSO BY TODD A. DeMITCHELL

- *Educators at the Bargaining Table: Successfully Negotiating a Contract That Works for All*
- *Labor Relations in Education: Policies, Politics, and Practices*
- *Negligence: What Principals Need to Know to Prevent Liability*

ALSO BY TODD A. DeMITCHELL AND RICHARD FOSSEY

- *The Challenges of Mandating School Uniforms in the Public Schools: Free Speech, Research and Policy*
- *School Dress Codes and the First Amendment: Legal Challenges and Policy Issues*
- *The Limits of Law-Based School Reform: Vain Hopes and False Promises*

ALSO BY TODD A. DeMITCHELL AND MARK A. PAIGE

- *Threading the Evaluation Needle: The Documentation of Teacher Unprofessional Conduct*

203

About the Authors

Todd A. DeMitchell (BA, MAT, University of La Verne; MA, University of California, Davis; EdD, University of Southern California; and Postdoctorate, Harvard Graduate School of Education) is the John & H. Irene Peters Professor of Education and Professor of Justice Studies at the University of New Hampshire, where he previously held the Lamberton Professorship of Justice Studies. He was also selected as a Distinguished Professor by the university and received an Excellence Teaching award from the College. Prior to joining the faculty at the University of New Hampshire, he spent eighteen years in the public schools as an elementary school teacher, principal (K–8), director of personnel and labor relations (K–12), and superintendent (K–8). He sat at the bargaining table representing two school districts. He has published eight books—six with Rowman & Littlefield. He has over 200 publications including law reviews, peer-reviewed journals, professional journals, chapters, and commentaries. His research has been cited in top law school law reviews, in peer-reviewed journals, and in cases and motions before state and federal courts including the U.S. Supreme Court.

CONTRIBUTING AUTHORS

Jacob A. Bennett—Sidebar, "NLRB and Charter Schools" (chapter 3) (BA, Wesleyan University; MFA, Goddard College; ABD, University of New Hampshire) is a doctoral candidate studying higher education leadership and policy at the University of New Hampshire. Topics of research and writing include organizational culture and change, labor relations and collective bargaining, and the work experiences of adjunct and other contingent faculty.

205

Before enrolling in the doctoral program, Jacob taught composition and literature at La Salle University, and published poetry, translations of poetry, and reviews of books of poetry. His first peer-reviewed article in the field of higher education policy—titled "A Limited Review of the Post-*Heller* Fate of 'Campus Carry': Preemption and Constitutionality in New Hampshire and Beyond"—considers case law around "campus carry" policies and prohibitions, and is forthcoming from the *Journal of College and University Law*.

Nathan Fellman—Sidebar, "Transition: Union President to Administrator" (chapter 5) (BA, George Washington University; MS, Southern New Hampshire University; EdS, University of New Hampshire) is a doctoral student at the University of New Hampshire. He also works full time as an assistant principal of a middle school in a district where he has been working as an educator for fifteen years. Prior to entering administration, he served as a union negotiator and union president. Since becoming an assistant principal he has been appointed as administrative liaison for negotiations with the teachers' association.

Joseph J. Onosko—Coauthor of chapter 8 (BA, MA, PhD, University of Wisconsin, Madison)—is an associate professor in the UNH Education Department, specializing in social studies education, school reform, and inquiry-based learning. Recent publications with UNH colleague, Todd DeMitchell, appear in the *Southern California Interdisciplinary Law Journal*. One examines the tension between a parent's right to raise a child versus the community's right to create a future citizen, and the other examines recent judicial and legislative attacks on teacher tenure. Professor Onosko has been a vocal critic of federal educational reforms, including his widely read "Race to the Top Leaves Children & Future Citizens Behind: The Devastating Effects of Centralization, Standardization, and High Stakes Accountability," which appeared in the public-access online journal *Democracy & Education*. For ten years he codirected *History in Perspective*, a 2.7 million-dollar professional development project for K–12 NH and Maine U.S. history and humanities teachers. He also chaired the rewriting of the U.S. and world history standards for the New Hampshire K–12 Social Studies Framework. Recently, Joe co-taught a UNH course with Philosophy Department colleague, Timm Triplett, entitled "Teaching Philosophy in K–12 Classrooms."

Lightning Source UK Ltd.
Milton Keynes UK
UKHW010622100120
356701UK00002B/208/P